One Nation, Divisible

One Nation, Divisible

How Regional Religious Differences Shape American Politics

Mark Silk and Andrew Walsh

ROWMAN & LITTLEFIELD PUBLISHERS, INC.
Lanham • Boulder • New York • Toronto • Plymouth, UK

ROWMAN & LITTLEFIELD PUBLISHERS, INC.

Published in the United States of America
by Rowman & Littlefield Publishers, Inc.
A wholly owned subsidary of The Rowman & Littlefield Publishing Group, Inc.
4501 Forbes Boulevard, Suite 200, Lanham, Maryland 20706
www.rowmanlittlefield.com

Estover Road
Plymouth PL6 7PY
United Kingdom

British Library Cataloguing in Publication Information Available

Library of Congress Cataloging-in-Publication Data

Silk, Mark.
   One nation, divisible : how regional religious differences shape American politics /
Mark Silk and Andrew Walsh.
      p. cm.
   Includes index.
   ISBN-13: 978-0-7425-5845-8 (cloth : alk. paper)
   ISBN-10: 0-7425-5845-2 (cloth : alk. paper)
   1. Religion and politics—United States. I. Walsh, Andrew. II. Title.
   BL2525.S54 2008
   201'.720973—dc22   2008008124

Printed in the United States of America

⊗™ The paper used in this publication meets the minimum requirements of
American National Standard for Information Sciences—Permanence of Paper
for Printed Library Materials, ANSI/NISO Z39.48-1992.

For Tema and Cathy

Putting it together

Contents

Preface

$\mathcal{G}$eographical diversity is the hallmark of religion in the United States. There are Catholic zones and evangelical Bible Belts, a Lutheran kingdom and a Mormon Zion, metropolitan concentrations of Jews and Muslims, and (in a different dimension) parts of the country where religious affiliation of whatever kind is very high and parts where it is far below the norm. This religious heterogeneity is inextricably linked to the character of American places. From Boston to Birmingham, from Salt Lake City to Santa Barbara, even the casual observer perceives differences of public culture—in architecture, in the media, in the life of the community—that are related to religion.

Yet when the story of religion in American public life gets told, the variegated landscape tends to be reduced to a series of black-and-white snapshots of the spiritual state of the union, of piety along the Potomac, of great watersheds or swings of mood that raise or lower the collective religious temperature. Whatever the virtues of such a monochrome national narrative—and we believe they are considerable—it fails to disclose a great deal. The central claim of this book is that religion in American public life has distinct regional variants, each of which needs to be understood on its own terms. Each has social, cultural, and political concomitants and consequences. Because of religion, the United States is one nation, divisible.

Making the case for a regionally differentiated approach to American religious history a generation ago, Jerald Brauer of the University of Chicago Divinity School wrote: "Regionalism is as susceptible as any other construct to distortion or to abuse. However, if taken seriously on its own terms and not employed as the single motif to explain American religious history, it can be a most useful tool in helping to explore the complexity of that history."[1] For our part, we do not claim that religion is the master key that will unlock all

ix

the secrets of American history, nor, indeed, that it plays the same kind of public role in all regions of the country. Regions have different religious ecologies, based both on the numerical strength of the religious groups on the ground and on how these groups have interacted with each other over time in places subject to different social, economic, and environmental circumstances. In some regions, religion has come to serve as a shaping force; in others, as a subtler conditioning agent. Our principal object is to draw a series of portraits that show what the ecology looks like in each case and how it behaves. But we have no interest in decomposing a national story into eight separate narratives and leaving it at that. Because the national story is not independent of the regional dynamics, we call attention throughout to the interplay of regional and national religious attitudes, impulses, and rhetoric. In the final chapter, we briefly essay a retelling of the recent history of religion in American public life that incorporates the regional dimension. As the famous red-and-blue maps of the 2000 and 2004 presidential elections made clear to everyone, U.S. national politics has in recent years manifested strong geographical divisions. We believe that the story we have to tell has important new light to shed on the nature of those divisions.

One Nation, Divisible is the capstone of *Religion by Region*, a project of the Leonard E. Greenberg Center for the Study of Religion in Public Life at Trinity College that represents the first comprehensive effort to relate religion to region in America. Edited volumes on each of eight regions of the country were published between 2004 and 2006. It is important to emphasize how much of a collaborative effort this ninth volume is. Its eight predecessors featured seven outside co-editors: Randall Balmer, Philip Barlow, Patricia O'Connell Killen, William Lindsey, Wade Clark Roof, Jan Shipps, and Charles Reagan Wilson. They have been our primary collaborators and we are profoundly indebted to them for everything from helping to conceptualize each volume to selecting the teams of contributors to contributing their own analytic essays. To the 44 other authors, we can only express our thanks and appreciation for work done well and on schedule. The measure of our debt lies in the extent to which we have taken advantage of their ideas, research, and prose. Although this is not a long book, it reflects a large and ambitious undertaking—one that we could not have undertaken alone. For any errors we have introduced, through misunderstanding or wrongheadedness, we sincerely apologize.

That said, *One Nation, Divisible* is both less and more than a summary of what has gone before. Much of interest and importance has had to be left out. In particular, we would point to the regional accounts of those minority faith communities whose increasing numbers have so enriched American society over the past generation. It is no disrespect to them to point out that few have made the kind of impact on public life that warrants more than passing attention here. On the other hand, we have updated, extended, and in a few cases introduced new themes into the stories of religion in regional public life. Being able to stand on our authors' shoulders has helped us gain some fresh perspectives, as has the ongoing saga of America's religious politics, which has taken some notable turns in just the short couple of years since the rest of the project was put to bed. The retelling of the national story in the final chapter lay outside the purview of the regional volumes and the conclusions flowing from it are ours alone. Not that this is meant to be the last word on the subject of religion and region in the United States. To the contrary, from the beginning of the Religion by Region project, our object has been to open discussions about religious regionalism that have, for the most part, not existed. Our aspiration has been to put down enough in the way of first words to get the discussions going.

Special thanks are owed to David Bodenhamer and his associates at the Polis Center in Indianapolis, who created the *North American Religious Atlas* (NARA) database that was essential to getting a fix on the demographics of religion in America; to Barry Kosmin and Ariela Keysar, now of the Institute for the Study of Secularism in Society and Culture at Trinity College, whose *American Religious Identification Survey* (ARIS) provided an essential alternative mode of accounting for the religious commitments of Americans; and to John Green, director of the University of Akron's Bliss Institute and fellow at the Pew Research Center, both for providing critical empirical data on social attitudes and religious voting patterns and for his analyses of exit poll data for articles in *Religion in the News*. For an explanation of how these data were compiled, see the Appendix.

A project of such scope does not come cheap and we are deeply grateful to Lilly Endowment, Inc., and to Leonard E. Greenberg for making it possible. Above all, we are grateful to Trinity College, without whose institutional commitment, now 12 years and counting, this entire enterprise would have been no more than a will-o-the-wisp.

Mark Silk
Andrew Walsh
Hartford, Connecticut
January 2008

Religion by Region

$\mathcal{W}$hat are regions in America? They are not political units, nor do they all possess the same degree of clarity on the map or in the minds of their inhabitants. The Civil War imparted a powerful collective identity to the eleven states of the Old Confederacy. New Englanders know exactly which states make up their region and recognize a common consciousness even when they don't belong to Red Sox Nation. In the Pacific Northwest, ideas of regional solidarity up to the point of secession have been entertained over the years by way of such imagined entities as the State of Jefferson, Ecotopia, and Cascadia, yet the geographical boundaries of the region are far from fixed. People who live in the Middle Atlantic states do not conceive of themselves as "Middle Atlantics." Midwesterners answer to the name, but will question whether there is enough in common from Toledo to Topeka, from Peoria to Pierre, to represent something worth talking about. And so on. A minimalist definition might be that regions are portions of the country, more or less familiar, that beg the question of their coherence. What is certain is that any comprehensive regional analysis needs to begin as an exercise in identification.

Our division of the country into regions is largely conventional: New England, the Middle Atlantic, the South, the Midwest, the Mountain West, the Pacific, the Pacific Northwest. The only novelty is what we call the Southern Crossroads—a region roughly equivalent to what American historians know as the Old Southwest, comprising Louisiana, Texas, Arkansas, Oklahoma, and Missouri. Since we have committed ourselves to covering every state in the Union (though not the territories—e.g., Puerto Rico), Hawaii has been included in a Pacific region with California and Nevada, and Alaska in the Pacific Northwest.

1

Because our interest is driven by population density and culture rather than ecology and land use, we have drawn some regions in ways that geographers will find odd or at least unfamiliar. The reason that Nevada has been assigned to the Pacific is that 90 percent of its people live within 10 miles of the California border. Idaho has been taken out of its customary place in the Pacific Northwest because most Idahoans live in the heavily Mormon southern part of the state, thereby linking it more closely to Utah than to Oregon and Washington. We could have gone further and assigned northern Idaho (along with western Montana) to the Pacific Northwest—or, to take another example, created a Southwest region of Roman Catholic predominance running from southern Louisiana through south Texas, across New Mexico and Arizona on into southern California. But to generate regions of maximum religious homogeneity by separating Louisiana's Cajun Catholics and Texas' Latino Catholics from the white evangelicals in the northern parts of those states would have been self-defeating. States are—by the laws they pass, the politicians they elect, and the loyalties they nurture—central arenas of American public life. They had to be kept intact.

But then, why regions? With no common governing institutions to point to, do we have empirical grounds for claiming that what we are dealing with here are little more than contiguous aggregations of states? Secular census data do not help much. To be sure, we can point to some regions (the Middle Atlantic, the Pacific) where immigration is high, and to others (New England, the Midwest) where it is relatively low. Race and ethnicity, too, vary markedly from region to region: The proportion of African Americans in the South and Southern Crossroads far exceeds that in New England and the Pacific Northwest. Yet from income and education levels to age, gender, and marital patterns, the regions do not differ very much. Where they do differ, to a remarkable degree, is in their religious profiles. Here's what these look like.[1]

THE MIDDLE ATLANTIC: NEW YORK, NEW JERSEY, PENNSYLVANIA, DELAWARE, MARYLAND, DISTRICT OF COLUMBIA

The Middle Atlantic region—New York, New Jersey, Pennsylvania, Delaware, Maryland, and the District of Columbia—is, at 65.8 percent, the second most heavily "churched" region of the country, exceeded only by the Southern Crossroads. About half the Middle Atlantic's adherents are Catholic; that is well below the percentage in New England, but far above that in the South. The Middle Atlantic is roughly one-third more Catholic than the nation as a whole. The Hispanic portion of the region's Catholic population is considerably lower than in the Pacific, the Mountain West, and the Southern Cross-roads, pointing toward an important difference in immigration patterns. The only states in the region with a substantial number of Hispanic Catholics are New York and New Jersey, where the Hispanic population regardless of religious identity constitutes 15 percent and 13.3 percent of the population respectively. In the other Middle Atlantic states, Hispanics number less than five percent. In sum, the Catholic concentration in the region runs northeast to south, from two-fifths of the population in New York and New Jersey, to less than one-third in Pennsylvania, to under one-fifth in Delaware and Maryland.

The other groups with a higher proportion of the population in the Middle Atlantic than in the country as a whole ("overrepresented," in demographer's lingo) are Jews and Muslims. Jews have a long history of settlement in the region, but have declined slightly as they intermarried with non-Jews and integrated into American society, and as younger members of the community migrated out of the region. Region-wide, Jews constitute 5.7 percent of the population, or three times the national average. Like Catholics, they are most numerous in New York and New Jersey (8.7 percent and 5.6 percent), but stronger in Maryland than in Pennsylvania or Delaware. Above all, Jews cleave to the major metropolitan regions of New York City, Philadelphia, Baltimore, and Washington, D.C. For their part, Muslims have grown from a very small base as a result of immigration and conversion (particularly of African Americans) in recent years. They now constitute 1.4 percent and 1.2 percent of the population in New York and New Jersey, and, most strikingly, represent over 10 percent of the population of the District of Columbia.

Protestants tend to hew to their ancestral roots in the region: mainliners, members of the denominations that first established themselves in the colonial era, outnumber evangelicals by better than two to one—the only region in the country where this is the case other than New England. Indeed, only in New England do evangelicals constitute a smaller proportion of the population than in the Middle Atlantic. On the region's bottom rim, in south-central Pennsylvania, rural Maryland, and the District of Columbia, evangelicals approach 20 percent of the population. Altogether, Protestants become thicker on the ground as you move away from New York and New Jersey.

NEW ENGLAND: CONNECTICUT, RHODE ISLAND, MASSACHUSETTS, VERMONT, NEW HAMPSHIRE, MAINE

Sixty-eight percent of all religious adherents in New England are Roman Catholics, making it by far the most Catholic region in the country. Most are clustered in three metropolitan corridors in the region's southern portion: from

New Haven westward along Long Island Sound (New England's contribution to the tristate New York metropolitan area); from Hartford north to Springfield; and from Providence north through Boston and Worcester into southern New Hampshire. Migration across the border from Massachusetts has raised the proportion of Catholics in New Hampshire in recent years. Because Hispanics are strikingly underrepresented in the region, New England Catholicism retains its powerfully Anglo—or, more accurately, Irish—cast.

Northern New England is at once more rural and more religiously unaffiliated than the region's three southern states. There, indeed, the unaffiliated (or, more precisely, the uncounted[2]) predominate: 50.6 percent in New Hampshire, 57.2 percent in Vermont, and 62.1 percent in Maine, as opposed to 31.8 percent in Massachusetts, 34 percent in Rhode Island, and 35.6 percent in Connecticut. Thus, while New England's overall unaffiliated rate of 38.5 percent is close to the 40.5 percent national average, the region embraces two distinctly different religious zones.

New England may be famous as the place established by Calvinist Protestants (called Puritans) to be a light unto the nations, but nowadays Protestants come in a poor second to Catholics in number of adherents. Mainliners range from a low of 5.9 percent of the Massachusetts population to a high of 10 percent in Vermont; overall, they outnumber evangelicals by nearly three to one. The second largest Protestant grouping consists of the historically African American churches, making this the only region of the country where African American Protestants outnumber white evangelicals. Still, members of these churches total less than three percent of the population. All told, New England is the least Protestant region of the country.

Jews have a strong presence in the region, at three percent exceeding all regions of the country other than the Middle Atlantic. Massachusetts' 4.3 percent Jewish population gives the Bay State the fourth highest concentration of Jews after New York, New Jersey, and Washington, D.C. Across the region, they cluster in metropolitan Boston and Hartford, and in New York City's Connecticut suburbs.

Because of New England's early global intellectual and commercial contacts, there have been practitioners of Asian religions in the region since the middle of the nineteenth century. After immigration reform in the mid-1960s, Hinduism, Buddhism, and Islam began growing rapidly. Buddhism of various types is particularly strong in Vermont, representing three percent of all residents in three of the state's rural counties. Massachusetts is the region's hotbed for Hindus, ranking eighth in the nation with 20 Hindu congregations. The region's Muslim population is considerable in the urban south and negligible in the rural north. Very few Muslims reside in New Hampshire, Rhode Island, and Maine, and virtually none live in Vermont. In fact, only

South Dakota has fewer Muslim residents than Vermont. Connecticut is New England's Muslim stronghold, with nine out of every 1,000 residents practicing Islam (fifth in the nation), and Massachusetts is a close second with seven out of every 1,000 (ninth nationally).

THE SOUTH: VIRGINIA, WEST VIRGINIA, KENTUCKY, TENNESSEE, NORTH CAROLINA, SOUTH CAROLINA, GEORGIA, FLORIDA, ALABAMA, MISSISSIPPI

It is hard to overstate the extent to which evangelical Protestantism sets the South apart from all other regions of the country. This does not have to do merely with the 25.7 percent of southerners who are counted as belonging to Baptist, Pentecostal, and other churches normally identified as evangelical. Many of the 17.5 percent of southerners who belong to the mainline Protestant denominations—Methodists and Presbyterians above all—deserve to be counted among the evangelicals, based on their beliefs and religious culture. Then there are the members of the historic African American Protestant denominations, Baptist and Methodist, whose beliefs and worship style are nothing if not evangelical. Leaving the mainliners aside, white evangelicals and the historic African American denominations represent 63 percent of all religious adherents in the region—significantly higher than the 54 percent in the Southern Crossroads and far above all the other regions, which range from 36 percent in the Pacific Northwest down to 10.6 percent in New England.[3] Altogether, the South is just about as evangelical as Utah is Mormon.

The rest of the region's religious demography helps underscore this dominance. Only eight percent of Southerners are Catholics, and 41 percent of them live in Florida alone; through the rest of the region, Catholics number less that five percent of the population—by far the smallest proportion of Catholics anywhere in the country. In addition, it is noteworthy that 40.3 percent of all southerners are unaffiliated/uncounted. Given the South's Bible-Belt identity, that is surprisingly close to the national average of 40.6 percent. Yet only 10.7 of Southerners answer the question, "What is your religion, if any?" by saying "None." In contrast to all other regions of the country, where the ratio of these "Nones" to the unaffiliated/uncounted is between 1:2 and 1:3, in the South it is nearly 1:4. Why are uncounted and unaffiliated southerners less likely than other Americans to say they have no religion? Partly, this may reflect the numbers of Southerners—especially in Appalachia—who belong to independent evangelical churches that do not report their membership numbers. It also seems to be the case that Southerners feel under more cultural pressure than other Americans to identify themselves as religious.

To be sure, evangelicalism does not dominate everywhere in the region. South of the Florida panhandle and in the booming Virginia suburbs of Washington, D.C., it is but one tradition among many. Nor is evangelicalism itself uniform across the southern heartland. Baptists represent the largest religious denomination in most counties of the region but their greatest strength reaches from southern Appalachia into the deep-south states of Georgia, Alabama, and Mississippi. Methodists are particularly strong along the western border of Virginia, in the Carolinas, and in eastern Mississippi. The mountains of east Tennessee were an important hearth for white Pentecostalism, while the deep south of Mississippi and nearby Memphis nurtured black Pentecostalism. The Churches of Christ, a theologically conservative and morally strict group that grew out of the Presbyterians, are one of the numerically largest and culturally most powerful groups from middle Tennessee down through north Alabama and north Mississippi.

The South has its religious minorities. Jews, who have been in the region for centuries, are the most numerous—though like the Catholics they are disproportionately concentrated in sub-panhandle Florida. Hindus, Muslims, Buddhists, Mormons, and Hispanic Catholics have all established a presence in the South, but the numbers remain limited. When it comes to the country's non-Christian minorities, the South has the next-to-least religious diversity in the country, after the Southern Crossroads.

THE SOUTHERN CROSSROADS: LOUISIANA, TEXAS, OKLAHOMA, ARKANSAS, MISSOURI

The Crossroads—Louisiana, Texas, Arkansas, Oklahoma, and Missouri—looks like the South plus Roman Catholics. At 18.6 percent of the population, Catholicism claims more than twice the share of the demographic pie as it does in the South, as well as a more dispersed and longstanding presence in the culture. Missouri and Arkansas were home to French Catholics early in their histories and St. Louis became a magnet for German Catholics later on. The southern tier of Louisiana is Cajun country, settled by French Catholic refugees from Nova Scotia in the eighteenth century. Texas was originally Mexican territory and south Texas is more heavily Mexican-American now than it was 100 years ago. Today, indeed, half of all Catholics in the region are Latino. Altogether, the proportion of Catholics in the Southern Crossroads approaches the national average of 22 percent of the population.

But the Crossroads is also chock-full of evangelicals. Here, white Baptists dominate; there are as many of them as there are Catholics in the region. Next in line come the members of the historically African American Protestant denominations, which claim 15 percent of all church members. Since a majority of African Americans are Baptists, that makes this far and away the region's most populous tradition. Taken together, Baptists and Catholics account for over half of the Crossroads population. The region also counts the largest proportion of members of Pentecostal/Charismatic/Holiness churches in the country—a reflection of the fact that this fastest growing of Christian traditions worldwide was birthed here. Claiming 8.1 of the population, these churches approach the size of mainline Protestantism, and equal it if the historically African American Pentecostal dominations, notably the Church of God in Christ, are included. The tradition is particularly strong in a swath of counties extending across the southern tier of Missouri across northwest Arkansas and into Oklahoma, as well as along the southern reaches of the Texas Gulf coast. It is a tradition strong among Latino Protestants, a group more numerous in the Crossroads than any other region but the Pacific. Eighteen percent of all Latino Protestants in the United States reside in the Southern Crossroads region—mostly in Texas, whose population is almost one-third Latino.

Among the mainline Protestant denominations, United Methodists have the largest constituency in the Southern Crossroads with more than half of all mainline Protestants in the region—although, as in the South, many Methodists deserve to be counted in the evangelical camp. Overall, mainliners are somewhat thinner on the ground than in the South. Methodists, Presbyterians, and Episcopalians together total 6.8 percent of the population, as opposed to the South's 8.6 percent. But the mainline Disciples of Christ denomination, which grew out of the Restoration movement of the early 1800s, maintains a distinct presence in the region, with .8 percent of the population and fully 21 percent of all Disciples congregations nationwide.

The Crossroads is the least religiously diverse region in the country when it comes to members of minority religious traditions. It is, in fact, the only region in the country where the identification level of Jews, Mormons, Muslims, and members of Eastern religions each does not exceed half of one percent of the population. It is next-to-last (slightly ahead of the South) in the proportion of adults who say they have no religion, and dead last by a significant margin in the proportion of unaffiliated/uncounted adults (less than one-third of the population).

THE PACIFIC: CALIFORNIA, NEVADA, HAWAII

Catholics constitute by far the largest religious community in the Pacific region, with 28.7 percent of the population. Nearly eight points higher than in the American population at large, it is, after New England and the Middle

Atlantic, the third most heavily concentrated Catholic region in the country. As a result of migration from Latin America, the proportion has been growing. From 1971 to 2000, the region's Catholic population increased much faster in Nevada (260 percent) and California (155.8 percent) than in the country as a whole (38.3 percent). It is in the Pacific region that the "Latinization" of American Catholicism is most in evidence; indeed, Hispanics are now approaching 60 percent of the region's self-identified Catholic population.

By contrast, the mainline Protestant presence in the region has been declining, and considerably so, over the past half-century. Mainliners now account for only 4.6 percent of the region's population—the lowest in the nation. They are, in fact, outnumbered by evangelicals by 70 percent to 30 percent, the highest of any region outside the South and Southern Crossroads. There are more evangelicals than adherents of both the mainline and African American Protestant denominations combined, which is the reverse of what holds for the country as a whole. But unlike the South and the Crossroads, where Southern Baptists make up the large Protestant majority, the Pacific counts far more Pentecostals and independent, nondenominational Christians than Baptists. As with Latino Catholics, so with Latino Protestants; they constitute 19.5 percent of all Protestants, the largest proportion in any region of the country.

Eastern religions have a larger following in the region than elsewhere in the country (2 percent of the population). In fact, 29 percent of all Eastern religions' followers in the United States reside within the region. It is noteworthy that more residents of the Pacific identify with Eastern religions than with any of the mainline Protestant denominations—the only region of the country where that is the case. According to the ARIS survey, there are nearly twice the number of Buddhists as Hindus in the region. Thanks to the large number of Buddhists of Japanese descent, Hawaii has by far the largest proportion of adherents of Eastern religion; at 5.7 percent, they represent the second largest religious sector in the state.

Jews (2.9 percent), Mormons (1.9 percent), and Muslims (0.7 percent) are all over-represented in the region. Of greater importance, however, is the over-representation of Nones—those who identify with no religion. In this respect, residents of the Pacific are typical westerners, coming in slightly ahead of the Mountain West, somewhat behind the Pacific Northwest, and well in advance of other regions of the country. Rural southern California tends to have higher rates of affiliation than the north, thanks to larger percentages of both Latinos and white evangelicals. The proportion of unaffiliated/uncounted ranges from 29 percent in San Benito, a county in the Coast Range Mountains south of San Jose with a 44 percent Latino population, to 80.8 percent in Calaveras, the old mining district made famous by Mark Twain's "Jumping

Frog" story. Overall, California, at 46.2 percent, ranks behind both Hawaii
(55.4 percent) and Nevada (61.4 percent) in unaffiliated/uncounted.

THE PACIFIC NORTHWEST:
OREGON, WASHINGTON, ALASKA

Nowhere in the United States is religion thinner on the ground than in the
Pacific Northwest. Together, Washington and Oregon lead the nation in the
number of Nones.[4] At 25 percent of the population, they are more than
twice as numerous as the largest single religious body in the region, and
close to twice the proportion of Nones in the country as a whole (14.1 percent). In terms of the religiously affiliated, Oregon ranked dead last among
all states at 35.2 percent, followed by Washington with 38.1 percent and
Alaska with 39.8 percent. The region's overall 37.2 percent adherence rate
is the lowest in the country, more than 22 percentage points below the national average. Because nearly two-thirds of its population is unchurched,
the Pacific Northwest is frequently described as secular and godless. As one
former Catholic archbishop reportedly put it, "There are no Christians
here; they are all pagans." Yet the picture is more complicated than that, for
more than two-thirds of the adults in Oregon and Washington identify
themselves as having a religion. The gap between actual adherents (those
whom religious bodies carry on their rolls) and identifiers (those who associate themselves with a religious community of some kind) is larger in the
Pacific Northwest than anywhere else in the United States. In fact, this "gap
group"—those who identify but do not affiliate—is the largest segment of
the population of the Northwest, and the wild card in any assessment of the
role of religion in the public life of the region.

 As in most regions of the country, Catholics are the largest single religious
group but in the Northwest Catholicism is far from the dominant tradition that
it is in New England or the Middle Atlantic. At 11.3 percent of the population,
Catholics occupy only half the space they do in the country as a whole. On the
other hand, the Holiness/Wesleyan/Pentecostal and "Other Conservative
Christians" groups, which rank second (4.7 percent of all who affiliate in the region) and third (4.0 percent) respectively in the region, rank only fifth (2.8 percent) and sixth (2.8 percent) nationally. Baptists are the fifth largest group in the
Northwest (2.6 percent of the population), but are second nationally (8.5 percent). Taken together, these data show that the Northwest is the only region
outside the South and the Southern Crossroads with as many evangelicals as
Catholics. But from Virginia to Texas the largest number are Baptist, while in
the Northwest the bulk are Pentecostal and nondenominational Christian.

Mormons come in fourth (3.0 percent) in the Northwest, as opposed to tenth (1.5 percent) nationally, and (not surprisingly) are proportionally stronger in the eastern than the western parts of Oregon and Washington. Indeed, Northwesterners on the east side of the Cascade Mountains tend to be more religious generally—more rural and traditional—than those on the west.

Testifying to the region's location on the Pacific rim, Eastern religion ranks higher (eighth) than every mainline Protestant denomination other than Lutheranism, and numbers twice as many adherents as Judaism. Altogether, the mainline denominations count 7.2 percent of Northwesterners as members, although more than twice as many—16.5 percent—actually identify with a mainline church. Since there are comparatively few blacks in the Northwest, the historically African American dominations register at just 1.8 percent of the region's population (only the Mountain West ranks lower), compared to 7.4 percent nationally. Finally, Muslims are slightly less well represented in the Northwest (ranking eighteenth) than in the nation as a whole (fifteenth).

THE MOUNTAIN WEST: ARIZONA, NEW MEXICO, UTAH, IDAHO, COLORADO, WYOMING, MONTANA

This is the United States' preeminent oasis, or archipelago, region. It is characterized by a great deal of "empty" (i.e., unpopulated) space dotted with a few urban concentrations, often several hundred miles apart. From our perspective, the Mountain West is best understood as comprising three sub-regions, distinguishable less by geography and secular demography than by religion and culture: Arizona and New Mexico to the south; Utah and Idaho to the northwest; and Colorado, Wyoming and Montana to the northeast. The differences among them go back a long way.

New Mexico and Arizona (together with southern Colorado) have a strong Catholic concentration. This derives in part from the area's proximity to Mexico, from which immigration has given nearly all border counties from Texas to California a Catholic coloration. But the Catholic presence is also long-standing: Catholic missionizing and settlement of the Rio Grande valley began in 1598 and has been continuous ever since. This has sometimes led to exotic variants—most importantly, syncretism with Native American religion. Strong evidence also exists of crypto-Jews, descendants of refugees from Spain, in the area since the colonial period. Recently, the traditional Catholic presence has been massaged by three migratory streams whose impacts have conflicted: new arrivals from Mexico and Central America; mainline Anglo-American Catholics who have been part of the net migration into the southwest (more to Arizona than to New Mexico, though both states have experienced it); and a wide range of white Protestants who arrived beginning in the 1950s as part of the broad population move to the Sunbelt. In-migration has put Arizona on a multicultural path similar to southern California, bringing the state's affiliated Catholic population down to 43.2 percent of the religiously affiliated and 19 percent of the population as a whole. Meanwhile, with 58.4 percent of all of the religiously affiliated and 37 percent of the population as a whole, Catholicism continues to dominate New Mexico.

The northwestern subregion (Utah and Idaho) is home to the largest, purest concentration of a single religious group anywhere in the country. By contrast, Mormons constitute only 9.5 percent of the population of Wyoming and less than five percent of the other Mountain states. Fully two-thirds of Utah's population is Mormon, and besides the 4.3 percent who are Catholic, no other religious body or grouping in the state reaches one percent of the population. The proportion of unaffiliated/uncounted, 23.5 per cent, is among the lowest in the country. Mormons also dominate the religious scene in Idaho, but to a considerably lesser degree; at 24.1 percent of the population, they outnumber Catholics, the next most populous group, by nearly 2.5 to 1. Not quite half of all religious adherents in the state are Mormon, while half of all Idahoans are unaffiliated/uncounted.

As for the northeastern sub-region, it is characterized by the largest portion of religiously unaffiliated people—significantly below the Pacific Northwest but upwards of 50 percent of the population. Among the religiously affiliated, the Catholics dominate with between 30 percent and 40 percent and a wide array of other groups weighted a bit differently depending on the state. Mormons are stronger in Wyoming and Montana, while Colorado is notable for its evangelical Protestants and devotees of Eastern religion. Taking the bird's-eye view of the region, the unaffiliated decisively outnumber everyone else everywhere except in Utah and New Mexico; but formal affiliation is less common than in any region other than the Northwest. Besides a lot of Nones, the region boasts an unusually high proportion of Mormons and a fairly average quantum of Catholics—but as one might expect from a cultural archipelago, these are distributed very unevenly around the region.

THE MIDWEST: OHIO, MICHIGAN, INDIANA, ILLINOIS, WISCONSIN, IOWA, MINNESOTA, NORTH DAKOTA, SOUTH DAKOTA, IOWA, NEBRASKA, KANSAS

The Midwest is the most balanced region in the country—which makes it stand out. Its religious layout is similar to the national population, more so than all other regions, in the proportion of adherents who are Catholic,

Baptist, Holiness/Pentecostal, and unaffiliated/uncounted. It is closer than most regions to national rates for Muslims, humanists, and unspecified Protestants. Its proportion of African American Protestants lies precisely in the middle of the pack, between the South and Southern Crossroads at the high end and New England and the Pacific Northwest at the low.

Not that everything is average in this region. The proportions of Mormons and members of Eastern religions are sharply smaller, and Jews moderately so. On the other hand, mainline Protestants are a stronger presence here than in any other region of the country. Twenty-five percent of Midwesterners identify with a mainline denomination (compared with 17 percent throughout the United States). The Midwest is the only region that counts a roughly equal balance of mainliners and evangelicals, 53 percent and 47 percent respectively. Evangelicals have long had a strong presence in southern Illinois and Indiana, and have been growing in strength in southeastern and south central Ohio. Lutherans rank disproportionately high in the region; at 14 percent of the population, they more than double their concentration in the country as a whole. Famously, they dominate the landscape of Minnesota and the Dakotas, and maintain a powerful presence in Wisconsin and Iowa as well.

Midwestern Catholics have a more distinctively Germanic tinge than Catholics elsewhere in the country. The "German Triangle" runs from Cincinnati to Milwaukee to St. Louis (a city not, on this regional accounting, in the Midwest proper but sitting on its border). Midwestern Catholics comprise as well a large number of descendants of eastern European immigrants, especially in and around Detroit and Chicago. And, of course, there's no shortage of Irish and Italians and—in Chicago, in particular—more recently arrived Latinos.

Of special note is what the historian and religious demographer Philip Barlow calls the Bible Suspender: a large vertical pattern of counties whose proportion of citizens attached to a church or religion exceeds 75 percent (and, as a penumbra, 65 percent). Descending south and slightly eastward from the Canadian border, the Suspender covers the whole of North Dakota and western Minnesota, proceeds through eastern South Dakota and northern Iowa, then twists somewhat westward, encompassing eastern Nebraska and most of Kansas before proceeding out of the region south into Oklahoma and Texas. What the Suspender reveals is that rates of connection to organized religion are, contrary to popular imagination, higher in a broad vertical swath in the Midwest than in the horizontal, mythic Bible Belt of the South.

CONCLUSION

The foregoing survey provides sufficient demographic data to suggest that such differences as exist among the public cultures of America's regions have something to do with religion—that, for example, the dominant presence of Catholics in New England, evangelicals in the South and Southern Crossroads, and Nones in the Pacific Northwest do much to shape the character of each of those regions. The chapters that follow attempt to show, region by region, how such shaping occurs. They do not argue that all regional distinctiveness derives from religion. Public cultures are the product of many other forces—geographic, ethnographic, economic. But religion is an essential and too often overlooked part of the mix. An adequate understanding of the way America works requires taking it into account.

• 2 •

The Middle Atlantic: Fount of Diversity

Since the earliest days of European colonization, the Middle Atlantic region has served as the proving ground for diversity. In 1609, Henry Hudson, an Englishman under contract to the Dutch West India Company, nosed the *Half Moon* into what would become New York harbor and opened the way for immigration. The first group of settlers to disembark at Manhattan were Walloons, French-speaking Belgians, followed soon thereafter by a modest influx of Netherlanders, Germans, and French. In the seventeenth century, no less than today, religious affiliation served as a badge of identity. Early reports filtering back to Amsterdam from New Netherland told of Huguenots, Mennonites, Brownists, Quakers, Presbyterians, Roman Catholics, even, according to a contemporary, "many atheists and various other servants of Baal."[1] English Puritans settled toward the eastern end of Long Island. Jews, seeking asylum, arrived in New Amsterdam from Recifé in 1654, following the Portuguese takeover of the erstwhile Dutch colony there. The English conquest of New Netherland a decade later added further to the diversity of the colony renamed in honor of the Duke of York; attempts by the new rulers to tame the religious and ethnic diversity of the colony met with considerable resistance.

Other colonies in the Middle Atlantic were also characterized by ethnoreligious diversity. Quakers and Scots-Irish Presbyterians, among many others, inhabited what is now New Jersey. Further south, the Swedes, flush from their crucial engagement in the Thirty Years War, sought to establish a beachhead in the New World with settlements along the Delaware River. Maryland was founded by Lord Calvert as a refuge for English Catholics but he recognized even from the beginning that Catholic settlers would have to accommodate believers from other traditions in order to

15

ensure toleration for themselves. In 1680, the English Quaker William Penn founded his "Holy Experiment" as a place of religious toleration that attracted Lutherans and Quakers, along with smaller groups such as Moravians, Mennonites, Amish, and Schwenckfelders.

The diversity in the Middle Atlantic persisted throughout the colonial period. When it came time for the framers of the Constitution to configure the relationship between church and state for the new nation, they looked not only to the notion of a "wall of separation" advanced by the Rhode Island Baptist Roger Williams but also to the Middle Atlantic multiplex ethnoreligious scene. The idea of doing without a state religion was alien to the eighteenth-century mind but New York had been functioning for decades with de facto disestablishment, proving that religious pluralism posed no threat to the secular order, and that government could function without the backing of a particular religion. Real liberty of worship in the American republic probably owes more to the fact that Pennsylvania's Holy Experiment actually worked than to any theory of church-state separation articulated by Thomas Jefferson.

Middle Atlantic diversity has continued unabated to the present. Waves of immigration in the nineteenth century—especially Irish (fleeing the potato famines) and, later, Italians—changed the character of Catholicism in the region and the growing Catholic presence led to a greater assertiveness in the public arena. Similarly, the arrival of Jews from eastern Europe toward the end of the nineteenth century led to tensions, and eventually to denominational differentiation within the Jewish community, a community that expressed a broad spectrum of approaches to assimilation into American society at large. By the middle decades of the twentieth century, however, the sharp edges had been rubbed off and the main ethnoreligious communities had settled into a regime of mutual familiarity and understanding nicely captured in the movies and television shows of Baltimore native Barry Levinson (most notably his 1982 coming-of-age film *Diner*).

In the wake of the Hart-Cellar Immigration Act of 1965, immigrants once again recast religious life in the Middle Atlantic. The abolition of the national quota system, which had been in place since 1924, opened the harbors of the Middle Atlantic to thousands of immigrants from Latin America and Asia. Catholic immigrants from Central and South America reshaped many parishes with their national shrines, saints, festivals, and religious practices. By the end of the twentieth century, Muslim mosques, Buddhist stupas, Hindu temples, Sikh gurdwaras, and Shinto shrines dotted not only the five boroughs of New York City but also Schenectady, New York, Allentown, Pennsylvania, and Elsmere, Delaware. According to the 2000 census, the Middle Atlantic ranked second among the regions of the country in foreign-born population. At 14 percent, this was substantially lower than the Pacific region's 25 percent but it encompassed greater geographical diversity. Where nine out of ten foreign-born residents of the Pacific came from either Latin America (55 percent) or Asia (34 percent), the foreign-born of the Middle Atlantic included nearly a quarter from Europe (as opposed to 8 percent in the Pacific) and more than three times as many from Africa (4.3 percent versus 1.3 percent). More than anything else, however, what sets the Middle Atlantic apart is a public culture in which religion serves less as a unique feature of personal identity than as one among a number of indicators—ethnicity, race, geography, social class, even sexual orientation—that mark out particular communities.

After World War II, when Americans began to think of themselves as a Judeo-Christian rather than a Christian country, it was the Middle Atlantic approach to religious pluralism that shaped the reconceptualization. New York City was where "Judeo-Christian" first came into common usage, via a series of conferences on Science, Philosophy, and Religion in Their Relation to the Democratic Way of Life, held during World War II at Columbia Teachers College. The term was imported to Washington by Dwight D. Eisenhower, who (having served as president of Columbia University) made this famous pronouncement at the Manhattan-based Freedoms Foundation on the eve of his election as president of the United States: "Our form of government has no sense unless it is founded in a deeply felt religious faith, and I don't care what it is. With us of course it is the Judeo-Christian creed but it must be a religion that all men are created equal."[2] But if Judeo-Christian was the umbrella term for common religious cause in the immediate postwar period, the charter of religious pluralism was Will Herberg's classic *Protestant-Catholic-Jew*, published in 1955.

Employing Marcus Hansen's Law of Third-Generation Return, Herberg argued that even as ethnic differences were disappearing in America, third-generation Americans were prepared to embrace the religious traditions of their immigrant grandparents (as their parents were not): "The newcomer is expected to change many things about him as he becomes American—nationality, language, culture. One thing, however, he is *not* expected to change—and that is his religion. And so it is religion that with the third generation has become the differentiating element and the context of self-identification and social location."[3] Herberg's postulate of the "triple melting pot" involved a triple sleight of hand—each component of which implicated the Middle Atlantic region. In the first place, only in the Middle Atlantic (and, really, only in New York City) could anyone have made a reasonable case that the religious scene was in fact shared on something like equal terms among Protestants, Catholics, and Jews. Second, the idea that religion constituted a fixed personal and social identity was far more plausible in the Middle Atlantic than it was in parts of the country where traditions of conversion and denomination-switching were common and widely recognized. Finally, it was precisely the close connection between ethnicity and religion in the Middle Atlantic generally—and in his own Jewish community in particular—that made it possible for Herberg to construe religion as the mechanism for preserving communal solidarity in an age when ethnic markers seemed to be in decline. To be sure, Herberg's theory did not remain uncontested, even on its home turf. Thus, in the introduction to the second (1970) edition of their 1963 volume, *Beyond the Melting Pot*, Nathan Glazer and Daniel Patrick Moynihan contended that race had superseded religion as the critical dividing line in the public life of New York City. If anything, Glazer and Moynihan (New York City natives both) simply sought to restore religion as one among several markers of communal identity in the public life of the city.[4]

During the Cold War, the Herbergian formulation suggested a way for Americans of different faiths to make common religious cause while retaining distinct, even mutually exclusive, communal identities. Today, in a country increasingly aware of its non-Judeo-Christians and its new immigrant streams, "Protestant-Catholic-Jew" may sound like a quaint reminder of a defunct and exclusionary religious regime. But in the Middle Atlantic, Herberg's theory still provides the best insight into the way religion functions in public life. It is a place where communal solidarity still matters a great deal, and where the community at large still tends to be conceived as an aggregation of communities more than of individuals. It is, moreover, a place where white Protestantism is still understood as quintessentially referring, as it did in the 1950s, to the mainline Protestantism of the white Anglo-Saxon Protestant; in fact, 70 percent of the white Protestants in the northeast (Middle Atlantic and New England) are mainliners, as compared to the other regions of the country, where they range from 20 percent to 50 percent. Finally, the Middle Atlantic is that part of the country where something like a power-sharing arrangement applies among the three Herbergian actors. A case in point is the balance of religious affiliation among the 15 top elected officials—governors and U.S. senators—of the five Middle Atlantic states as of the 2006 election: four Protestants, five Catholics, and six Jews.

THE PROTESTANT MOSAIC

One-third of the adults in the Middle Atlantic identify themselves as Protestants of one kind or another but that number understates the significance of the tradition in the region. Apart from Maryland, Protestants founded the seventeenth-century colonies that became the region's states. While formal religious establishments had short and checkered careers compared to the Standing Congregational Order in New England or to the Church of England in Virginia and the Carolinas, each of the Middle Atlantic colonies had multiple strong denominational presences throughout the era leading up to the Revolution. For several Protestant bodies, the Middle Atlantic is home turf—a place of residence for congregations, denominational leaders, and key support institutions such as colleges, seminaries, and denominational headquarters. To this day, the Middle Atlantic ranks second among all regions in the proportion of Lutherans, Episcopalians, Congregationalists, and Pietists and Anabaptists in the population. Collectively, the free denominations and traditions formed a de facto Protestant hegemony for the region's first 200 years. Even though this hegemony gave way before the immigration of Roman Catholics in the later nineteenth century, established Protestant institutions and cultural patterns continue to influence the character of the region.

Because Protestantism is a category that encompasses more theological, political, and ecclesiastical diversity than it rules out, it is always necessary to know what kind of Protestants one is dealing with and what role they play in the local religious ecology. In the Middle Atlantic, there are two main Protestant types, based on geography. To the east of the Alleghenics, Catskills, and Adirondacks lies a liberal zone; to the west, a conservative one. In upstate New York, western Pennsylvania, and western Maryland are towns and cities where Bible reading in the public schools persisted well into the 1960s and student prayer fellowships continue to flourish in public high schools, only somewhat tempered by the attempts of various civil liberties groups to do away with them. This area features large concentrations of Protestants who tend to vote more Republican in state and national elections than their downstate and eastern counterparts. But it is important to recognize that these "Bible believing" folks are not, for the most part, members of evangelical denominations. (Only when moving southward toward the Baltimore/Washington metropolitan area does the pattern begin to tip away from mainline dominance as more Southern Baptists are added into the denominational mix.) The evangelical churches are weak in the region because in the west one does not have to leave a mainline church in order to be part of a conservative and evangelical Christian fellowship. The Presbyterians, Episcopalians, and United Methodists of western Pennsylvania, for example, have been among the most conservative in their voting patterns within their respective denominational families when it comes to proposals for women's ordination, gay ordination, church recognition of gay marriage, evangelization of Jews, and the morality of abortion. It says something about this subregion that, in the current split in the national Episcopal

Church, the Bishop of the Pittsburgh diocese, Robert Duncan, has been a major player on the conservative side.

The cities of Pittsburgh and Buffalo help illustrate how politics, policy, and Protestantism are affected by the regional divide—and how it is more than simply a reflection of urban-rural differences. Pittsburgh was a trading city dominated in its early days by an elite of Scots-Irish Presbyterian merchants. In Buffalo, the local elites almost universally possessed English surnames when they founded the city's First Church of Christ in 1812. Through the nineteenth century, these two elites founded not only churches but libraries, schools, and other cultural institutions. Yet the success of their business enterprises brought in massive numbers of workers of neither Scots-Irish nor English stock—including large numbers of German and Irish Catholics and Slavic Catholics and Eastern Orthodox. Today, Protestantism in both cities is strongest in the outlying suburbs but huge church edifices and congregations remain from the heyday of their industrial elites—as does a conservative political tinge. Thus, whereas in Brooklyn and Philadelphia Al Gore recorded roughly four votes for every ballot marked for George W. Bush in the 2000 presidential election, in Allegheny (Pittsburgh) and Erie (Buffalo) counties, the margins were less than 60-40—comparable to Columbus, Ohio, or Davenport, Iowa. The strength of antiabortion sentiment in western Pennsylvania helps explain why it took an antiabortion Democrat, Bob Casey, Jr., to knock off two-term Republican incumbent Rick Santorum in the 2006 election for U.S. Senate.

East of the mountains, eastern Pennsylvania is where nearly every Protestant group—Lutherans, Quakers, Anglicans, Swiss Brethren, Presbyterians, Moravians, Mennonites, and German Reformed Christians—found an early home. Many went on to thrive in a place where no church or sect predominated and nearly all found the respect of their neighbors. In consequence, the state early on exemplified what would become the prevailing regional character of religious pluralism: a functioning ecology in which each community finds its niche under an umbrella of shared values. Thus, the western Pennsylvania conservative Anglo Protestants and the more moderate German-descended Protestants of eastern Pennsylvania have more in common with the other Protestants in their subregions than with their coreligionists on the other side of the mountains. What is particularly notable about Maryland and Delaware is the prevalence of Methodists. It was in these states that Methodism, a reform movement within the Church of England, was created as a separate American denomination at the end of the eighteenth century, and to this day nearly every community has a Methodist church, however small its congregation might be. Purveying a plainspoken gospel message offering an assurance of salvation, relying on itinerant clergy capable of sustaining small groups of the most modest means, Methodism was in its early days perfectly suited for a frontier society. Throughout the Middle Atlantic, where it retains a modest but ubiquitous presence, it helped shape a religious ecology of stable communities comfortable in their own skins and comfortable with their neighbors.

These days, no state captures the aboriginal community-based character of Middle Atlantic Protestantism better than New Jersey. In the highly dense, often impoverished urban areas, Protestants are likely to be members of historically African American churches, or first- or second-generation American members of charismatic churches. Leaders of African American churches have played such a key role in Democratic Party politics that their ability to get out the vote is widely viewed as a determinant of statewide and local election results. In places like Newark, Passaic, and Patterson, those filling the churches of colonial derivation (Episcopalian, Reformed, or Presbyterian) are likely to be Korean, Chinese, African, and Caribbean. In contrast to the radical Protestant ethnic diversity of New Jersey's cities are the suburban and small town Protestant churches whose members are white and native born— and possibly more Republican than white, native-born Protestants in any other part of the country. But these are moderate Republicans, notably pro-choice on abortion and supportive of gay rights. Theirs is a homeowners' Republicanism, grounded in a determination to resist the urban-inflected taxation, public works, and education-equalization policies of the Democrats in Trenton's statehouse. As in the rest of the region, but even more so, their religion is not so much an independent variable as part of a communal identity, inextricably entwined with race, class, ethnicity, and where one lives.

In the mind of the Middle Atlantic, Protestantism as a whole is still typified by these socially liberal suburbanites at the top of the pecking order. Indeed, it was here that the concept of the white Anglo-Saxon Protestant (WASP) emerged after World War II. The term was first formally deployed by political scientist Andrew Hacker, a native of New York City then teaching at Cornell University, in a 1957 article that makes clear it was then in wider use as academic shorthand ("in the cocktail party jargon of the sociologists").[5] A few years later, it was popularized by University of Pennsylvania sociologist and Philadelphia native E. Digby Baltzell in his 1964 volume, *The Protestant Establishment: Aristocracy and Caste in America.* Thus did the American elite become transformed, via Middle Atlantic rhetorical alchemy, into another of the region's ethnoreligious tribes like the Irish Catholics, the German Jews, and the Greek Orthodox. As Glazer and Moynihan put it in 1970, "It is a created identity, and largely forged in New York City, in order to identify those who are not otherwise ethnically identified and who, while a small minority in the city, represent what is felt to be the 'majority' for the rest of the country."[6] For sure, the demotion to tribal status did not efface WASP-dom's own hegemonic pretensions. These were exemplified in the National Cathedral of the Episcopal Church in Washington, D.C., constructed between 1907 and 1990, which came to function as the chapel of the United States in mourning. When thousands were killed in the attacks of September 11, 2001, it was in the National Cathedral that the nation's leaders gathered to pray, to grieve, and to pledge fidelity to the memory of those killed. Though the Roman Catholics and the Presbyterians also have self-described "national" ecclesiastical edifices capable of hosting large services of this type, it is the Gothic pile set in an archetypal English cathedral close that bills itself as "A National House of Prayer for All People."

Historically, New York City served as the more or less official capital of the country's pan-Protestant establishment. In the nineteenth century, it was where the Protestant denominations held their annual meetings, along with the interdenominational societies devoted to spreading the gospel, eradicating slavery, limiting the consumption of alcohol, and advancing the humane treatment of animals. In due course, many of the denominations made the city their headquarters, as did their umbrella organizations, the Federal Council of Churches and then the National Council of Churches, which represents most mainline Protestant bodies in an ecumenical council. For decades the Interchurch Center at 475 Riverside Drive was the home not only of the National Council but also of the Presbyterian Church (USA), the Reformed Church in America, the United Church of Christ, Church World Service, several international mission agencies, and the Board of Global Missions of the United Methodist Church. Several of these bodies moved to locations that were geographically more central to the rest of the United States in the 1980s and 1990s, but all continue to maintain a presence in New York.

The habits of pan-Protestantism helped establish a tradition of ecumenical cooperation and interfaith undertakings. These are so ingrained in the New York metropolitan area that what seems natural to representatives of even conservative Protestant groups can appear unintelligible and unforgivable to their co-religionists in other regions. The Rev. David Benke, the regional leader of the theologically conservative Lutheran Church-Missouri Synod (LCMS), found himself being ordered to apologize for mixing Christian and non-Christian beliefs at the nationally televised prayer service held at Yankee Stadium following the September 11 terrorist attacks. On September 23, 2001, he took part in the service, standing alongside representatives of other Christian, Muslim, Jewish, Hindu, and Sikh groups. Benke asked those in the stadium to join hands and pray with him "on this field of dreams turned into God's house of prayer." Though he ended his prayer "in the precious name of Jesus," Benke soon found himself charged with offenses that ultimately led to his suspension.

In a denominational decision reached the next summer, the Rev. Wallace Schulz wrote: "To participate with pagans in an interfaith service and, additionally, to give the impression that there might be more than one God, is an extremely serious offense against the God of the Bible." The New York press treated the story with outrage and LCMS adherents in the region expressed disappointment but clearly ecumenism in New York City extends farther than it does in some other parts of the country.[7]

In the life of the city itself, liberal ecumenism found expression in the Social Gospel, a movement of thought and action that was committed to help the poor and disenfranchised by Christianizing the social order of industrial urban capitalism. Its foremost figure was Walter Rauschenbusch, a Baptist pastor whose father came to the United States from Germany as a missionary and stayed to teach at Rochester Theological Seminary. Rauschenbusch's views were fundamentally shaped by his experience leading the Second German Baptist of New York in the gritty Hell's Kitchen neighborhood on the west side of Manhattan. It was, he believed, the church's responsibility to devote itself to social reform via practical efforts to meet the physical and political as well as the spiritual needs of the poor. Convinced that this work needed to proceed on a nondenominational basis, in 1892 Rauschenbusch organized the Brotherhood of the Kingdom to "infuse the religious spirit" into secular reform efforts. During the heyday of progressive reform, he made his views broadly influential throughout mainline Protestantism through such works as *Christianity and the Social Crisis* and *Christianizing the Social Order*.

As a national movement, the Social Gospel ran out of steam by the end of World War I but the basic social orientation of Protestantism in New York City to this day reflects its take on modern life. Protestantism in New York City is liberal, engaged, and political to the point of being confrontational. Nowhere is this more evident than in the city's leading black churches. From Adam Clayton Powell, Sr., to Calvin O. Butts III, a succession of pastors of the Abyssinian Baptist Church in Harlem, for example, have inspired a large following of middle-class blacks to see social and political causes as an essential part of Christian life. At the height of his power in the 1960s, Adam Clayton Powell, Jr., was one of the most visible members of the United States House of Representatives, serving as chairman of the House Education and Labor Committee. Rev. Floyd Flake represented the Sixth District of New York in the U.S. House from 1986 to 1997, all the while serving as senior pastor of the Allen African Methodist Episcopal Church in Jamaica, Queens. And Brooklyn native Al Sharpton, a Pentecostal minister and sometime road manager for the singer James Brown, became a significant political player in national Democratic politics.

Not that religious-political leadership in post-World War II New York was merely an African American phenomenon. As late as the 1980s, William Sloane Coffin, as pastor of the Riverside Church on the upper west side of Manhattan, used his pulpit and energized his congregation to push for a reduction of nuclear armaments and to resist the policies of the Reagan administration in Central America. Yet the retreat of mainline Protestantism in the waning years of the twentieth century left it to other clergy to lead the charge for moral reform and to resist various forms of evil in the city. In 1999, for example, it was Sharpton who took charge of organizing a rolling series of demonstrations to protest the killing by police of Amadou Diallo, an African Muslim. In due course, the protesters involved rabbis, imams, black Protestant pastors, and Catholic priests, and led to dramatic encounters between Butts and Mayor Rudolf Giuliani, and between Cardinal John O'Connor and city cops.[8] Significantly, the protests also enlisted members of a host of city tribes defined in other than religious terms: labor unions, gays and lesbians, academicians, antiwar activists. As the *Village Voice*'s Peter Noel described a March 26 demonstration in front of police headquarters, "It has been six hours since the Reverend Al Sharpton orchestrated the largest multiethnic sit-in of his 15-day campaign of civil disobedience."[9] Altogether, the Diallo affair resulted in Muslims achieving new status as one of the "ethnic" communities to be reckoned with in New York City politics.

New York City stands at one end of the spectrum of Middle Atlantic religious empowerment. At the other end, the religious order in Washington, D.C., is unstable and disempowered. The nation's capital is a majority African American city whose brief years of supposed home-rule have brought leaders up from the ranks of the black churches at odds with the 535 members of Congress who ultimately hold the purse strings. The power of the African American congregations in the city's neighborhoods is not the power to shape legislation but rather to maintain and sustain life in the midst of urban existence poised between government service jobs on the one hand and street crime and drug violence on the other. In recent years, there has been a large out-migration of African Americans and their churches from the district to the Maryland suburbs—most notably to Prince George's County, where over one-third of religious adherents now belong to historically African American denominations.

CATHOLIC PLURALISTS

Catholics have been present in the Middle Atlantic for nearly as long as Protestants (albeit as a small minority in the early days). Maryland was settled in 1634 by relatives and associates of a British convert to Catholicism, George Calvert, Lord Baltimore, who died in England the same year as the colony's founding. Calvert's "vision," according to the historian Thomas W. Spalding, entailed "interfaith harmony, public service, and attachment to such American principles as religious liberty and separation of Church and state."[10] The early years of the Maryland experiment indicated that Catholics fared best in British colonies when Christian fervor was at low tide. Although Catholics were prohibited from holding public office in Pennsylvania until 1775, the historian John Tracy Ellis still described the Catholic experience there as "the most pleasant and positive of any of the original thirteen colonies." The first permanent urban Catholic foundation in the British colonies was St. Joseph's Church, established on Walnut Street in Philadelphia in 1733. In 1789, John Carroll, scion of Maryland's leading Catholic family, became bishop of the nation's first "See," the diocese of Baltimore, which initially included the entire United States. Carroll's election by the 30 Catholic priests scattered around the country—as distinct from the customary papal appointment—was partly the result of diplomacy by Benjamin Franklin, U.S. Minister to France, and others with an interest in promoting the compatibility of the church with American democracy. For his part, Carroll was a "republican" who advocated the election of bishops by those he termed "the older and more worthy clergy."

The tidal wave of Irish immigration that hit American shores in the wake of the Great Famine of 1845 transformed Middle Atlantic Catholicism. Most of these refugees landed in New York, and most remained in the city and region, especially when compared with the vast numbers of German Catholic (and Protestant) immigrants who followed the Irish inundation and were much more likely to make their way to the nation's interior regions.[11] The Catholic Church played the central role in transforming the Irish arrivals from peasants into urban Americans. In the absence of public agencies dedicated to serving the newly arrived, the church tended to their material as well as their spiritual needs. The support was particularly welcome since the Irish did not receive the warmest of welcomes in Philadelphia, New York, or the smaller Middle Atlantic cities. In May of 1844, two Catholic churches were burned by nativists in Philadelphia's Kensington neighborhood and more than 20 people were killed in July of that year when a mob of thousands attacked members of the state militia guarding St. Philip Neri Church in nearby Southwark. In New York, the Irish-born bishop John Hughes announced that if any Catholic churches in the city were burned, "New York would be another Moscow." His churches went unharmed. The most powerful American prelate of the mid-nineteenth century, Hughes laid the cornerstone of Manhattan's massive St. Patrick's

Cathedral in 1858, triumphantly proclaiming before a crowd of more than 100,000 that New York's Irish Catholics could "laugh to scorn" those who ridiculed their customs and religion. If any site can be considered the symbolic capital of Catholicism in America today, it is St. Patrick's.

Ethnic parishes were the principal vehicle of Catholic Americanization, a paradox rooted in the nature of ethnic and neighborhood politics in the urban northeast. For immigrants did not simply replicate the traditions of the old country but created new hybrid forms of identity: Italian Americans, for example, initially identified themselves almost entirely with a village or at most a region of Italy, but found themselves part of a much larger collectivity in American cities. Members of these newly constituted ethnic groups—including Poles, Slovaks, Lithuanians, Germans, and Hungarians—sought to worship with their compatriots in a parish led by a pastor who shared their language and culture. The first Italian American parish in the United States, St. Mary Magdalen da Pazzi, was founded in Philadelphia in 1857; by the early twentieth century Italian Americans outnumbered the Irish in many of the largest cities in the region, including Jersey City, Newark, and New York City. The "inland" dioceses of Pittsburgh (1843), Albany (1847), Buffalo (1847), and Scranton (1868) were established under Irish American bishops but quickly attracted a larger percentage of eastern European immigrants than their counterpart dioceses on the eastern seaboard. Ethnic conflicts with Irish bishops in the interior Middle Atlantic grew common by the late nineteenth century.

Notwithstanding the influx of other immigrant streams, the Irish stranglehold on the hierarchy in the Middle Atlantic was near total from the midnineteenth century to the mid-twentieth. This "hibernarchy" tended to view Irish American parishes as simply "American" with all others classified as "national." Interethnic discord was a major element of the "Americanism" controversy of the late nineteenth century—a conflict that pitted largely Irish American bishops against Germans and others who believed the Church was adapting too readily to the American environment at the expense of cultural traditions imported by non-Irish immigrants. The Germans, located mostly in the Midwest, were the most vocal in resisting the "Americanizing" impulse of Irish American bishops, calling on Rome to condemn Americanism and finding substantial support for their cause.

The most influential spokesmen for the Americanist camp was Cardinal James Gibbons of Baltimore, a son of Irish immigrants who emerged during the late nineteenth century as the leader of the national hierarchy. In 1884, Gibbons presided over the Third Plenary Council of Baltimore, which mandated a parochial education for every Catholic child and produced a new catechism that became standard nationwide. Gibbons objected to intervention in U.S. Catholic affairs by "officious gentlemen" in Europe, promising: "Loyalty to God's church and to our country—this [is] our religious and political faith." In 1889, Gibbons secured the Vatican's approval to establish the Catholic University of America in Washington, D.C., and this institution remained a center for Americanism even after Pope Leo XIII condemned it as heresy in a letter to Gibbons in 1899. In 1919, Msgr. John A. Ryan, a faculty member and protégé of Gibbons', drafted a *Bishop's Program on Social Reconstruction* that signaled the American church's commitment to the pursuit of social justice for all Americans, harking back to the activist, optimistic Maryland tradition of Calvert and Carroll.

While historians of American Catholicism have been preoccupied with Americanism as an ecclesiastical controversy, a more enduring, nontheological version of Americanism emerged among the urban laity in the Middle Atlantic region in the late nineteenth and early twentieth centuries. Immigrant Catholics, whether Irish, German, Italian, Polish, or Latino, carried to the United States a great variety of street entertainments and a zest for holiday and carnival rooted in folk traditions. Not only could these things be commercialized but they also reflected an untroubled acceptance of gaiety that made possible an enormous range of other commercial pastimes. Mass-circulation newspapers, nickelodeons, movie palaces, and commercial radio broadcasting outlets all targeted Catholic audiences. These new institutions in turn reflected Catholic sensibilities, which were never shaped in isolation but were the product of interactions with other urban groups, particularly Jews and—especially in the years following World War I—African Americans. This model of popular Catholicism as highly interactive was particularly evident in New York City. The connections between Jews and Catholics on the streets of lower Manhattan, for example, prefigured the almost reflexive tendency of Jewish producers in Hollywood to "synthesize the Christian religion in the person of an Irish priest," as Daniel Patrick Moynihan once put it.

The story of post–World War II America involves a narrative of suburbanization, by which an urban immigrant style of Catholicism yields virtually overnight to a homogenized, post-ethnic pastoral retreat. Certainly, Middle Atlantic Catholics were well represented in the suburban experiments that blossomed in the potato fields of eastern Long Island and the meadows of South Jersey. A larger number, however, remained behind in core cities and older, inner-ring suburban neighborhoods. Tied to parish churches and schools in a way their white Jewish and Protestant neighbors were not, ethnic Catholics found themselves on the front lines of the postwar crisis of the cities—particularly in opposition to struggles for fair housing and integrated schools and access to employment for waves of African American migrants from the South. Yet Middle Atlantic Catholicism was not only about a rejection of postwar social reforms.

The role of John F. Kennedy's administration in advancing the cause of civil rights and social justice more broadly is well known, but the centrality of Kennedy brother-in-law Sargent Shriver has often been overlooked. Where the Boston-bred Kennedy kept his Catholicism under wraps, Shriver was an extraordinarily devout "public Catholic" in the tradition of his Maryland ancestors. His paternal grandfather was a former seminary classmate and close friend of Cardinal Gibbons and the young Shriver served as an altar boy at Masses celebrated by Gibbons at the Shriver family's summer home in rural Maryland. By the time he married Eunice Kennedy in 1953, he was well established as a leading Catholic activist. His leadership of the Peace Corps under President Kennedy, and later of the War on Poverty in the Lyndon B. Johnson administration, was deeply grounded in the traditions of Catholic social thought. Like so many Catholic public figures, Shriver was also deeply influenced by the Second Vatican Council (1962–1964), whose key documents called on Catholics to embrace the aspirations and sufferings of the entire world, including the non-Christian world.[12]

The Catholic idealism represented by Shriver also shaped movements for better relations between white and Latino Catholics of all colors in the cities of the Middle Atlantic. By the mid-1950s, Puerto Ricans made up fully one-quarter of Catholics in the Archdiocese of New York, but church leaders proved incapable of responding to this challenge until a young European-bred priest named Ivan Illich decided to tailor his ministry to the needs of Puerto Ricans in the Washington Heights parish he served. The federal Immigration Reform Act of 1965 led to even more profound demographic changes in Middle Atlantic Catholicism. Hudson County, New Jersey, once the redoubt of Irish and Italian Americans, gave rise to a Latino majority by the 1990s. Within this Latino population there was also extraordinary diversity, with the Cuban Americans who had been present in Union City and west New York and the Puerto Ricans long established in Jersey City now joined by large communities of immigrants from Ecuador, Guatemala, and Mexico, among many other countries. Jersey City is also home to a very large and deeply Catholic Filipino community that worships alongside Korean Americans at St. Aloysius Church on West Side Avenue. Similarly diverse parishes are now found in urban centers throughout the region. (The Roman Catholic Church no longer designates parishes as "national" or "ethnic," but encourages cooperation among groups within parishes.)

The "liminality" of Middle Atlantic Catholic life in the 1960s and 1970s—poised awkwardly between urban ethnic tradition and the liberating potential of social mobility—was treated in some remarkable literary works of the period, from Tom McHale's *Principato* (1970), set in south Philadelphia, to Mary Gordon's *Final Payments* (1978), whose characters are rooted in Queens, New York. These works and others treated characters pulled between the inheritance of ethnic separatism and the ambivalent "freedom" represented by geographical, social, and sexual mobility—a testimony to the "in-between" character of Middle Atlantic Catholic life. New England society was so stratified, anti-Catholicism so deeply embedded, and Irish, Italian, Portuguese, and French-Canadian immigrants so numerous and so heavily concentrated in urban areas that Catholic separatism was virtually inevitable. In the Midwest, German Catholics may have battled Irish bishops over the latter's alleged Americanism but they themselves lived alongside Protestants in cities, small towns, and rural communities, and never worried about being considered un-American. Forging a middle path, Middle Atlantic Catholicism has been both engaged with the broader culture and conscious of its distinctiveness. The emerging field of American Catholic studies draws much of its energy from the experiences of Middle Atlantic scholars, raised during the lengthy postwar era of Catholic transformation and committed to their religious tradition while deeply attracted to a form of cultural pluralism that Middle Atlantic Catholics helped create decades ago.

In the wake of the sex abuse scandal that began in 2002, the closing of schools and parishes was certain to aggravate the disaffection of many Catholics with the institutional church and its leaders. While dioceses of the Middle Atlantic may not have suffered as badly or received as much attention as the Boston Archdiocese, the effects of the scandal were deeply felt and ongoing. In Philadelphia in particular the fallout from the scandal was substantial; as high-level diocesan administrators faced scrutiny for decisions made during the regime of former Cardinal Anthony Bevilaqua. Other dioceses, particularly Metuchen, New Jersey, under the leadership of Bishop Paul Bootkoski, earned high praise from abuse victims and their advocates. The nation's first memorial to sex abuse victims was dedicated in April 2004 at St. Joseph's Church in Mendham, New Jersey, where a 400-pound basalt millstone was installed on the grounds of the church by the current pastor, Msgr. Kenneth Lasch, to commemorate more than a dozen victims of Rev. James Hanley, who was assigned to St. Joseph's in the 1970s and 1980s. The millstone recalls the passage from the Gospel according to Matthew in which Jesus asserts that whoever harms children would be better off "to have a millstone hung around his neck and [be] thrown into the depth of the sea."

Msgr. Lasch evoked a tradition of Middle Atlantic Catholicism in which the realities of suffering and conflict were acknowledged and confronted. But the current church leadership in the region does not generally recognize this long tradition as a source of strength. Many prominent bishops currently serving in the region were sent there from other parts of the country and do not share the experience of their constituents. Ideological rigidity has come to be equated with obedience to the *magisterium*, the universal church's teaching authority. For example, when Archbishop John Myers (an Illinois native) suggested that Catholics supporting abortion rights no longer receive holy communion, State Senator Bernard Kenny of Hoboken—a deeply devout Catholic—announced that he was leaving to join the Episcopal Church. Kenny's painful defection powerfully symbolized the deep rupture within the Church.[13]

In September 2004 the Roman Catholic Archdiocese of New York confirmed speculation that Democratic presidential candidate John Kerry—a Roman Catholic who like virtually all national Democratic figures supports abortion rights—would not be invited to the Alfred E. Smith Memorial Foundation Dinner, a highly visible charity event hosted each October by the leader of the archdiocese, currently Cardinal Edward Egan. (For the sake of balance, President George W. Bush was not invited either.) Presidential candidates are customarily invited to the dinner, though Bill Clinton was not in 1996 due to his support of abortion rights. As the 2004 election approached, pundits noted that where Catholic politicians had once struggled for acceptance from voters outside the church, their greatest challenge now came from within, as bishops sought to reaffirm church teachings on moral issues by highlighting the unorthodoxy of prominent public figures, nearly all of them Democrats.

To be sure, Catholic politics in the Middle Atlantic region had always been contentious, including internally. When John F. Kennedy appeared at the Smith Dinner in October 1960, his "religion problem" entailed not the suspicions of non-Catholics but the fairly active hostility of the dinner's host, New York's Cardinal Francis Spellman, the nation's most powerful prelate. Spellman's unhappiness at the prospect of being eclipsed by Kennedy as the nation's leading Catholic was but one among his numerous grievances with the young presidential candidate. Kennedy rose above Spellman's tepid introduction at the dinner and delivered a witty, self-deprecating speech that confirmed his stature as a cosmopolitan figure seemingly unencumbered by Catholic tribalism. But there is little question that a decision to bar John Kerry from attendance at the Al Smith dinner violated the Catholic spirit embodied by Smith himself. The first Roman Catholic to secure the presidential nomination of a major party, Smith was the quintessential Catholic urban Democrat, a multiethnic (Irish, Italian, and German) product of the streets of New York whose faith was grounded in a practical spirituality shaped by the cultural diversity of his upbringing. From the vantage point of New York City in 1928, Smith's appeal was irresistible—but the rest of the country, still infected with anti-Catholicism, didn't see it that way.

More than half a century after Smith's failed presidential run, another Catholic governor of New York State, Mario Cuomo, addressed an issue Smith was never obliged to face. Speaking at the University of Notre Dame in September 1984, Cuomo asserted that "as a Catholic, I have accepted certain answers as the right ones for myself and my family," including a belief that abortion is morally wrong. Yet Cuomo went on to argue that "the Catholic who holds political office in a pluralistic democracy . . . bears special responsibility . . . to help create conditions . . . where everyone who chooses may hold beliefs different from specifically Catholic ones—sometimes even contradictory to them."[14] The theological legitimacy of this position was, and continues to be, deeply contested but there is no doubt that Cuomo's views were authentically grounded in his early days in Ozone Park, Queens, where an Italian American immigrant community defined itself as part of a multiethnic, multireligious metropolis, and indeed, made the celebration of such diversity a constitutive element of Catholic spirituality. A subsequent Catholic Republican mayor of New York City, Rudolph Giuliani, shared this spiritual worldview with Cuomo. In the hours after the attacks of September 11, 2001, Giuliani insisted that New Yorkers would demonstrate respect for members of all religious traditions precisely by virtue of being authentic New Yorkers, which is a medium through which Giuliani expresses his fidelity to his brand of urban Catholicism.

The tension between exemplars of this tradition and church leaders in the Middle Atlantic is real, and is most likely to endure. In 2004 John Kerry carried all the states of the Middle Atlantic, heavily Catholic as they are, despite the clear if unofficial opposition of most of the region's Catholic prelates. Kerry was, however, singularly unimpressive in his handling of the "Catholic issue," which by 2004 entailed not his fitness to run for president as a Catholic but his ability to ground his positions in a sensibility that was recognizably Catholic, if not to bishops then at least to a substantial portion of the church community. Kerry failed badly on that score, not only because he seemed untutored in church teachings but, even more, because his experience in the largely religion-free political culture of New England did not equip him to carve out the kind of positive public religious identity that the country demands of its presidents. A New England liberal, he lacked grounding in the multiethnic political culture of the Middle Atlantic—a politics that made space for a non- or even an anticlerical Catholicism, and opened the door to an "Americanism" that has its roots in the first Catholic settlement in the region.

JEWISH HEARTLAND

In numbers and influence, the Jewish communities of the Middle Atlantic region so predominate within the overall American Jewish population that their story is inseparable from that of American Jewry as a whole. The key to understanding American Jewish life, in its national as well as its Middle Atlantic manifestations, is the fact that America has afforded Jews as individuals, and Judaism as a religion, an unprecedented degree of freedom and equality. The seedbed for this circumstance is the Middle Atlantic generally, and above all New York, where Jews voted and were eligible to be elected to office throughout the eighteenth century. Indeed, at the time of the American Revolution, New York was the only colony with no restrictions on Jewish voting and office-holding. Only after the Revolution would other states gradually modify their constitutions to eliminate political bias against non-Christians. The federal government, established under the Constitution of 1787—written in Philadelphia and originally based, it should be recalled, in New York City—included no Christian phraseology and barred any religious test for holding office. It thus brought into existence, at least on the federal level, "a government where all Religious societies are on an Equal footing," as requested in a letter to the Constitutional Convention from Jonas Phillips, a leading member of Philadelphia's Jewish community.[15]

Since then, American Jews have tended to congregate in the Middle Atlantic, both because that was where most immigrants landed and because the region's dynamic economy provided jobs and upward mobility. The great majority of Jews living in the region are descendants of two waves of immigration from eastern and central Europe. The first consisted of the two million Jews, primarily from Russia (including much of what had been Poland), Romania, and the Hapsburg Empire, who entered the United States between the 1880s and 1914, the bulk of whom settled in or near their Middle Atlantic ports of embarkation. This migration was largely cut off by World War I and the restrictive immigration laws adopted in the 1920s. The second wave was made up of refugees from, and survivors of, the Holocaust, amounting to some 300,000 Jews; these too tended to settle in the region.

The demographic predominance of the Middle Atlantic region was most pronounced in the first half of the twentieth century, reaching some 70 percent of the American Jewish population in the 1930s. Since World War II, migration to the Sunbelt—particularly California and Florida—has cut into Middle Atlantic hegemony, reducing the proportion to between 45 and 50 percent. At nearly six percent of the Middle Atlantic population, Jews today are more than three times as thick on the ground as they are in the rest of the country. Within the region as in other parts of the country, they have over the past half-century migrated away from small towns and mid-sized cities—indeed, from all cities proper—and into the suburbs of the largest metropolitan areas. A 2002 demographic study of Jews in the New York City area showed that for the first time in well over a century there were fewer than a million Jews living in the city proper.[16] But the New York City metropolitan area as a whole is home to a third of all American Jews, some two million people—almost 10 percent of the total metropolitan population. The Philadelphia-Wilmington (Delaware)-Atlantic City (New Jersey) area contains the country's fourth largest concentration of Jews, a total of 285,000, while Washington, D.C., and its suburbs come in eighth with 215,000, and Baltimore tenth with 106,000. Over 41 percent of America's Jews reside in these four metropolitan areas.

But the Middle Atlantic is even more significant for American Jewish life institutionally than it is demographically. The region is home to a plethora of national and local voluntary organizations—large and small, religious, philanthropic, cultural, social, and political. Of those dealing with what is known as "community relations" (the non-Jewish world), 27 out of 29 have Middle Atlantic headquarters. Of Israel-related organizations (many of them set up to raise money for specific Israeli institutions), 85 out of 88 are Middle Atlantic. And of the Jewish religious and educational bodies, 52 out of 61 are located there.[17] New York, the effective capital of Jewish America, is home to almost all the national Jewish agencies engaged in community-relations work and/or combating anti-Semitism, although in recent years these have established Washington offices as well. They include, most importantly, the American Jewish Committee, American Jewish Congress, the Anti-Defamation League as well as the coordinating bodies of the American Jewish community: the Conference of Presidents of Major American Jewish Organizations, which represents 52 national agencies largely on matters relating to Israel and the Middle East; United Jewish Communities (formerly the Council of Jewish Federations), which seeks—not always successfully—to coordinate the allocations to Jewish domestic and overseas causes of monies collected by Jewish philanthropic federations in local communities; and the Jewish Council for Public Affairs (JCPA, formerly the National Jewish Community Relations Advisory Council), which tries (again, with mixed results) to develop consensus positions on domestic and international issues of concern to American Jews for advocacy use by local Jewish community-relations agencies.

Washington has, in fact, grown in importance in Jewish public life. The most politically effective American Jewish organization, the American Israel Public Affairs Committee (AIPAC), is headquartered there. With convenient access to the U.S. administration and Congress, AIPAC is the primary pro-Israel lobby in the country, with grassroots members in every state and congressional district. Also based in the capital are the National Jewish Democratic Council and the Republican Jewish Coalition, which engage in outreach to Jewish voters on behalf of the two major parties while at the same time apprising party leadership of Jewish concerns. Hillel, which services Jewish college students on hundreds of campuses around the country, is headquartered in Washington as well. Not to be underestimated in symbolic importance is the United States Holocaust Memorial Museum, which is federally chartered and located near the National Mall in Washington. First proposed by the Carter Administration in 1980 and opened for visitors in 1993, its creation and location signify the central role that the memory of the Nazi Holocaust plays in American Jewish life and the clout that the Jewish community wields in national politics.

The actor Marlon Brando, in a 1996 television interview, claimed that "per capita, Jews have contributed more to American—the best of American—culture than any other single group." The Middle Atlantic has produced most of the great American Jewish writers, and much of their work reflects that background. The line goes from New Yorkers Abraham Cahan (himself an immigrant), to Henry Roth, Phillip Roth (Newark, New Jersey), Bernard Malamud, Chaim Potok, Cynthia Ozick, and Isaac Bashevis Singer, another immigrant.[18] But it is in American popular culture that Middle Atlantic Jews have had their greatest impact. From Irving Berlin to Stephen Sondheim, the world of Broadway has been "inescapably Jewish."[19] It was in the heavily Jewish lower east side of New York that movie theaters got their start, and although the motion picture industry moved to Hollywood in the 1920s, its movers and shakers were almost all Middle Atlantic (mostly New York) Jews. The first "talking" picture, of course, was *The Jazz Singer* (1927), in which Al Jolson portrayed the son of a lower east side cantor who must choose between following in his father's footsteps or entering the new world of jazz music. Likewise, radio and television features a strong Middle Atlantic Jewish presence, including executives like William Paley (CBS) and David Sarnoff (NBC) as well as innumerable comics. All in all, American popular culture has become so saturated with media-generated "Jewish" humor that it is no longer easy to tell "Jewish" and "American" apart.

With the numbers, the institutions, and the cultural throw-weight, Middle Atlantic Jews are the country's most "Jewish" Jews. This is clear from the measures of Jewish identification employed in the 2000–2001 *National Jewish Population Survey*, which (in accord with U.S. Census designations) subsumes the Middle Atlantic into a "Northeast" region that includes the substantially smaller Jewish communities of New England. These measures are: having at least half of one's closest friends Jews; attending a Passover Seder; lighting

Shabbat and Hanukkah candles; fasting on Yom Kippur; keeping a kosher home; having visited Israel; and contributing money to a Jewish cause. However, northeastern Jews are somewhat less likely than Jews in some other regions to belong to a synagogue or to other Jewish organizations, undoubtedly because the density of Jewish population makes such formal membership less necessary for the establishment of Jewish connections. That strong Jewish self-identification does not require synagogue membership points to the distinctiveness of Judaism over against Christianity. From its origins in the Middle East, Judaism retains a strong sense of peoplehood, such that it has proved impossible to entirely separate the "religious" from the "ethnic" dimension of this ancient form of communal identification. Not that there haven't been attempts to do so.

Of the three main branches of American Judaism—Reform, Orthodox, and Conservative[20]—Reform Judaism emerged first, in early nineteenth century Germany. Like the Reformation of Martin Luther and John Calvin from which it takes its name, Reform conceived its mission to be purging from Jewish practice what it considered medieval accretions, and returning to Biblical Judaism, by which it meant the emphasis of the Hebrew prophets on moral behavior rather than ritual. It spread rapidly in the United States with the immigration of Jews from central Europe in the nineteenth century. Based in that most German-American of cities, Cincinnati, it established its strongest presence in the heartland, whose often tiny Jewish communities felt most comfortable accommodating themselves to their non-Jewish neighbors with a form of Judaism that, in worship style and daily life, most resembled Protestant Christianity. In turn, "Orthodoxy" quickly became the banner for those Jews determined to preserve traditional Jewish liturgical and legal traditions. Over time they proved themselves a heterogeneous lot, ranging from those, like the Hasidim, who reject any contact with modern culture, to the so-called Modern Orthodox, who espouse a synthesis between Western culture and traditional religious observance.

Conservative Judaism evolved in late-nineteenth and early-twentieth century America as a middle stream among Jews eager to retain tradition but in modernized form. Conservative congregations afforded their members a traditional yet decorous Hebrew worship service featuring a measure of English in the liturgy, mixed-gender seating in contrast to Orthodox segregation of men and women, and a liberal interpretation of Jewish law (including a readiness to look the other way on violations of law such as driving on the Sabbath). In the years after World War II, Conservative Judaism outstripped Reform to become the largest of the three religious streams. It appealed to the children and grandchildren of eastern European immigrants because it embodied the ethnic folk religion of American Jews without discouraging assimilation to postwar suburban America. It was perfectly suited to the Middle Atlantic religious regime, and nowhere was it stronger. Beginning in the 1960s, however, the contradictions inherent in a movement dedicated to both tradition and change became evident. A campaign to ordain women, though ultimately victorious, led to defections from the old, and more are likely to occur from ongoing efforts to eliminate all barriers to the equality of gays.

In fact, between 1990 and 2000, the Conservative movement experienced a precipitous 10-percentage-point decline, from 43 to 33 percent, among the two-thirds of Jews nationwide declaring a religious or communal affiliation to the community, according to the 2000–2001 *National Jewish Population Survey*. On the left, Reform resumed its place as the biggest of the branches, increasing its share of the affiliated from 35 to 39 percent, while, on the right, Orthodoxy (which most observers had relegated to a slow death a few decades earlier) was thriving, its share of affiliated Jews up from 16 to 21 percent. The national rise in Orthodox identification was greatest in the Middle Atlantic. In the New York metropolitan area alone, the Orthodox portion of *all* Jews (as opposed to just the communally affiliated) rose from 13 to 19 percent between 1991 and 2001. Institutionally, this Orthodox surge has led to a proliferation of Jewish day schools and kosher eating establishments. Professional staff positions within the national Jewish agencies have increasingly been filled by young Orthodox men and women, both because Orthodoxy provides the largest pool of committed and knowledgeable applicants and because those doing the hiring do not share the anti-Orthodox prejudices that animated their predecessors in previous decades. It has also not gone unnoticed that large public events sponsored by the Jewish community, such as the annual parade for Israel down Fifth Avenue in New York City, the meetings of AIPAC (the primary pro-Israel lobby) with political figures, and the mass rally for Israel that drew thousands to Washington, D.C., on April 15, 2002, have been attended by large numbers of Orthodox activists, who often constitute a majority of the participants.

The new prominence of the Orthodox element has brought with it a heightened Orthodox sense of triumphalism as well, creating tensions with other Jews. One common complaint is that Orthodox families send their children to Jewish day schools rather than the public schools, and yet use their numbers to gain representation on local school boards, which they then exploit to benefit the day schools. Another—which Orthodox Jews vehemently deny—is that the Orthodox treat other members of the faith as if they were not authentic Jews, making them feel guilty for keeping their businesses open and driving on the Sabbath, and discouraging their children from playing with Jewish boys and girls who do not attend day schools. On several college campuses in the Middle Atlantic region, the representation of Orthodox students is so high and their Jewish activity so intensive, that complaints have been raised by non-Orthodox students who feel excluded from the Jewish campus community. And unlike the more liberal pattern of many of their predecessors a generation ago, Orthodox rabbis today will not participate in joint programs with their Reform and Conservative counterparts—a policy that the Orthodox justify on the grounds that they do not wish to suggest that the other movements are legitimate. It is no surprise that this argument enrages the non-Orthodox. In certain neighborhoods, existing non-Orthodox Jewish communities have attempted to discourage Orthodox "invasions."

No less remarkable than the growth of Orthodoxy has been the jump in religiously unaffiliated Jews. Between 1990 and 2001, the percentage of those with at least one Jewish parent who considered themselves Jewish by religion dropped from 80 to 68 percent nationwide. Two major explanations were offered: the rise in marriage between Jews and non-Jews and the secularization of the Jewish community.[21] The 2002 survey of Jews in greater New York shows how deeply Jewish movement away from religion has affected the bellwether of the Middle Atlantic region. The 10 percent who identified as "nondenominational" or "just Jewish" in 1991 grew to 15 percent in 2002, while the percentage of those describing themselves as "secular" or having "no religion" jumped from 3 percent to 10 percent. Thus, those not identifying with a religious stream almost doubled in the course of the decade, from 13 percent to 25 percent. Not that the lives of Jews unidentified with one of the religious movements or who call themselves secular are necessarily devoid of Jewish substance. In New York, for example, the steep rise in these categories has gone hand in hand with slightly higher rates of performance of certain Jewish rituals—such as lighting Sabbath candles or maintaining a kosher home—or by indulging in the vogue of mysticism through participation in independent Kabbalah "centers" offering classes and mediation sessions. Finding self-fulfillment in such practices does represent a species of authentic Jewish identification; whether it sustains a sense of Jewish peoplehood is another question.

THE POLITICS OF DIVERSITY

In the 1980s, south Asians began streaming into Middlesex County, New Jersey, where the Garden State Parkway crosses the New Jersey Turnpike in the middle of the state. Coming from urban enclaves in Queens and Jersey City as well as directly from India, they ranged from affluent professionals to those of modest means. Like the Irish, Italian, and Hungarian Catholics who preceded them, they came in search of the Middle Atlantic dream of good schools, safe neighborhoods, your own single-family home—and ethnoreligious solidarity. What they brought with them, above all to the suburban townships of Edison and Woodbridge, was an intense and alien ethnic subculture. As *Washington Post* reporter Kalita Mitra describes it in her book, *Suburban Sahibs*:

> In Edison neighborhoods around dinnertime, the smell of curries and cardamom wafts over freshly manicured lawns. In the commercial center in the Iselin section of Woodbridge, specifically along Oak Tree Road, parking is nonexistent, so Toyotas and Hondas double-park and blast the latest Bollywood songs. Hindu and Sikh temples dot highways and side roads, carved out of former homes, churches, office spaces, and toy factories. On weekend mornings, the clapping and chanting inside reach one's ears even before entering.[22]

Push-back was not lacking from the indigenous population. There was vandalism of cars and businesses, name-calling, and even physical assaults on individuals by gangs of white youths. Oak Tree Road was derisively christened "Little Calcutta." On the governmental front, the Edison Township Council passed a series of ordinances in the early and mid-1990s to limit the celebration of Navratri, a Hindu festival organized by the local Indo-American Cultural Society. The festival, drawing thousands to Edison's Raritan Center over four weekends in October, was dedicated to a Hindu goddess's epic victory over evil and involved singing and dancing into the early hours of the morning. The Society took the Township Council to court and won rulings in 1996 and 1997 that overturned the ordinances on religious freedom grounds.

Meanwhile, the demographic influx continued apace. Between the 1980 and 2000 national censuses, the Asian population of Edison grew from 2,000 to 30,000, reaching one-third of the population—of which the majority, some 17,000, were south Asian. Middlesex County as a whole acquired the largest proportion of Asians (18 percent) in the entire Middle Atlantic region. So it was no surprise that in 2001, a local lawyer named Pareg Patel was elected to the Edison Township Council, eventually ascending to its presidency. Also in 2001, Upendra J. Chivukula became the first Indian American to be elected to the New Jersey General Assembly. But the twenty-first century did not bring only communal sweetness and light. During their time of struggle, the Indians of Middlesex found a staunch supporter in the mayor of Woodbridge, James McGreevey, and when McGreevey ran for governor in 2001, he looked to the Indian community to return the favor. To that end, he signed up a dubious character named Rajesh "Roger" Chugh, an ex-cabby and sometime travel agent who put the arm on Indians rich and poor for $1 million in campaign contributions, earning the nickname, "McGreevey's money machine." After McGreevey was elected, Chugh became an assistant commissioner in the secretary of state's office, but was forced to resign in 2003 when the Bergen *Record* published an exposé that included accusations that he had defrauded several airlines. That was a year before McGreevey himself resigned, acknowledging that he was gay amid a corruption scandal. Welcome, Indian Americans, to New Jersey politics.

As the saga of the Middlesex south Asian community shows, the Middle Atlantic has not lost its distinctive approach to religious pluralism. Like immigrants to the region before them, Buddhists, Muslims, Hindus, Latino Catholics and others have built themselves into ethnoreligious communities and, not without a certain amount of fighting on the ground and in the courts, made a place for those communities in the rough-and-tumble of public life. In the Middle Atlantic, a region not unfamiliar with the ravages of ethnic conflict—English *versus* Dutch, Catholic *versus* Protestant, Irish *versus* Italian, Jew *versus* African American—the pluralist imperative was forged out of numberless confrontations and tempered by such mediating institutions as schools, government, the media, and (not least) places of worship. Small wonder, then, that institutions remain important in the region, for they have helped to build and continue to sustain a remarkable measure of comity in the midst of pluralism. Middle Atlantic pluralism is about the daily negotiation of religious and ethnic boundaries. It's an imperative that was born amid the Protestant diversity of the seventeenth century, that expanded to include Catholicism and Judaism in the nineteenth and early twentieth centuries, and that came into its own following World War II. But while it once looked like the American future, it has more recently seemed like a receding past.

Partly, that is because the Middle Atlantic isn't what it used to be. In demographic terms, its share of the national population shrank from 22.3 to 16.5 percent between 1950 and 2000; in the 1990s, it grew at less than half the pace of the nation as a whole (6.1 versus 13.2 percent). More importantly, the national religious institutions that emblemized its national religious leadership no longer matter the way they once did. The National Council of Churches is a shadow of its former self and the flight of Protestant denominational headquarters from New York City to the hinterland likewise points to the region's declining significance in American Protestantism. Meanwhile, the National Conference of Catholic Bishops, which in the wake of the Second Vatican Council was a force to be reckoned with in the land, became in the era of Pope John Paul II a more reticent body, discouraged from uttering the collective voice of the American church leadership on matters of faith, morals, and public policy. In the Jewish world as well, the denominational bodies no longer wield the influence they once did and the major national organizations suffer from shortness of funds and a hollowing out of staff.

On the interfaith front, the three legs of the Herbergian dispensation no longer seem connected to an impulse to pursue some common causes. Where once anti-Communism and civil rights were great thematic concerns, now the opportunities for alliance tend to be episodic and ad hoc—a Diallo protest here, a 9/11 service there. Protestant, Catholic, and Jewish leaders are far less concerned with performing ensemble in the common space than with shoring up their own flocks. For the Protestants, the shrinking of the mainline seems all but irreversible. For the Catholics, there's the ongoing challenge of reconfiguring the church in the backwash of the pedophile cover-up scandal. For the Jews, it's the prevailing anxieties over "continuity"—in numbers, in the education of the next generation, in the State of Israel.

So while the Middle Atlantic is still the heartland of ethno-religious community, of religious institutions that matter, of the hard work of creating a pluralism that is truly plural, it is less itself than it once was. It has ceased to be the country's model, instead now standing as just one region among many, and a rather anomalous one at that. With few white evangelicals on the ground, and a culture far removed from theirs, it has become, with New England, a place where the dominant religious politics of the past quarter century has been hard to comprehend, a place where the public rhetoric of the religious right falls harshly on the ear. Yet, after the 2006 midterm election, the deepening blue states of the Middle Atlantic find themselves back in the congressional driver's seat, with reason to hope that the rest of the country is coming back in their direction. In the post-Bush era, will this region once again rise to the occasion?

· 3 ·

New England:
Steady Habits, Changing Slowly

$\mathcal{N}$ew England has always stood apart in the American mix and the six New England states—Maine, New Hampshire, Vermont, Massachusetts, Rhode Island, and Connecticut—still share a lively, deep-rooted, and coherent identity. With only five percent of the U.S. population and two percent of its land mass, it is the country's smallest region geographically and its second smallest in population—13.9 million, according to the 2000 U.S. Census. While New England's population rose five percent between 1990 and 2000 (almost all of that due to immigration), the overall U.S. population rose at a much faster 13 percent clip. Most of the region's inhabitants are clustered around three metropolitan corridors: from Providence north through Boston and Worcester into southern New Hampshire; from Springfield to Hartford; and from New Haven westward along Long Island Sound, the area that makes up Connecticut's contribution to the tri-state New York metropolitan region. But many of the region's 67 counties are overwhelmingly rural and rural folks outnumber urban dwellers in both Vermont and Maine. Given these disparities, it makes sense to conceive of New England in terms of two distinct subregions: a rural north and an urban south.

The region has a reputation for being lily white and that reputation is largely deserved, especially in the rural north. African Americans constitute less than one percent of all residents of Maine, New Hampshire, and Vermont, and at least 96 percent of the population in each of those states is white. But the picture in the urban south is different. African Americans are a sizeable minority in Connecticut (nine percent of the population), Massachusetts (five percent), and Rhode Island (four percent). And 93 percent of the immigrants who arrived in New England between 1990 and 2000 came to one of those three states. Like African Americans, Latinos are strikingly underrepresented in New England. Only 30 percent of foreign-born New Englanders hail from Latin America (the lowest figure of any region in the country) and Spanish is spoken in just six percent of all households. Still, Latinos comprise nine percent of the population in Connecticut and Rhode Island, and seven percent in Massachusetts.

To the casual observer, religion appears to play no obvious role in the public life of New England. In fact, however, three salient religious characteristics are constitutive of its distinctive regional identity. First is the overwhelming Roman Catholic presence. According to NARA, nearly seven out of ten New Englanders who claim a religious identity are Catholics. In addition, New England's Catholic population is more homogeneous than that of any other American region. Although there are many descendents of immigrants from French Canada and Italy and new immigrants are arriving from Latin America, the Caribbean, and elsewhere, New England Catholicism was and continues to be dominated by Irish Catholics.

Second, mainline Protestantism remains a significant force in a region where moderate and liberal mainliners outnumber conservative Protestants by almost three to one. Beyond the question of their numbers, mainline Protestants are active custodians of New England's intensely local civic culture, which is focused on the town, an institution accorded virtually sacred status. The mainline churches—so frequently symbolic presences on the town green—nourish a sense of connection to the region's distinctive colonial past, when Congregationalism was the established state religion in many parts of the region for almost two hundred years.

Finally—and related to the first two—the region's life still bears the marks of the long struggle between Protestants and Catholics that began in the 1840s, when massive immigration by Catholics from Ireland opened. Within a few decades, Catholics outnumbered Protestants in New England. But the deep-rooted cultural and economic advantages enjoyed by the Yankees made them formidable combatants. They gave ground grudgingly and used a wide range of tools to maintain their ascendancy, beginning with economic and political power but eventually employing the public schools, public libraries, and museums among other social service and cultural organizations, to hem in Catholic communal power. Catholics responded with aggressive self-assertion, but—fatefully—they preferred to build a self-sufficient, entrenched, semi-detached subculture anchored in the region's industrial towns and cities. Over time, Catholics "took over" many Yankee institutions—the public school systems most notably—but the lag was often very lengthy. In the meantime, New England developed a dual institutional culture, where separate and contending "Catholic" and "Protestant" schools, colleges, hospitals, orphanages, cemeteries, and even professional and cultural associations came to seem perfectly natural. This vigorous rivalry persisted for more than a century and was resolved, in the decades after World War II, not with outright victory, but with a kind of truce—a truce in which those on both sides still take some care not to upset the delicate balance of forces. In this mood, religion is treated as a force with great divisive potential. In New England, it is therefore addressed obliquely in public, or not at all.

This nuance of regional culture is not widely appreciated outside New England. One of the first major signs of trouble in Howard Dean's early front-running campaign for the Democratic Party's 2004 presidential nomination arose from his difficulties with public discussion of religious faith— something all American presidential aspirants must handle competently. "I'm still learning a lot about faith and the South and how important it is," Dean, the former governor of Vermont, ineptly remarked in January of 2004, just a few days before the Iowa caucuses. Widely criticized—perhaps mocked is a better term—for his fumbling attempts to characterize his quite possibly non-existent religious beliefs, Dean later told a group of reporters traveling with him on a campaign plane, "I'm a New Englander, so I'm not used to wearing religion on my sleeve and being open about it." Dean's explanation didn't persuade many people on the national stage, but in the context of New England it had the ring of truth. The region's politicians have little to gain by triggering the polarizing animosities that sometimes, on some issues, lie close to the surface.

It would, however, be a mistake to see New England public life as an unending, unchanging, behind-the-scenes wrestling match between Catholics and mainline Protestants. The Jewish and African American Protestant communities, roughly comparable in size, have been energetic and well-organized actors in New England for decades. Other forces for change are also making themselves felt at several levels. New populations are moving into the region, including people of color, although they are doing so more slowly than in many other parts of the nation. Conservative Protestants, once virtually invisible and still few in number, are increasingly visible. In smaller numbers, Muslims, Hindus, Buddhists, Sikhs, and other practitioners of non-Western religions are now present in many parts of the region. But these groups are just beginning to make themselves felt in the region's public life.

Overall, the most dramatic changes that have taken place in recent decades have worked within the major blocks of New England's population. The biggest shift since the mid-twentieth century has been the movement of the Catholic population up the socioeconomic ladder and out of cities to the suburbs. Prosperous suburban Catholics, who now make up New England's Catholic core constituency, mix easily with middle-class Protestants and secular citizens, and often vote like them. While Catholic and mainline

Protestant identities still hold, many in both groups are more loosely tied to their institutions than was once the case. For those seeking to understand the current state of religious influence in public life, the $64,000 question may well be: Why is there so little difference between the voting patterns of New England Catholics and secular New Englanders?

ROMAN CATHOLICS:
MAJORITY FAITH WITH A MINORITY MINDSET

In the long historical drama of religion in New England, Roman Catholicism is not the first act—or even the second or third—but Catholics have dominated the region's population for more than a century. Though the first Catholic parish in the region, Holy Cross Church (later cathedral) in Boston, had been organized in 1789, that community remained a small and marginal one until the 1840s. Thereafter, immigration and natural increase swelled the Catholic population. Today, there are 11 dioceses in New England, each one centered in and named for the major city of the surrounding area. For lay Catholics, the primary association with the church is not with these higher administrative structures, but rather with their local parish church, of which there are just over 1,600 in the region. This number varies constantly as new parishes open and older ones close, corresponding roughly to the movement of the Catholic population. Many parishes have schools, at the elementary and secondary level, and other entities—hospitals, nursing homes, charitable and social service agencies, colleges and universities—that fill out the rest of the New England Catholic landscape.

Given this impressive institutional presence and its hierarchical structure, the Catholic Church in New England can seem monolithic but its very size, geographic spread, and internal diversity undermine so easy a characterization. Catholicism in this region, as elsewhere, seems at first glance to be an absolute monarchy, ruled by an all-powerful king (i.e., the bishop) whose word is law for his docile and obedient subjects. In fact, the Catholic Church is more like a feudal kingdom, with many fragmented sources of authority and power, both central and local, which must constantly accommodate themselves to one another. A more realistic view of Catholicism in New England, therefore, takes into account internal diversity and differences.

In the mid-nineteenth century, the region's ports, close to Europe, were natural landing points for ships of passage. But the open stretches of farmland that attracted settlers to the Midwest and West did not exist in New England. Instead, immigrants found work in the growing cities and the burgeoning light industries of the region, a circumstance that made New England Catholicism largely a church of the urban working class. No less daunting to immigrants, the region already had well-established social, political, and religious structures, ruled by Protestant elites who were perhaps the most homogeneous population anywhere in the country. Yet immigrant adherents of the Roman Church came and stayed in the region, often in numbers that seemed staggering to contemporaries and remain no less impressive in retrospect. Whereas only about 2,000 immigrants had come through Boston in 1820, for example, the number of new arrivals at that port skyrocketed to almost 120,000 in 1850, and close to half of those came from one country (Ireland). Other parts of New England saw similar influxes. The number of Catholics in Connecticut grew from fewer than 10,000 in 1840 to nearly 80,000 by 1890. Between 1835 and the end of the century, Catholics in New Hampshire increased from fewer than 1,000 to more than 100,000. Yankee New Englanders found that they could comprehend the impact of this social change only by recourse to the language of natural disaster: Immigration was a "flood" or a "tidal wave"— metaphors that hardly spoke of welcome.

For all its size and social impact, Catholic immigration to New England was noticeably different from that in other parts of the country in its relative lack of diversity. The Irish predominated through the early twentieth century, though the region's proximity to Quebec also meant that there were periodic influxes (especially into Maine, New Hampshire, and Vermont) of French Canadians—a group that was far less common elsewhere. German Catholic immigrants, by contrast, were never very numerous in the region. Italians and eastern Europeans of several nationalities eventually arrived in larger numbers, but their presence was for the most part confined to particular localities. It was thus possible in many parts of New England to think of Catholic ethnicity in relatively uncomplicated terms: There were the Irish, and then there was everybody else. In other parts of the country, contending ethnic parties were more evenly matched, the outcome of internal Catholic Church conflict more unpredictable, and the passions therefore more inflamed. In New England, Irish dominance of the Catholic Church was never really open to question.

Catholic immigrants, their children, and their grandchildren experienced some enduring tensions in relation to their New England surroundings. These were expressed most often in the form of a persistent oppositional mindset within the Catholicism of the region. Because the Yankee population had often been overtly anti-Catholic, immigrants and their descendents might understandably visualize the world as divided neatly into "us" and "them." There had been examples of genuine bigotry—most notably the rioting mob that destroyed a convent and school of Ursuline Sisters in

Charlestown, Massachusetts, in the summer of 1834—enough to sustain among Catholics a nagging sense that they were unwelcome outsiders who always had to be on guard against slights and disadvantage. But by the 1960s, large numbers of Catholic voters in New England were described by one political scientist as "Al Smith Democrats": those who believed that government should help the "underdog" and that they *were* the underdog, even after they had climbed to the top of the political and economic ladder.

More significant than the plain facts of growth and diversification among New England's Catholic population was the ongoing social impact of those processes. Until the middle of the twentieth century, the Catholic Church in this region, as in other parts of the country, was an overwhelmingly working-class institution. In the setting of homogeneous working-class neighborhoods, immigrants retained their Catholic identity and practice. French Canadians in New England, for example, continued to be active church members in far higher numbers than their relatives who remained behind in Quebec. Moreover, this grounding of the church in the working class proved remarkably long-lasting. In the 1950s, Boston's archbishop, Cardinal Richard Cushing, claimed that no bishop in the region could boast of parents who had gone to college, and that continued largely to be the case half a century later.

As the twentieth century proceeded, however, the social transformation of New England Catholic lay people was dramatic. Playing out the stereotypical American story of upward mobility, Catholics used the institutions they had built to promote their own advancement across the generations. Church-affiliated colleges with undergraduate, graduate, and professional schools opened new paths to white-collar jobs, and Catholics eagerly took advantage of them. Figurative movement up the social and economic scale for New England Catholics was often accompanied by physical movement out of the cities to the suburbs. The institutions of the Catholic Church followed this population movement to the suburbs, leaving in place its urban infrastructure of churches and schools even as it built a parallel set of facilities in the surrounding towns. Between 1950 and the end of the century, the number of parishes in the diocesan headquarter cities remained roughly constant, while the number of parishes in the outlying towns grew steadily. But by the first decade of the twenty-first century, with the number of priests falling rapidly and church attendance off, many dioceses began to close underutilized urban parishes. In 2005, pressed by the priest shortage, falling attendance, and the post-2002 financial crisis, Cardinal Sean O'Malley announced the closing of a quarter of the parish churches in the Archdiocese of Boston.

The impact of suburbanization on Catholic religious practice and, by extension, on Catholic worldview has also been marked. Suddenly, the local parish church was not a building one passed a dozen times a day—on the way to school, to work, to the market—a place of silent retreat where one might drop in briefly for a quick "visit" of prayer or lighting a candle. Rather, the church was now a place one intentionally got into the family car and drove to for some specific purpose and, when that had been accomplished, drove home again. Both "The Church" and the local parish church remained important markers of identity but they receded to a more compartmentalized place in Catholic mental geography. According to surveys, the number of Catholics who attend Mass at least once a week ranges between 30 and 40 percent—well below what it was a generation ago—and may have dropped under 20 percent in the Boston area in the wake of the clergy sexual abuse crisis of the early 2000s.

The most important factor to keep in mind in thinking about New England Catholics today is that religious identity and behavior have become essentially voluntary. In contrast to their forebears, they feel free in everyday life to choose whether or not to adhere to a religious tradition. Many choose Catholicism, and they do so for various, often multiple, and sometimes changing reasons. It is the tradition that they know best and that anchors their identity; it is the tradition that marks their significant life events from birth to death, its multiple strands of doctrine and theology offer them resources for spiritual growth; and it is the religion whose worldview fits with their own sense of how to be a good citizen and how they try to shape a good society. But regardless of the reasons why people choose to be Catholic, and no matter what kind of Catholic they are—liberal or conservative, traditional or progressive, mystical or social activist—the most certain statement that can be offered about them is that they are notably independent and self-assured about their Catholicism. This does not mean that their faith and religious identity is weak, or that their confidence in the church as an institution is weak. It means rather that in choosing *to be* Catholic they are also choosing *how* to be Catholic.

THE CATHOLIC POLITICAL TRAJECTORY

If New England seems the quintessentially Catholic region of the country, it is the way Catholics came to influence the politics of the six states that has been the most visible public expression of that dominance. It did not happen all at once, of course, and it took almost three-quarters of the twentieth century before all of the region's states had elected a Catholic as governor for the first time: Rhode Island in 1906, Massachusetts in 1913, New

Hampshire in 1936, Connecticut in 1940, Maine in 1954, and finally Vermont in 1972. On the local level, the triumph of Catholic urban political machines in the first half of the century is now the stuff of legend. Figures like John "Honey Fitz" Fitzgerald (maternal grandfather of President John F. Kennedy) and James Michael Curley in Boston embodied Catholic political success, relying on a solid electoral base and the enduring Catholic influence within the Democratic Party. But these urban political machines had a distinctive regional character, in that they generally remained small, fragmented, and always at odds as much with one another as with Yankee Republicans. Bosses in the cities of New England typically controlled small neighborhoods only: Within those wards, each leader was supreme, but outside it he was nothing. As a result, alliances among contending factions were always necessary and constantly shifting. In New England, individual politicos were out of office at least as often as they were in and they were constantly making and breaking alliances with one another in search of a supremacy that always proved temporary.

Despite such fluidity, the Catholic impact on public policy was tenacious and cumulative. In the first half of the twentieth century, Catholics achieved sufficient numerical strength at the polls to ensure that their views were embodied in public policy and the political influence of religious leaders might be considerable. Boston's Cardinal William O'Connell, for example, single-handedly killed an effort to establish a state lottery in Massachusetts in 1935. A bill creating the lottery was speeding through the legislature, destined for easy passage, until O'Connell's condemnation of it as immoral ("out-and-out gambling") appeared in one evening's papers; by the next afternoon, the measure had been voted down by a 4-1 margin. In 1948, O'Connell's successor, Richard Cushing, mounted a hard-nosed, sophisticated, and successful campaign to beat back a referendum question that would have liberalized the state's birth control laws. In Connecticut at the same time, a solid phalanx of Catholic Democrats in the state legislature, working closely with the offices of Bishop Henry O'Brien of Hartford, succeeded in blocking similar efforts in successive legislative sessions, thereby sending birth control reformers to the courts. The resulting U.S. Supreme Court case, *Griswold v. Connecticut*, in 1965 laid the groundwork for a constitutional right to privacy that formed the core of the Court's 1973 *Roe v. Wade* decision, which legalized abortion nationwide.

The election of John Kennedy as president of the United States in 1960 seemed like the pinnacle of political success for New England's Catholics, and so it was. Apparently settling once and for all the "Catholic question" about the religion of candidates for the presidency, Kennedy's victory signaled that Catholics had achieved full acceptance, both regionally and nationally. In reality, the triumph was more an ending than a beginning. Catholic politicians, conforming voluntarily to the Protestant model of nonsectarian public life, increasingly distanced themselves from positions taken by their church's leaders and found that they often could gain significant support by doing so, especially among middle- and upper-middle-class voters.

This evolution was most clearly evident in the trajectory of abortion politics in the region. In the period immediately before the *Roe* decision, New England Catholic politicians were uniform in their opposition to expanding access to abortion. Even after *Roe*, the region's most prominent Catholic officeholder, Senator Edward Kennedy of Massachusetts, was still condemning abortion as "not in accordance with the value which our civilization places on human life." Within two years, however, he had shifted his position to that of being "personally opposed" to abortion but unwilling to "impose" that belief on others in public policy. And by the time of his 1996 reelection campaign, he was condemning his Republican opponent for precisely that position, now expressing instead his full support for "a woman's right to choose"—all this in spite of his church's unshaken opposition to abortion. In taking this path, Kennedy was simply proceeding along the same trajectory as his constituents, for if New England Catholic voters were ever "priest-ridden" (the abiding bogey-man of centuries worth of New England Protestants), they certainly aren't now. Exit poll surveys of political opinions from the last three presidential elections show that white Catholic New Englanders are far more likely to be pro-choice (45.7 percent) or moderate (18.9 percent) on abortion than pro-life (35.4 percent)—a good deal more pro-choice than white Catholics in the rest of the country.

MAINLINE PROTESTANTS: CUSTODIANS OF COMMUNITY

Despite their venerable tradition of social as well as religious leadership, the sense of social prominence that still envelopes mainline Protestantism in New England is sustained more by lingering memories than by any active feature of contemporary community life. In recent decades the 1.4 million adherents of New England's mainline Protestant churches (the United Church of Christ [UCC], Episcopal, American Baptist, United Methodist, Evangelical Lutheran, Presbyterian, and Unitarian Universalist) have become used to a kind of ghostlike invisibility in the towns and cities where they work and worship. They are known quantities and taken for granted. With buildings located in the most prominent locations in the center of town and members typically deeply involved in local decision-making, these churches visibly and symbolically hold a great portion of the local social and cultural capital. Those who today serve or minister in one of these "congregations on the green" still feel a sense of responsibility for this heritage of community leadership.

There are, to be sure, notable variations in the state of mainline Protestantism within the region. The most obvious is a major division between rural northern New England and the urbanized states of southern New England. In the North, mainline Protestantism has encountered grave challenges as many congregations have dwindled past the point where they can support clergy. In the large and medium-sized cities of Massachusetts, Connecticut, and Rhode Island, by contrast, the picture is more mixed. Many historic downtown churches continue to flourish but congregations in city neighborhoods are disappearing because of inexorable population change. And in the vast suburban reaches of southern New England, mainline churches often continue to play a vibrant and central role in community life.

With membership in a decline that began forty years ago, church people in the mainline denominations realize that their position of leadership is by no means secure or even stable. But with 150 years experience of swimming against the demographic tide, there is little sense of panic. Mainline congregations still see themselves as primarily local institutions dedicated to issues touching the people close to home, in the town in which they are located. They maintain their skill at mounting and sustaining cooperative ventures, a characteristic that magnifies their public presence. This public style first showed itself in the nineteenth century, especially in urban areas, when Protestant leaders began to cooperate with one another to counter the surging and monolithic presence of Roman Catholicism. It is a cooperative impulse that continues to function at two levels: first, in formal ecumenical organizations and, secondly, in cities, towns, and neighborhoods where mainline congregations often take the lead in forming collaborative, nonprofit organizations to address important community needs and issues, from providing day care to giving poor children opportunities to attend college.

For most of the twentieth century, enthusiasm for ecumenism as a formal movement toward church unity ran especially high in New England. The ecumenical organizations achieved their peak impact in the years after the Second Vatican Council, when Protestants and Catholics began to talk openly with one another and to live together in the suburbs. But after the mid-1980s many perceived a decline in enthusiasm for formal ecumenical ventures, partly because local activism couldn't resolve global or national divisions among Christians. As the century closed, "conciliar ecumenism" was having trouble charting its course between two mutually exclusive options: to grow by approaching non-Christian groups, such as Jewish and Baha'i congregations, which would turn the councils into interfaith groups, or instead to expand support by inviting evangelical or other conservative Christian churches into membership—if they could be enticed to join. Both options would mute the mainline style of engagement in civic problem solving.

If conciliar ecumenism is weaker than it was a generation ago, the second aspect of the New England Protestant style of collaboration—focusing on the development of local ministries and partnerships—is unambiguously thriving. Scholars such as Robert Wuthnow of Princeton University and Mark Chaves of Duke University have demonstrated that mainline congregations are significantly more likely to maintain several connections to community and social service ventures than are Catholic or evangelical Protestant congregations. And the spirit of mainline Protestantism still permeates New England's nonprofit sector. Mainline Protestants are still the main source of volunteer directors for New England social, cultural, and educational nonprofits. And all over the region Protestant-led collaborative ministries abound. A good example is Center City Churches, a nonprofit agency sponsored by 12 downtown Hartford churches (11 of them mainline) that operates an astounding variety of educational and social service programs in partnership with a large number of groups, ranging from the Hartford Public Schools to the United Way.

In the ecumenical enterprise, the mainline often enjoys alliances with the relatively small but well-organized communities of Jews and African American Protestants. Both communities are concentrated in southern New England, especially in the Boston area and the major cities of Connecticut. Both have always been pioneers in civil rights organizing and both have followed strategies of organized community representation by means of federations and ministerial alliances. By and large, the Jewish community has welcomed New England's recent tradition of a religiously neutral public sphere, regarding that as a major advance in civil and democratic rights, while African Americans remain wedded to a church-based style of political and social mobilization. The two communities also face some anxiety about spreading out in New England's suburban landscape. The fear, not unjustified, is that the consequence will be a loss of group cohesion and political impact.

CONSERVATIVE PROTESTANTS:
PROSPERING ON THE MARGINS

For much of the twentieth century, conservative forms of Protestantism were almost entirely absent from New England. Indeed, demographically, culturally, and politically, conservative Protestants still have a weaker hold on New

England than on any other region in the United States. According to NARA, only about 27 percent of the region's Protestants and 37 percent of its Protestant congregations are evangelical; in terms of people, that's 381,000 evangelical Protestants and 165,000 Pentecostal and Holiness adherents in the region's six states. But these modest numbers actually represent a revitalization of conservative Protestantism in the region. The new vitality of conservative Protestantism flows from two sources: the activities of Protestants migrating into New England and the now significant regeneration of pockets of conservative Protestantism that survived after the overwhelming majority of the region's Protestants moved to theologically moderate and liberal "mainline" orientations in the early twentieth century. This revival began soon after World War II, fueled by population movement and by deliberate mission efforts launched from other parts of the nation by an array of evangelical, fundamentalist, Pentecostal, and Holiness groups.

The Southern Baptist expansion into New England serves as a good illustration of the scope and limits of conservative Protestant movement into the region. Until the end of the 1950s, there were no Southern Baptist congregations at all in the region. By 2003, 230 congregations with about 35,000 members were recorded in the Baptist Convention of New England (BCNE), the Southern Baptist umbrella organization for the region. Initially, the Southern Baptist movement came to New England as a result of population movement initiated by Uncle Sam. For example, the region's first Southern Baptist church was organized by U.S. Air Force families transferred in 1958 from Strategic Air Command bases in Louisiana and New Mexico to Pease Air Force in New Hampshire. The church gathering at Pease sparked efforts to establish more Southern Baptist churches in New England, led mostly by transplanted southerners serving at Army, Air Force, Navy, and Coast Guard bases and stations around the region.

Eight of these congregations joined to establish the New England Baptist Association in 1962, with the energetic support of the Southern Baptist Convention's national Home Mission Board. By 1967, 20 congregations were in place. By 1983, there were 114 Southern Baptist churches and missions in New England with more than 13,000 members, and the movement no longer relied chiefly on members of the military and other southern transplants for its growth. During this period of surging growth, Southern Baptist churches spread out from their original clusters around major military bases and the facilities of large, national, manufacturing corporations, and took root in small towns in northern New England and in the broad arc of suburbs around Boston, as well as in suburban Connecticut. By 1988, the New England Baptist Convention had 160 member congregations and was aiming to double in size by the mid-1990s. Suddenly, however, the rate of congregational growth slowed. In addition, like the region's other conservative Protestants, the Southern Baptists experienced dramatic and unanticipated change in the composition of their membership. Those who responded most readily to Southern Baptist mission efforts were now non-English speaking immigrants, and not suburban whites.

The NEBC repositioned to embrace the opportunity and by 2003 about half of its 230 member congregations were non-English speaking. The Greater Boston Baptist Association, for example, includes nine Haitian, three Brazilian, and four Latino churches, as well as churches composed of immigrants who speak Chinese, Portuguese, Greek, Korean, Arabic, Khmer, and Tagalog, among its 51 congregations. As a result of this trend, the Southern Baptist movement now looks quite different in rural northern New England than in the urbanized South. In northern New England, Southern Baptist churches tend to be small, English-speaking, and mostly of native stock. In Massachusetts, Connecticut, and Rhode Island, the movement is now growing fastest in poorer, older, urban centers and first-ring suburbs, among immigrants.

This broad trend is shared by other conservative Protestant groups, including independent congregations, small evangelical and fundamentalist denominations, and Pentecostal and Holiness groups. The Assemblies of God is now probably the largest conservative Protestant denomination in New England. Between 1992 and 2002, it grew from 319 to 359 churches. While that represented a slowing of the congregational growth rate during the 1980s, the number of adherents increased faster, rising by 32 percent from 51,464 to 67,859. Assemblies congregations are concentrated in Connecticut and Massachusetts, where the denomination has a large number of Spanish-speaking and other immigrant combinations, a pattern that began to take shape as early as the 1970s. Other Pentecostal groups are now present as well, including the West Coast-based International Church of the Foursquare Gospel, which has 61 congregations, more than half in Massachusetts. The Church of the Nazarene, the largest of the Holiness groups in the region, has 171 congregations and also operates one of the region's two Christian colleges, Eastern Nazarene College.

The second major stream of conservative Protestant growth stems, at least indirectly, from the tiny group of conservative Protestants who survived the great Protestant realignment of the early twentieth century. In the years after World War II, a few New England churches and other institutions connected with the national revival of evangelicalism began to expand. To cite the most notable example, Boston's Park Street Congregational Church and its minister, Harold Ockenga, became important to the movement as a whole, and helped nurture local growth. Also critical to the revival were a number of small, existing evangelical educational institutions in the region.

In the 1950s, Gordon College, a small Boston institution founded in 1889 to train missionaries, moved to a 500-acre campus on Boston's North Shore and began to grow. Within a few decades, it had emerged as one of the nation's most prominent Christian liberal arts colleges. Along the way, it spun-off a separate, graduate-level institution, now called Gordon-Conwell Theological Seminary, which has become one of the largest seminaries in the nation. Evangelical, but not denominational, Gordon and Gordon-Conwell have identified themselves mostly with the Reformed (Calvinist) tradition from which New England Protestantism sprang. Their influence is now widespread in the region and among many conservative and moderate constituencies. One of the most important aims of the schools has been to encourage the revival of evangelical faith within mainline Protestant congregations. And, at this point, hundreds of mainline congregations in New England—Baptist, Episcopalian, Presbyterian, United Church of Christ, and others—are led by ministers and lay leaders produced at Gordon or Gordon-Conwell.

Another revitalized organization that has gained wide influence is Vision New England, which was founded in 1887 as the Evangelistic Association of New England, a collaborative venture of seven denominations. The group now provides about 5,000 New England congregations from 80 different denominations with a variety of ministries and services. The organization itself is clearly evangelical—it subscribes to the National Evangelical Association's statement of faith—but its style and many of its programs are inclusive. Vision New England also organizes elaborate networks and training programs for clergy and lay leaders, including those working in ministries targeting men, women, children, the elderly, the deaf, the disabled, small groups, family life, and those in prisons.

Given New England's religious demography, it is hardly surprising that conservative Protestants have not been a major force in New England politics. Even in the region's most politically conservative state, New Hampshire, students of religion and politics haven't found much connection between the activities of religious and political conservatives. However, an emerging and distinctive feature of conservative Protestantism in New England is its willingness to work closely with Catholics on public policy matters, and even to say nice things about Catholicism. Conservative Protestant efforts to make a common front with Catholics on issues like abortion and gay rights date all the way back to the beginning of the religious right in the late 1970s. Today, there is a pervasive sense among politically active evangelicals that the public world is properly divided between people of faith and those without faith. In 2004, as the Catholic bishops mounted a large-scale campaign to block gay marriage in the wake of a Massachusetts Supreme Judicial Court decision mandating it, their chief and most effective public allies seemed to be conservative Protestant-oriented groups like the Massachusetts Family Institute. Such collaborations intensified as a coalition of religious conservatives that included the Mormon governor of Massachusetts, Mitt Romney, as well as the Catholic hierarchy and Protestant conservatives struggled valiantly if ultimately unsuccessfully to persuade state constitutional conventions in 2004 and 2007 to send the question of gay marriage to a referendum.

ON COMMON GROUND

In another time of change in New England, the nineteenth-century worthy Oliver Wendell Holmes (the famous jurist's father) gleefully compared the sudden collapse of the region's ancient Calvinist "Standing Order" to the disintegration of a rickety old "one hoss shay" underneath the parson driving it. It was, Holmes estimated, precisely 1855 when New England's old order "went to pieces all at once,—All at once and nothing first,—Just as bubbles do when they are burst." That homogeneous Yankee New England was supplanted by the long contention between Yankee and Catholic. Curiously, this sectarian model of communal life broke apart almost as dramatically as its predecessor—in about 1960. It did so along with that paladin of a new and more vigorously neutral church state order, John F. Kennedy. Along with a whole generation of upwardly mobile, suburban New England Catholics, Kennedy sincerely adopted the New England Protestant model of a democratic public realm where citizens did not impose sectarian demands on one another in order to preserve civic peace. Religious values would remain important, but function at the level of the individual, the family, and the voluntary religious community.

   This "New England model" of pluralism had its moment on the national stage in the mid-twentieth century, when it seemed persuasive to many Americans, including the federal judges who shaped the series of landmark "separation of church and state" decisions that marked the years between the late 1930s and the 1960s. But by the late 1960s, it was clear that what worked for New England was generating vigorous opposition in other places. As the twenty-first century opened, there was no denying that change was creeping into old New England, encouraged by both immigrants from other parts of America and from the four corners of the world. And yet, the region's long-running and distinctive regional public culture still seemed pretty sturdy, as did its religious underpinnings. For their part, New England Protestants still benefited enormously from their connection to the region's institutional history and to its symbolic life. A regional civil religion, complete with sacred landscapes, rites, and institutions—including professional sports franchises—nourished the region's identity and remained closely tied to the public posture of the heirs of the Standing Order. At the heart of this civil religion was the institution of the town, which gave form to local life and identity. Tiny Connecticut remained a commonwealth of 169 towns, each jealously asserting its right to home rule, no matter how far the state might lapse into suburban sprawl. Almost all of these towns remained demonstrably tied to a "First Church" and usually to some sort of town green, complete with a Civil War memorial and an ancient cemetery close at hand. As it had been since the Grand Army of the Republic marched home from Appomattox, Memorial Day remained the occasion of great civic celebration, when everyone from vets and pols to Little Leaguers, Brownies, and the public works department all paraded down Main Street to the accompaniment of high school and middle school bands in a grand display of municipal solidarity.

The forms of local government crafted by Puritans in the seventeenth century—the boards of selectmen and the annual town meetings—still endure in New England. These civic forms were shaped by and for Protestants but others now inhabit them fully. Catholics, Jews, African American Protestants, and soon, perhaps, Latino Catholics and Protestants, have all made comfortable adjustments to a social and political geography mapped by town and by an ideal of very local democracy. It is worth emphasizing that the notion of the New England town as an organic, democratic entity that bestows a common local identity on residents and transcends their religious identities was developed by and for Protestants. The town acquired this inclusive spin during the late nineteenth and early twentieth centuries, when the descendants of the Puritans redefined its symbolic meaning in an attempt to persuade the Catholic hordes that the town—the public sphere—stood for democratic values transcending the bounds of sectarian identity, for a realm where citizens meet together to work for the public good.

At a second level, New England's white mainline Protestants still exercise social and political leadership because they arrived first in the location where everyone else would seek to follow them: into the suburban middle class. They remain a highly mobilized group, who participate often in the political process; indeed, they lead the nation in voter registration, with 93 percent registered, according to ARIS. Further, according to exit polling from recent presidential elections, it is mainline Protestants (and those with no religious affiliation) who do most to define the region's distinctive voting patterns—with strong liberal preferences on social issues like abortion, gay rights, welfare spending, national health insurance, and environmental policy.

The above notwithstanding, New England's mainline Protestants are also important because they cast a lot of votes for Republican candidates.

Those whose acquaintance with the region's voting patterns is limited to presidential elections may be surprised but Republicans often win certain kinds of elections in New England. As recently as 2004, five of the six New England governors belonged to the GOP. Outside of New Hampshire, few of these Republicans are conservatives by national standards. But New England voters often elect Republicans, especially as governors, to serve as a check on the Democratic legislatures they also tend to elect. Surveys show that in a region where a plurality of voters is registered Democrats, mainline Protestants are still far more likely to be registered as Republicans or Independents—46 percent and 29 percent respectively, according to exit polls taken at recent presidential elections. Only 25 percent are Democrats. Even those of "low commitment"—who attend worship less than once a week—are considerably more likely than the regional average (42 percent versus 34.5 percent) to register as Republicans. Since New England's mainline Protestants are, by and large, social moderates and liberals, their insistence on registering as Republicans remains a commentary on their persistent collective identity, their disinclination to identify themselves with the party that was, historically, the political home of Irish Catholicism.

GOODBYE TO ALL THAT

Catholic participation in New England's public life, and particularly Catholic voting behavior, remain distinctive too. And because of the overwhelming size of the Catholic population and electorate, the Catholic vote goes a long way toward deciding New England elections. In the middle of the twentieth century, the voting pattern was quite clear. New England Catholic voters were overwhelmingly Democratic; they were enthusiastic supporters of the New Deal, especially as it benefited them; and quite often they were responsive to the leadership of the Catholic clergy and hierarchy in public matters. In the early twenty-first century, Catholics, teamed with the region's African American Protestant, Jewish, and secular voters, give the national Democratic Party one of its strongest, most reliable regional voting bases. Exit polling in presidential elections since 1992 shows that 47 percent of New England Catholics identify themselves as Democrats—a higher percentage than any other regional group of white Christians in the United States. A further 23 percent are Independents.

One of the most surprising revelations contained in the exit poll data is that in New England, "high-commitment" Catholics—those who attend Mass at least once a week—are more likely to describe themselves as both

Democrats and liberals than Catholics who attend worship less frequently. Fifty-two percent of New England's high-commitment Catholics are Democrats—well above the national average for high-commitment Catholics of 45 percent. (In the region with the next highest percentage of high-commitment Catholic Democrats, the Mid-Atlantic, 48 percent identify themselves that way; in most other regions the percentage is below 42 percent.) To heighten the contrast, only 42 percent of New England's low-commitment Catholics call themselves Democrats. In addition, 33 percent of the region's high-commitment Catholics describe their political ideology as liberal, in contrast to the national average of 29 percent. On the issues front, New England Catholics—both high- and low-commitment—are slightly more likely than their national peers to support gay rights. The two groups are not divided on a number of ideological issues—half or more of both groups support liberal positions on national health insurance, more welfare spending, and environmental protection. Both are also lukewarm in their support for school vouchers.

However, the two groups of Catholics diverge on the two most divisive social issues. Low-commitment Catholics are far more likely to support gay rights (67 versus 56 percent) and abortion rights (61 versus 29 percent) than those who attend worship at least once a week. New England Catholics who attend Mass less than once a week are also far more likely to be pro-choice than low-commitment Catholics at large, 50 percent of whom are pro-choice. In fact, the views of New England's low-commitment Catholics on these controversial issues align more closely with those of mainline Protestants and African American Protestants than with their high-commitment co-religionists. Interestingly, the region's low-commitment Catholics are also less liberal on economic issues, and often hold a mix of views strikingly similar to the views of mainline Protestants (with 32 percent of low-commitment Catholics, 35 percent of low-commitment mainline Protestants, and 33 percent of high-commitment mainline Protestants favoring less welfare spending). Forty-three percent of low-commitment Catholics describe their ideology as conservative, compared to 43 percent of low-commitment mainline Protestants and 41 percent of high-commitment mainline Protestants.

While the exit polling cited here does not provide all the information one might wish for, it seems reasonable to conclude that the high-commitment New England Catholics who are such loyal Democrats are probably older and residents of core urban areas. Low-commitment Catholics, whose opinions are liberal on issues of personal morality and more moderate to conservative on economic issues, seem to be moving toward the norms for New England's educated, middle-class, suburban Protestants. This suggests that the overlap between mainline Protestants and upwardly mobile, loosely attached Catholics is growing, and that a stable middle ground is now shared by New England's two old ethnoreligious antagonists. The exemplar of this evolution is arguably U.S. Senator John Kerry of Massachusetts, the Democratic presidential candidate in 2004, whose Catholic identity, Brahmin social and educational credentials, and liberal politics are all familiar features of the New England scene, but are combined in ways that reflect changes since 1970. Catholic but not Irish—his paternal grandfather was a Czech Jew who converted to Catholicism (a fact that he himself was not aware of until recently)—Kerry represents the style and perhaps the substance of the low-commitment style of Catholicism that has become so important in New England. Educated at St. Paul's School and Yale, a member of the elite undergraduate club Skull and Bones, Kerry encountered few of the barriers that hindered most ambitious New England Catholics growing up before the late 1950s. (It didn't hurt that his mother was a Forbes, one of Massachusetts' elite Brahmin families.)

Kerry's movement into the higher realms of New England political life was straightforward. After service in Vietnam and a prominent role in the anti-Vietnam War movement, he enrolled at Boston College Law School—the Catholic law school that is the royal road to Massachusetts political life. He then served as a state prosecutor, district attorney, and lieutenant governor before being elected to the U.S. Senate in 1982. Through his rise, no one connected him in any particular way to the Catholic Church or to its social teachings, nor had he ever been as engaged by public discourse about Catholic doctrines in the manner of Senator Eugene McCarthy of Minnesota or Gov. Mario Cuomo of New York. But neither did anyone in Massachusetts question his commitment to Catholicism. As is the case with most New England Catholics, Kerry said little publicly about his faith. Asked early in the 2004 campaign about his religious formation, he alluded briefly to his service as an altar boy, and on Ash Wednesday appeared on the campaign trail with a dark smudge on his forehead. His Catholicism was simply a matter of fact, in the New England style. On his campaign website, Kerry dealt characteristically with the religion issue in the first paragraph of his biography by stating, "John Kerry was raised in the Catholic faith and continues to be an active member of the Catholic Church." That was it.

If Kerry's Catholicism is important enough to be in the first paragraph of his campaign biography, that doesn't mean that he—or the vast majority of other Catholic political figures—lines up often with the Church hierarchy on such public policy matters as abortion, same-sex marriage, or even capital punishment. To do so would be to become unelectable in "Catholic" New England. Kerry has plenty of company in the Senate; Connecticut's Christopher Dodd, Vermont's Patrick Leahy, and Edward Kennedy of Massachusetts are prominent pro-choice Catholic Democrats. It is only fair to observe that almost all of the region's prominent Catholic Republican elected officials—former Connecticut Gov. John Rowland and former Massachusetts governors Paul Cellucci and Jane Swift, for example—have also been pro-choice. How powerful can the Catholic Church be and how Catholic can those public officials be, if the church's positions on matters like abortion and same-sex marriage are flouted so consistently? The answer is a bit complicated, but it goes to the heart of any explanation of the role of religion and public life in contemporary New England.

The most direct response is that Catholic power in New England is limited, but quite real, and that the chief restrictions on Catholic power are enforced by the region's Catholics themselves. A fuller account must take note of the fact that, at least for the moment and especially among low-commitment Catholics, Catholic identity is more about participation in the Catholic community—in the sacraments, in the life of the parish—than it is about public policy. In addition, it seems indisputable that many of New England's Catholics have accepted the argument about public life and religious culture advanced by the region's Protestants as they attempted to divert a Catholic takeover of the region. First evident in the 1960 presidential campaign, this shift was made manifest in the very agitated Massachusetts debate over same-sex marriage.

In late 2003, the state's Supreme Judicial Court ruled that the restriction of marriage rights to heterosexual couples violated the rights of gay and lesbian couples to equal protection under the constitution of the commonwealth. Four years of complex political wrangling followed, as a coalition of religious conservatives, backed by then governor Mitt Romney, attempted to win a majority vote in the Massachusetts General Court—the state legislature functioning as a constitutional convention—to authorize a public referendum on a constitutional amendment banning gay marriage. In the course of this lengthy struggle virtually all of the state's religious actors were mobilized. Leading the vigorous opposition to the legalization of same-sex marriage was Archbishop Sean O'Malley of Boston and the other Catholic bishops of the commonwealth. In the weeks preceding special constitutional conventions in February and March of 2004, the bishops attempted to activate their flocks to lobby the legislature to block gay marriage. They paid for a mailing to one million Massachusetts households and organized a huge network of rallies and meetings, from parish halls to the Boston Common. They also forged alliances with a variety of like-minded religious groups—most especially conservative Protestants and African American Protestants but also smaller bodies including Orthodox Jews, Eastern Orthodox Christians, Muslims, and others. Opposing them was a smaller but very vocal group of mainline Protestants and Reform and Conservative Jews. Romney, a Mormon, sided with those arguing for an anti-gay marriage amendment to the state's constitution.

Caught in the middle were the 199 members of the legislature, functioning now as delegates to the convention. During this period, the New England journalistic convention of avoiding explicit discussion of the religious identities of lawmakers fell away. (Almost 70 percent of them, it turned out, were Catholics.) A two-day session of the convention that ended in deadlock in February 2004 offered an interesting barometer of religious politics in the Bay State at the dawn of the new century. According to the *Boston Globe* and the *Boston Herald*, the largest single group of legislators (about 80) were aligned with the Archdiocese of Boston's position that neither same-sex marriages nor civil unions should be permitted. A group of 44 lawmakers, almost all of them Catholic, opposed same-sex marriage but wanted to send a measure legalizing civil unions to referendum. Another group of 55, including many mainline Protestants and all 13 of the Jews in the legislature, supported gay marriage.

During the debate, polls—supported by interviews in many news articles—suggested that opposition to gay marriage and/or civil unions was far stronger in the legislature than in the general Massachusetts population. Senator Kerry, not yet the Democratic nominee for president, staked out a position against same-sex marriage but in favor of civil unions, reflecting polling in Massachusetts that showed strong support for gay rights in most religious constituencies dating back to the early 1990s.

Mainline Protestants and many Jews rushed to exploit this division between the Catholic hierarchy and laity, often using a logic familiar from earlier battles to restrict Catholic influence. "We respect the right of the Catholic Church to set its own policies and its own definition of marriage but the Catholic Church does not have the right to impose its religious beliefs on others," Rabbi Devon A. Lerner, cochairman of the Religious Coalition for the Freedom to Marry, told the *Globe* on January 17. "Equal civil marriage will not force priests, or any clergy, to change their beliefs or practices—our laws of separation of church and state guarantee that."

During this discussion many Catholics, both inside and outside the legislature, frequently invoked Lerner's distinction between what they believed as Catholics, and what should be civil law. The *Hartford Courant* followed canvassers for "Love Makes a Family," a pro-same-sex marriage advocacy group, as they knocked on doors in suburban West Hartford. "I'm Catholic, and that's not in the belief structure, but if you're talking about civil marriage, I don't have a problem with that," Jay Corbalis told the paper. The same day, the Lowell, Massachusetts, *Sun* interviewed State Representative Kevin Murphy, "a product of Catholic schools who attends Mass faithfully." Murphy, the

Sun reported, would vote against constitutional amendments banning same-sex marriage because he understood the Supreme Judicial Court's action as a civil rights decision. "I obviously weighed what my church felt, but I also have to understand that as a public official, I represent all of the constituents of my district. I have to do what I believe is the right thing for all my constituents." Other Catholic legislators also applied this "inside/outside" logic. Thus, the Associated Press noted that state Senator Martin Montigny would vote for gay marriage despite his church's teachings. "As a Catholic, I would never vote to diminish the sanctity of the church sacrament of marriage," Montigny said. "As a human being, I will never deny someone their equal rights. It is my belief that the only requirement of civil marriage is enduring love and respect." For many Catholic legislators and voters, it made a kind of local sense to express solidarity with Catholic understandings of sacramental marriage, while still voting to amend the constitution to permit civil unions for homosexuals, even if that left Archbishop O'Malley sputtering with frustration.

In 2004, the attempt to send gay marriage to referendum failed to win a majority of the convention by two votes. Over the next several years, anti-gay-marriage activists failed in their efforts to pick off pro-gay-marriage legislators at the polls and to stem the tide of legislators moving toward pro-gay-marriage positions. In 2007, the eroding position of anti-gay-marriage proponents was illustrated when another proposal to send the question to voters failed to garner even one quarter of the convention. That meant that, constitutionally, Massachusetts' unique-in-the-nation legal allowance of same-sex marriage could not be repealed by referendum any earlier than 2012, and to all intents and purposes seemed a permanent part of the social order. Through the debate, it became clear that the Catholic Church's opposition to civil unions as well as to same-sex marriage was a minority position that could not prevail. In 2005, the *Boston Globe* reported that a poll showed that 49 percent of Massachusetts Catholics endorsed gay marriage and an overwhelming majority backed civil unions. With survey data indicating that the Catholic laity were so closely aligned with the thinking of non-Catholics in the region, the prospects for the church's ability to influence public policy anywhere in the region seemed limited. It seemed like the consummation of religious politics, New England style.

· 4 ·

The South: In the Evangelical Mode

In 1949, the famous bluegrass duo of Lester Flatt and Earl Scruggs introduced a song about a wayfarer who happens upon a gathering in the center of a town. He hears "a welcome voice biddin' me come and share their preachin', prayin', singin'." He feels "so much at home amid the nameless throng" that he is able to "lay the burdens down" and become a redeemed part of "an old-time meeting down on the public square."

The South has changed a lot over the past six decades. Its notoriously broken-down, predominantly agricultural economy has been transformed by Sunbelt boom into an engine of job growth. Gone is the regime of de jure racial segregation and extrajudicial violence that kept the children and grandchildren of slaves separate and unequal and sent them streaming north in search of decent employment and some measure of civic equality. Now the stream of out-migration has reversed and it is in the states of the Old Confederacy that the number of African Americans is increasing most rapidly—by an astonishing 58 percent in the 1990s alone. Meanwhile, a population that for centuries traced its origins almost exclusively to western Europe and west Africa has been joined by new ethnic groups, especially Latinos, who have made their presence felt across the region. And from the margins of power, the Republican Party has ascended to political dominance.

But the force of evangelical Protestantism, of which Flatt and Scruggs' "Preachin', Prayin', Singin'" is a classic expression, remains intact. From the little frame churches in the countryside to the out-sized brick meeting houses in the cities to the huge Christian campuses in the suburbs, the South continues to serve up its religion of sin and salvation. As dim and dirty a thing as human nature is, evangelicalism promises free grace toward redemption to the individual who makes the right choice. In the South, however, evangelicalism is not only about the individual soul. Flatt and Scruggs' lost wayfarer is saved via a public event expressing the faith of a community. Evangelical churches orient their resources toward evangelistic and missionary work designed to further the Great Commission announced in the New Testament: to go forth and convert the world. If the central theme of Southern evangelicalism has been an imperative drive toward personal conversion and the moral life afterward, it is also bound up with the hope that the faithful will be at ease not only inside the churches but also out in the community at large.

THE WHITE WAY

Evangelicalism emerged among the socially marginal in the southern colonies in the late eighteenth century. At the turn of the nineteenth century, frontier revival broke out on the border between Kentucky and Tennessee, spreading its message of the need to be born again, throughout the largely unchurched frontier areas of the region. Baptists, Methodists, and Presbyterians were all part of this spiritual fervor. Making their peace with the dominant social patterns of the region, including slavery, they soon converted much of the elite to this passionate faith. It was through shaping the moral lives of individuals that they aspired to influence the public—the kingdom of God on earth would come through personal moral reform. And in due course, they began identifying their kingdom with the South itself.

The emergence of a distinctive southern identity coincided with the rise to dominance of evangelicals in the years after 1820. Sectional conflict crystallized fears of political vulnerability within the nation, just as the South was recognizing that slavery was the basis not only of much of its economy but also of its social order. At the beginning of the 1830s—when northern abolitionists began attacking the morality of slavery and the Nat Turner slave rebellion terrified Virginia—the white South turned to its religious leaders to articulate a Biblical defense of their "peculiar institution." Citing Paul's admonition that servants obey their masters, these worthies advanced the claim that chattel slavery had coexisted with Christianity from the beginning. They also succeeded in making the Bible the fundamental text of southern life in general; it was the Good Book that, soon enough, could be found everywhere, from the seats of state government to the humblest backwoods cabins. The inerrantist view of Scripture that prevails in evangelicalism today has its roots in this era, when southern evangelicals came to see themselves as both the moral custodians of their own culture and its public defenders against outside attack. In splitting off from their northern brethren to form separate denominations in the 1840s, Baptists and Methodists (and Presbyterians during the Civil War) created the first institutions of a southern civil religion that asserted a God-ordained regional identity based on white supremacy. These institutions long outlasted the war to provide ongoing structures for white southern identity and for mobilizing the faithful for public crusades. While the southern Methodists and Presbyterians eventually reunited with their northern counterparts, the largest and most important of the South's denominational bodies, the Southern Baptist Convention (SBC), remains a thing unto itself.

The southern white churches developed a social ethic that turned them into pillars of the region's civil order. Southern Presbyterians spoke for other Protestant groups in asserting the doctrine of the "spirituality of the church," which would long remain a justification for churches and religious leaders to refrain from participating in many progressive social causes—yet it was always selectively applied. Southern ministers, building on their Bible-based proslav-. ery arguments, declared from the pulpit that the South's cause was a holy war against northern atheists. They blessed troops marching off to war and cared for soldiers in battle. They led prayer groups, preached revivals, and performed mass baptisms. They interpreted Confederate victories as God's blessings and Confederate defeats as divine chastisements, all the while proclaiming days of fasting and thanksgiving. In a word, the war provided for the full flowering of the religious construction of (white) southern identity.

After the war, evangelicals expanded their influence in the South's public life as the region struggled to maintain its sense of itself in the face of catastrophic defeat. The late Confederacy was sacralized through the development of a Religion of the Lost Cause that cast the failed Southern secession as a tragic holy war for regional self-determination. Meanwhile, whites eagerly created a self-image of social solidarity that was expressed in their churches' support for the political disenfranchisement of the black population and Jim Crow segregation laws. Emerging as the largest and most dynamic of the denominations, the Baptists became the region's unofficial established church, responsible for ensuring that religion never ceased to be as an essential dimension of regional identity. In due course—with the passing of the Confederate generation, the engagement of southern soldiers in the Spanish-American War and World War I, and the election of a son of the south (Woodrow Wilson) as president—white southerners did begin to identify again with the United States as a whole. This did not mean surrendering a sense of their region's spiritual distinctiveness, however. It was the south's special destiny, they thought, to bring redemption to the nation and beyond. As Southern Baptist leader Victor I. Masters wrote in 1918, "Evangelical faith has had here its best chance in the world to show what it can do for a civilization."[1]

There was no challenging the cultural hegemony of the mainstream evangelical denominations in the first half of the twentieth century. Episcopalians and Lutherans might hanker after a place to buy a drink, but when Baptists and Methodists and Presbyterians decided to press for laws prohibiting the sale and distribution of alcohol, they prevailed. Southern states and counties passed blue laws to regulate Sunday conduct, and gaming laws as well as Prohibition gave the force of law to evangelical moral standards. Public schools were like ancillary evangelical institutions, with local pastors serving as school chaplains and denominational Sunday school teachers leading students during the week in Bible reading and prayer. Not that there were no threats to this standing order. Always, the violence, intemperance, and religious indifference of the Southern white male were there to be combated and domesticated. By the 1920s, however, the norms themselves of Southern life were under challenge. More southerners were living in cities and being exposed to national jazz age culture. The increased availability of textbooks in the public schools acquainted the southern public with the ideas of Charles Darwin; in 1925, Dayton, Tennessee became the focal point of efforts to legally proscribe the teaching of his theory of evolution. To the nation at large, the Scopes Trial dramatized the conflict between science and religion and fostered the image of the South as a backward, benighted Bible Belt. Yet even as the forces of fundamentalism retreated from the national culture to establish their own associations, educational institutions, and broadcasting presence, the South succeeded in keeping Darwin and company at bay.

What fundamentally altered the southern way of life was the civil rights movement after World War II. Among whites, the movement's immediate effect was to inspire opposition, both physical and spiritual. To the conservative southern mind, the northern authorities pushing integration were nothing short of godless. Denouncing *Brown v. Board of Education*, the 1954 Supreme Court decision ending public school desegregation, in a speech to the South Carolina legislature, Rev. W. A. Criswell of Dallas' First Baptist Church, the largest Protestant congregation of the era, threw down the gauntlet: "Let them integrate. Let them sit up there in their dirty shirts and make all their fine speeches. But they are all a bunch of infidels, dying from the neck up."[2] As for activist black ministers like Martin Luther King, Jr., they were guilty of violating the spirituality of the church. Seeing death to their fond hope that the South would remain "white man's country forever," segregationists revived the Religion of the Lost Cause: state flags were altered to incorporate the old Confederate battle flag and new white supremacist organizations like the Citizens' Councils were created to keep black people in their place. In a popular diatribe embodying the conservative white South's "massive resistance" to *Brown*, Georgia Gov. Herman Talmadge fused the patriotic symbols of southernness and Americanness: "It will take courage . . . of the kind our fore-fathers showed when they signed the Declaration of Independence, the kind of courage they showed at Valley Forge, . . . at Gettysburg, and during the Reconstruction Era after the War Between the States."[3] Meanwhile, the old tragic sense of a lost plantation paradise gave way to visions of spiritual redemption and triumph. Picturing his denomination as strategically positioned within the divine purpose, one Southern Baptist pastor warned that the "future of our denomination, our nation, and perhaps the world depends on our stewardship of the gospel now." U.S. Senator James O. Eastland, a Methodist from Mississippi, was explicit: "The future greatness of America depends on racial purity and maintenance of Anglo-Saxon institutions, which still flourish in full flower in the South." In their struggle against civil rights, the journalist Robert Sherrill observed, southerners were "not just waging a political and economic war against change, but a religious war."[4]

THE BLACK WAY

African American religion originated in a melding of African and Christian beliefs and practices. In the eighteenth century, hundreds of thousands of enslaved people from different regions of Africa poured into colonial South Carolina and Georgia to clear land, drain swamps, and cultivate rice, sugar, and cotton. Those who survived the harsh conditions developed a new way of life, borrowing culturally from each other and from Europeans. White evangelical missionaries—Methodists, for the most part—conducted revivals and established churches among the enslaved people and they responded, endowing the gospel of salvation with the spirit-filled spirituality they had brought with them from Africa.

Indulgent masters allowed their slaves to worship together, but usually under white supervision, for the plantation owners worried far more than the evangelists about unsupervised slave gatherings, and rightly so. And while Methodist missionaries and regular ministers allowed blacks to preach, they only slowly sanctioned separate black churches. First in Philadelphia and later in New York, African Americans withdrew from predominantly white Methodist churches in order to control their own religious lives. In 1816, a number of black Methodist churches united under the leadership of Richard Allen to form the American Methodist Episcopal (AME) Church; six years later, others organized themselves into the American Methodist Episcopal Zion (AMEZ) Church. Both denominations harbored powerful anti-slavery convictions that ratcheted up the fears of white southerners. In reaction, the white denominations of the South launched a newly invigorated mission to the slaves.

The missionaries promoted a paternalistic vision of a biracial evangelical community, with white religious leaders assuming new responsibilities for the fate of slave souls. In fact, the generation before the Civil War experienced the one moment in southern religious life when blacks and whites enjoyed the same ritual and spatial setting—listening to the same sermons, partaking of communion together, and sharing church disciplinary procedures. Such settings were segregated to be sure but the interaction within biracial churches represented a foundation for later spiritual commonalities among blacks and whites in the South and provided the historic basis for moral commonalities on some contemporary public issues. At the same time, it is crucial to recognize that the way blacks understood the evangelical message was radically different from what was intended by the slave owner-sanctioned preacher anxious to achieve social control. For blacks, the Christian message embodied a profound vision of liberation and equality that was at once spiritual and endowed with a measure of millennial hope that it could be earthly too.

After the Civil War, southern blacks withdrew from biracial worship to establish their own churches; these combined existing white evangelical denominational forms with worship traditions rooted in the slave quarters and a notable sense of black spiritual destiny. As the central institution of African American culture generally, the "black church" helped maintain the African American community, and provided it with what public presence it had during the grim reign of Jim Crow. The AME Church especially was responsible for generating a distinctive civil religion designed both to uplift black people and (in a way parallel to white evangelicalism) to enable America to live up to its national ideals. The editor of the AME's official organ, the *Christian Recorder*, believed that the separation of the races was keeping the United States from becoming "the great field of training for . . . solving the great problem of a universal brotherhood, the unity of the race of mankind, and the eternal principles of intellectual, moral, and spiritual development." By forcing America to come to terms with racial difference, by pushing white America toward the acceptance of racial equality, African Americans would help fulfill the nation's as well as their own destiny.[5]

At the end of World War II, southern blacks came home from fighting Nazi racial ideology in Europe unwilling to tolerate an analogous ideology at home. Truman's progressive civil rights policy, which included desegregating the armed forces, together with the Supreme Court's 1944 *Smith v. Allwright* ruling ending the white primary (and later, *Brown*) convinced blacks that God was making "a way out of no way." Just as Richard Allen and the other founders of African Methodism had protested racial bias in church, so there had been black ministers throughout the Jim Crow era who used Christian principles to demand political and economic freedom, and employed religious media and denominational networks to attack racism. Yet this activist tradition should not obscure the African American churches' longstanding history of passivity when it came to social issues, or at least their preference for urging restraint and "moral suasion" rather than directly confronting racial oppression. Over the years, people in and out of African American communities had criticized conservative church leaders as cop-outs who substituted promises in the heavenly future ("pie in the sky when you die") for freedom and justice here and now. During the civil rights era, young radical activists ridiculed such preachers with lyrics set to the spiritual "Down by the Riverside": "Goin' to leave my shufflin' shoes, down by the parson's door."

Martin Luther King, Jr., himself grew up in Atlanta's mainline Ebenezer Baptist Church, where his father served as pastor. In 1960, "Daddy" King initially opposed the candidacy of John F. Kennedy, both because of traditional Protestant worries about Catholic power and because of the historic ties of African Americans in the South to the Party of Lincoln. (It took the civil rights revolution to bring Southern blacks firmly into the Democratic camp, even as, over a longer period, it pushed Southern whites into the Republican one.) Ebenezer was for its part a conservative institution with a conservative, middle-class congregation that did not want to rock the boat, though it took responsibility for providing for the social welfare of Atlanta's African American community. While the younger King and others demonstrated the effectiveness of greater militancy, leaders of the National Baptist Convention, the country's largest African American denomination, continued to argue that churches should not involve themselves in political activism regardless of how righteous the cause—the black version of the spirituality of the church. Nevertheless, black churches deserve a large share of the credit for the civil rights movement's achievements. During the struggle, they were always there to reinforce the principle of nonviolent disobedience, providing the participants and demonstrating the strength of Christian faith in the face of snarling dogs, police batons, and terrorist bombs. The documentary film *Eyes on the Prize* shows the face of a black woman in a civil rights meeting in Albany, Georgia, in the 1960s, singing and fanning herself with one of those cardboard fans once ubiquitous in southern churches. In a later scene, viewers see the same woman, now kneeling with others in prayer, moving with the spirit, in front of Albany's City Hall and jail. As she rises to be arrested, she is still waving that church fan. As Vincent Harding notes, that scene testified "in that simple motion to the fact that the religion that moved her life was one and the same in the church building and in the public square—and it would remain the same in the city jail."[6] Like the white evangelicals who, in the song, were "preachin', prayin', singin'," this church mother was kneeling, praying, and singing her faith on a southern public square.

In the national public square, before the Lincoln Memorial at the 1963 March on Washington, King gave the African American civil religion its finest expression. His "I have a dream" speech, the defining moment of the civil rights movement, was a soaring articulation of the messianic hope of black southerners that America would live up to its calling to represent an ideal brotherhood. As King later put it, the black community was to provide "a new expression of the American dream that need not be realized at the expense of other men around the world, but a dream of opportunity and life that can be shared with the rest of the world." America had a special role, noted the Birmingham civil rights minister Fred Shuttlesworth, for "once we got all the melting pot together here, and the hardest bit was to assimilate the blacks into it, then we could be an example for the world." By arguing that desegregation fulfilled the American purpose, this version of civil religion highlighted the idea of pluralism for all humanity. As a microcosm of the world's diversity, America was called by God to be an exemplar nation, even a redeemer nation, revealing how the rest of the world might live together as a family of nations. It was, in a real sense, the mirror image of the white evangelical vision of the Redeemer South, and its triumph sounded the death knell of the Lost Cause.[7]

FROM RACE TO GENDER

By the early 1970s, segregationists knew better than to air their views publicly. What had been mainstream thought was now extreme, and that included the Biblical justification of white supremacy. Even W. A. Criswell capitulated, confessing in 1970 that he had "come to the profound conclusion that to separate by coercion the body of Christ on the basis of skin pigmentation was unthinkable, unchristian and unacceptable to God."[8] But having given up their apologetics for Jim Crow, conservative southern clergy did not retreat from the public sphere. To the contrary, their day of maximum national prominence was just dawning. Nor was it an accident that this should happen following the demise of race as the central issue of southern life. While the end of legalized segregation may have signaled the imminent arrival of the Beloved Community for Martin Luther King, Jr.'s followers, for conservative white southerners "race mixing" remained a threat to right order in society. Equally threatening were the other changes in American culture associated with "the Sixties," including drugs and what came to be known as the sexual revolution. The religious right that would transform American politics over the next generation was rooted in a traditional southern evangelical defense of social hierarchy as necessary for a properly ordered liberty. No longer in a position to defend a discredited racial hierarchy, conservative clergy were needed now to elaborate a bold religious defense of patriarchy and "family values."

In the 1970s, a number of "anti-patriarchal" legal developments sparked the opposition out of which the religious right emerged. Of prime significance was the Equal Rights Amendment, which passed the U.S. Congress in 1972 by a wide margin. Although a large number of states ratified the amendment within a couple of years, by 1974 an active opposition was in the field claiming that the amendment would erase differences between the sexes and undermine the traditional family.[9] No region proved to be as resistant to the ERA as the South. Of the 10 southern states, only West Virginia, Kentucky, and Tennessee ratified the amendment, and the latter two both turned around and rescinded their ratification. Slower to gather strength was opposition to the Supreme Court's 1973 *Roe v. Wade* decision, declaring a woman's constitutional right to abortion, but by the early 1980s it was firmly ensconced at the top of the religious right agenda. In 1977, national attention was focused on a fight to overturn a Dade County (Miami), Florida, ordinance prohibiting discrimination on the basis of sexual orientation. The fight was successfully led by Anita Bryant, a sometime popular singer and spokeswoman for Florida orange juice, on the grounds that the ordinance violated "Christian beliefs regarding the sinfulness of homosexuality and the perceived threat of homosexual recruitment of children and child molestation."

To be sure, race was not entirely absent among the animating concerns of the nascent religious right. When the IRS set out in 1975 to revoke the tax exemption of Bob Jones University because the Greenville, South Carolina, school prohibited interracial dating, it brought such future leaders of the religious right as Jerry Falwell and James Dobson together for the first time in a public cause.[10] In 1979, Falwell, an Independent Baptist preacher from Lynchburg, Virginia, founded Moral Majority, Inc., which rapidly emerged as the religious right's first national marquee organization. Falwell, who during the 1960s had criticized black pastors in the civil rights movement for engaging their churches in politics, had come to believe that white religious leaders needed to go and do likewise. He himself had journeyed down to Florida to help in the fight against the Dade County ordinance. Although he claimed that what had alienated him from contemporary America was the Supreme Court's 1963 decision banning teacher-led prayer in public schools, by the time Falwell wrote the new movement's manifesto, *Listen, America!*, in 1980, his list of America's national sins was equally responsive to the cultural revolution of the 1960s. His top five sins were abortion, homosexuality, pornography, humanism, and the "fractured family," a catchall for divorced couples, unmarried couples living together, homosexual couples, and those living communally. In addressing education, Falwell made the case for private Christian schools, but despite the presence of "seg academies" across the South, race did not figure at all in his rationale. In place of segregation, the cause of ordering society now depended on a moral agenda that started with the education of youth, whether via Christian schools or in a public school system to which prayer had been restored.

At the heart of the religious right's concerns was the traditional understanding of sex and gender. Feminists, it was argued, were trying to destroy the family as God intended it. Concerned only with self-fulfillment, they denigrated women for choosing to be homemakers and mothers. When they should be promoting childbearing, they sanctioned a selfish agenda that included the right to kill unborn children. Those feminists who had children neglected them by going to work instead of staying at home and caring for them. Anti-scripturally, they refused to be submissive to men in both church and family. Feminists, per Falwell, had "never accepted their God-given roles." It was because of their "desire to eliminate God-given differences that exist between the sexes" that they were "prohomosexual and lesbian." Not surprisingly, they also promoted "secular humanism"—a philosophy that emphasized, as Falwell put it, "that within each individual there is a glorious talented personality . . . an inner divinity that he alone can bring out in himself," and which leads directly to moral relativism.[11]

The rise of the religious right had its strictly denominational side, institutionally and ideologically. In 1979, a group of conservative Southern Baptist men set out to win control of the Southern Baptist Convention (SBC). Theological modernism and political liberalism, they argued, were weaning Southern Baptists away from their historic defense of Christianity. The SBC needed to be put back in the hands of Biblical inerrantists—those who upheld the literal verity of the Bible. It took some time but in 1990 they achieved complete victory; after that year, moderates no longer showed up at the annual convention to contest elections or doctrinal statements. Behind the battle for control of the denomination there had been a classic struggle between those for whom human equality and autonomy reigned as fundamental principles, and those for whom communal norms and strictures and a divinely ordained hierarchy remained determinative of social life. For the latter, gendered patterns of hierarchy were fundamental to godly structures of religious, social, and political life. Southern conservatism had always intertwined race and gender hierarchies, particularly in its emphasis on social purity. Within the SBC, it had come time to separate the two and make gender the casus belli.

Meeting at their annual convention in Atlanta in 1995, the messengers (as SBC delegates are called) passed a resolution declaring that they "unwaveringly denounce racism, in all its forms, as deplorable sin" and "lament and repudiate historic acts of evil such as slavery from which we continue to reap a bitter harvest." It also apologized to all African Americans for "condoning and/or perpetuating individual and systemic racism in our lifetime" and repented of the "racism of which we have been guilty, whether consciously or unconsciously." Seeking forgiveness "from our African-American brothers and sisters," the messengers pledged to "eradicate racism in all its forms from Southern Baptist life and ministry." Then, meeting three years later in Salt Lake City, Utah, the messengers approved a change to the Baptist Faith and Message that endorsed "wifely submission" to husbands. Although this new language reiterated a time-honored position in southern religious life, its adoption was portentous. Never before had denominational leaders and representatives arrogated to themselves the power of making church law in private life (as opposed to theology and social policy).

No one could doubt what the new program was. By the early 1990s, conservatives had consolidated their power at the SBC's flagship school, the Southern Baptist Theological Seminary in Louisville. This brought about the near-total turnover of the faculty, including the forced resignation in 1994 of the theologian Molly Marshall. Had she not resigned, Marshall—the first woman to receive tenure at Southern and a supporter of women's ordination—would have been charged with "failure to relate constructively" to the SBC and alleged deviation from seminary positions on issues ranging from atonement and salvation to God and the Bible. Denying that gender had anything to do with the effort to dismiss her, the newly appointed president of Southern, R. Albert Mohler, Jr., acknowledged that "feminist theology, as distinct from the issue of the service of women in the church, is and has been one of proper concern related to Southern Baptist theological education." The seminary, Mohler said, would "not be open to a revision of basic Christian doctrine or of the text and character of Christian scripture in order to meet the demands of what is now considered the mainstream of feminist theology." For her part, Marshall denied that she was a "mainstream feminist theologian," insisting rather that the SBC's leadership felt threatened by the views of a woman who happened to be a theologian. What her ouster highlighted was the gender politics of the new regime.

The latter was no less evident in the troubles of the Woman's Missionary Union (WMU), the preeminent organization of Southern Baptist women. The WMU was organized in 1888 after years of opposition from SBC male leaders, who feared that approving a separate women's organization would lead to women speaking in public and would be an entering wedge for discussions of the burgeoning women's suffrage movement. Organized as an auxiliary to the SBC, the WMU was self-governing and self-supporting and it grew wildly from the start because both foreign and home missions were extremely popular causes with nineteenth century Protestant women. A century later, it continued to sponsor missionaries in the United States and abroad, educating and involving "women, girls, and preschoolers" in the missionary cause, raising funds, and publicizing the need for missions. On January 10, 1993, leaders of the WMU voted to support the missionary work of not only the SBC but also of the Cooperative Baptist Fellowship (CBF) and Mainstream Baptists, moderate groups formed in opposition to the SBC's new regime. Immediately, an SBC trustee accused the WMU of acting like an adulterous woman, while a member of the SBC's executive board suggested that the denomination might start another women's missionary organization under the control of national church leaders. When the WMU provided materials on missions to the CBF, the SBC leadership demanded that the women's group affirm "faithful and solitary support" for SBC missions or risk its position in the denomination. Three-time SBC president Adrian Rogers called for a takeover of the WMU and an end to what he termed the "feminization" of missions. Echoing fundamentalist concern about women's leadership, Rogers argued that "mission promotion . . . should be led by pastors and the leaders of the Brotherhood, a men's mission group."

In 1995, Mohler closed Southern's Carver School of Social Work, effectively ending (in the words of former WMU President Catherine Allen) "the only area of SBC theological studies in which women predominated." Mohler had concluded that "the tenets of social work are not compatible with biblical theology," the *Baptist Standard* reported on March 1, 2000. Ultimately, the WMU succeeded in having the Seminary return nearly $1 million in endowment funds earmarked for social work education. A number of WMU leaders left the organization to found, in December of 2001, Global Women, a group that actively embraced women in ministry and women missionaries. To explain the defection of so many WMU women, Catherine Allen, the new group's treasurer, cited the SBC's "misogynist missiology."

In 2001, the SBC changed its Faith and Message to assert that women pastors were not sanctioned by the Bible; shortly thereafter, its North American Missions Board announced that it would stop employing ordained women as chaplains and its International Mission Board (IMB) issued instructions that all missionaries endorse the revised standard. About the same time, Don and Esther Gardner of Birmingham, Alabama, applied to be Southern Baptist missionaries in Africa. They had both volunteered in African missions before, and the head of missions work in Africa had urged them to return. But as members of a congregation, Baptist Church of the

Covenant, that had a woman pastor, they had a problem with the revised standard. Rather than endorse it, they appended to their application lengthy explanations of the points of doctrine with which they disagreed. On September 10, 2002, the Gardners were informed that their application had been rejected. The president of the IMB, Jerry Rankin, told reporters that the Gardners had "made it very clear that they supported women pastors. It was discussed with them, and they did endorse their pastor." "We've been Southern Baptist all of our lives," Esther Gardner said in an interview. "It just hurt down deep in our gut."[12]

TO THE BARRICADES . . .

The cradle of the religious right was the Commonwealth of Virginia. For a decade, Falwell's Moral Majority was the means by which southern evangelicals, who historically had been suspicious of becoming religiously engaged in politics, eased their way into involvement in local and state issues like pari-mutuel betting as well as nationwide struggles over abortion and gay rights. The mantle of national leadership then passed to the Christian Coalition, which was established by the Virginia Beach-based Christian broadcaster Pat Robertson after his unsuccessful run for the GOP presidential nomination in 1988. Robertson, a convert to Pentecostalism whose father had been a conservative Democratic U.S. senator from the Old Dominion, hired a young Georgian Republican named Ralph Reed to be executive director and together they built the Christian Coalition into a formidable grassroots organization. Unencumbered by the ancient Baptist commitment to strict church-state separation, the Christian Coalition served as the beacon for faith-based politicking across the region. Besides these two marquee national outfits, a host of smaller organizations sprang up across the state to mobilize "values voters." Yet even in Virginia, the enthusiasm and passion generated by the religious right were not always matched by substantive victories. At the height of its political influence in the early 1990s, it did not have sufficient clout statewide to secure electoral victory for two of its leading figures: former Moral Majority leader Michael Farris, the Republican candidate for lieutenant governor in 1993, and talk show host Oliver North, the Republican candidate for U.S. Senate in 1994.

If the religious right discovered the limits of its power in Virginia, it learned the perils of internecine conflict in South Carolina. For years, ultraconservative Bob Jones University, located in Greenville, served as a launching pad for evangelical politicos in the Palmetto State. Yet in the late

1980s, Bob Jones Republicans joined with the state GOP establishment in repelling the advance of Pat Robertson's Christian Coalition and Robertson's own insurgent political campaign against then-Vice President George H. W. Bush. Over the next decade, intra-party skirmishing continued as Robertson's group sought unsuccessfully to take over the state party organization. Such setbacks notwithstanding, the Christian Coalition was extremely active on the campaign trail throughout the region during the 1990s, distributing its voter guides in white evangelical churches, which they gradually welded into a machine for turning out conservative GOP voters. Very often this proceeded in a stealthy way, as some candidates found it necessary to avoid too strong an association with the organization, lest they alienate moderates at the polls. Often a delicate balancing act had to be performed among older-style mainstream business Republicans, economic and social libertarians, and Christian conservatives.

The high-water mark of religious right success in Southern state politics may have come in the 2002 midterm elections in Georgia, in which voters turned out the incumbent Democratic governor and installed the first Republican since Reconstruction. The state legislature, which had been solidly Democratic, flipped to the GOP as well. A large part of the credit belonged to Ralph Reed, who, having left the Christian Coalition to start a political consulting firm in 1997, had taken on the chairmanship of the state Republican Party two years earlier. Working closely with the capable head of the state Christian Coalition, Sadie Fields, Reed succeeded in creating a seamless connection between the party apparatus and conservative white evangelical churches across the state. A good sense of what Reed and Fields wrought can be gotten from the following excerpts of a contemporaneous e-mail composed by a member of one those churches—a disgruntled Democrat in a sea of Republicanism.

> The "in crowd" at my church is all Republican and regularly encourage others in the church to attend the Christian Coalition meetings and rallies. They also ask for volunteers to help them in the election campaigns of Republican candidates. The Deacons and Pastor invite Republican candidates to come speak at our church, but never invite Democrats. . . .
>
> In all meals or meetings in the Church Fellowship Hall, whenever talk turns to politics and current affairs, the Church leaders always point out that the Republican Party is the one that represents "Christian values" and "Christian people" should always support them. During the Clinton presidency, there were 8 years of demonizing him and all things Democratic. If I ever spoke up in defense of a Democratic politician, I was talked down and sometimes actually yelled at by red-faced Deacons say-

ing that the Democrats are the work of the devil. Whenever I tried to point out church is not the appropriate place for secular politics, I've also been pooh-poohed . . .

It is now commonly accepted in the Christian community that the Republican Party is the Christian political party. . . . Because I am a Democrat, I have actually been pulled aside by fellow church members and told I'd better not let people in my church know that! . . .

Sunday morning before an election day, the so-called Christian Coalition's Voter Guide is distributed in the vestibule of my church (and hundreds of other churches across the state). The preacher always makes an announcement about it and exhorts everyone to be sure to pick one up as they leave the sanctuary. There is always a stack of these "voter guides" (which amount to Republican tickets) left in the vestibule, easily available to voters when they come to vote on Tuesday . . .

The Republican political activities continue year-round, no matter whether an election year or not. For an example . . . a so-called "Families and Freedom Rally" was held at Mt. Vernon Baptist [January 25, 2003] This was a fundraiser for "little people" at a cost of $20 per head. The program consisted of all Republican elected officials. . . . My own church actually sent a church van to carry people to this event, as they do for most of these things.[13]

After the election, Fields wrote her troops an e-mail thank you letter that began:

I received a call from the Governor's transition team last week requesting a meeting with me to discuss and plan how to best implement a pro-family agenda over the course of his administration. The Governor-elect is very in tune with our values, and wants to work with us on accomplishing our goals. I will be meeting with them either this week or the week after to discuss how we can work together on issues that are important to the pro-family movement in Georgia. While standing on principle, we must govern wisely and incrementally, and to that end I will work with the Governor's office to ensure that our agenda is reasonable and attainable.

The emphasis on making her movement's agenda dovetail with the work of the new gubernatorial administration is telling. After the 2002 election, Fields emerged as the unquestioned leader of the evangelical wing of the state GOP and a force to be reckoned with in Georgia politics as a whole. In 2004, she was widely acknowledged as the key figure behind passage of an amendment to the state constitution banning gay marriage.

Across the southern Bible Belt, the mobilization of white evangelicals through their churches was a notable feature of electoral politics—one traceable by the numbers. In the 2002 election, 51 percent of white evangelicals who said they attend church frequently (once a week or more) turned out to vote in the South (and Southern Crossroads), as opposed to 43 percent in the rest of the country. (Less frequent church-attending evangelicals actually turned out in smaller numbers in South.) Given that frequent church-attending evangelicals contributed twice the proportion of Republican votes in the South than elsewhere (41 percent versus 21 percent), the impact of mobilization was substantial. Just as labor unions during the Great Depression became the institutional power base of the Democratic Party in America's industrial heartland, so white evangelical churches had, by the turn of the millennium, become the GOP's institutional power base from Virginia to Texas.[14]

Looking back at Jerry Falwell's 1980 manifesto *Listen, America!*, it is striking how little the agenda of the religious right changed in the course of a generation. Same-sex marriage was added to the dangers on the homosexual/lesbian front, home schooling supplanted Christian private schools at the leading edge of educational reform, and "secular humanism" more or less dropped off the list of conservative talking points. Otherwise, the only significant additions to the agenda after 1980 were the teaching of evolution in the public schools, which returned to the national spotlight in the 1980s, and the display of the Ten Commandments in public spaces, which emerged in a rolling series of disputes in the 1990s. Thanks to this fundamental consistency, white evangelicals in the South became about as united as any group in the country on moral and social issues—or at least as united as any who attended church regularly. They used the language of "family values" and "what would Jesus do," and Southern politicians ignored them at their peril. To be sure, the pols often failed to deliver, and sometimes it was because the (largely evangelical) populace didn't really want them to. Divorce rates remained high in the South, as did levels of drug and alcohol abuse. But evangelicals had never been unacquainted with sin. The important thing was to uphold the right moral norms.

In the early years of the new millennium, white evangelicals across the South powerfully influenced but could not expect to control public life. Politicians were obligated to speak to issues important to evangelicals, and moral issues—"moral values"—were a part of electoral campaigns. But voters did not always support the evangelical party line (assuming there was one). This was especially true regarding gambling and the lottery, where practical considerations of economic development and funding for education often superseded moralistic pronouncements. Evangelicals placed many of their own in seats of political power at local and state levels, but there they had to forge coalitions, and often moved more to the center in order to avoid being out-voted and exiled. This was particularly true in states like Florida and, increasingly, Virginia, where greater ethnic and religious diversity made it difficult to run exclusively on a hard-core religious right platform.

It is important to recognize the extent to which the transformation of white evangelical churches into organs of political mobilization for the GOP was based on observation of black churches. Beginning with Falwell's political awakening in the 1970s, Southern evangelical politicos imitated the black church not just in the way they energized their troops and got them to the polls, but in how they constituted white congregations as homogeneous po litical communities. This is an example of the hybridized black-white culture of the South, in which both sides imitate even as they don't quite acknowledge their debts to the other.

For its part, the black church did not abandon political engagement after the 1960s. Surveys through the 1980s showed that, overwhelmingly, African Americans wanted their churches to be actively involved in civil rights, and in due course, more than half of the South's black churches established some sort of relationship with civil rights organizations and began participating in civil rights activities. Indeed, in the wake of the civil rights revolution, African American churches in the South became powerful instruments of political mobilization. Serving as the primary means for politicians to reach into African American communities, mainline Baptist and Methodist churches in particular offer forums for candidates and vital election networks. In 1973, for example, black ministers in Atlanta played a key role in the election of Maynard Jackson as that city's first black mayor. Their strategy relied heavily on using their churches to turn out the vote. White candidates also now plug themselves into the African American church network. Former Virginia governor Douglas Wilder, an African American, claims that it was because he introduced white Democratic senator Chuck Robb around at black churches that Robb managed to eke out reelection in the decidedly Republican year of 1994.[15] In December 2003, six weeks before South Carolina's Democratic presidential primary, Rev. James Darby counted the candidates who had already appeared at his Morris Brown African Methodist Episcopal Church in Charleston: Joseph Lieberman, John Kerry's sister, John Edwards twice, Howard Dean twice, Wesley Clark, and Al Sharpton. "We are being treated like the belles of the ball," Darby exclaimed.[16]

To be sure, as African Americans have joined the mainstream, the kind of political monopoly enjoyed by the church has suffered some erosion. In 2002, for instance, Artur Davis—a graduate of Harvard College and Harvard Law School—was elected as Alabama's first African American congressman since Reconstruction thanks not only to the black churches but also to extensive use of secular opinion shapers, websites, and e-mail. No one should, however, underestimate the importance of the churches when it comes to electoral politics—and to the capacity of the black clergy to influence black elected officials in the South.

. . . AND BEYOND

On February 26, 2004, the Georgia House of Representatives fell three votes shy of the two-thirds majority needed to put Sadie Fields' constitutional ban on gay marriage on the November ballot. Thereupon, black church leaders went into action, holding rallies, meeting with the press, and lobbying black legislators. One of the latter, Democrat Randal Mangham of Decatur, felt extreme pressure from Bishop Eddie Long, pastor of the 25,000-member New Birth Missionary Baptist Church, even though Long did not confront him directly. "But he's my pastor," Mangham explained. "I go to church there. He doesn't have to call me. He speaks from the pulpit." Sounding like any white evangelical, John Timmons, pastor of Calvary Missionary Baptist Church near Savannah, declared, "Marriage is just between a man and a woman. That's the way God ordained it, and that's the way it should be." On March 31, four members of the House Legislative Black Caucus switched their votes and the measure passed. Afterwards, *Atlanta Journal Constitution* editorial page editor Cynthia Tucker, comparing the ban to the defense of slavery, lamented that this had been "a triumph for bigotry based on the Bible." But this time, it wasn't just white voters who bore the responsibility. "Homophobia oozes across lines of color, linking black America with white in a common contempt masquerading as morality," wrote Tucker, herself an African American.[17] Tucker's disgust notwithstanding, the biracial character of the anti-gay coalition was not a masquerade. The fact was that African American churches in the South embraced many of the same moral values as their evangelical white counterparts, the two groups representing a shaping force of public life in the region.

For gay marriage was not the only issue on which African American Protestants were out of sync with the liberal views of their political allies in the national Democratic Party. On abortion, African Americans in the South were pro-life (48.3 percent) more than pro-choice (37.6 percent)—marginally further to the right than they were nationwide (46.4 percent pro-life and 38.9 percent pro-choice). Like their white Southern counterparts, African American churches opposed state lotteries. Altogether, with their tradition of community outreach, they continued to function as multipurpose institutions—but with a more conservative cast than in the wake of the civil rights movement. A generation earlier, roughly two-thirds of the black clergy indicated a positive response to the radical liberationist theologies of writers like Gayraud Wilmore, James Cone, and Pauli Murray; now, only a third claimed to be so influenced.[18] The shift could most clearly be detected in the megachurches that had become significant players in the religious life of the South for African Americans as well as whites. Black pastors of such churches as Atlanta's World Changers Ministries had built congregations of as many as 20,000 people who gathered in buildings that could be sports arenas to hear preaching about God's plans for the worldly success of believers. To the faithful there, the issues were not the old ones of social and political engagement but individual conversion, pious behavior, respectability—and wealth. In a version of the traditional white evangelical belief in social amelioration through personal redemption, these "prosperity ministries" stressed that if the individual rose, the broader African American community would do the same.

It was here that the black church seemed susceptible to George W. Bush's faith-based initiatives, particularly in his administration's early days, when the slogan "compassionate conservatism" was still on Republican lips. Although many black leaders and activists were skeptical of the GOP, seeing the effort as merely designed to silence prophetic voices in their communities, the promise of making government funding available for churches active in community projects but reluctant to suppress the evangelistic dimension of their social ministries held real appeal for some of the most ambitious and successful African American pastors. Moreover, without losing the sense of black consciousness that had long been a prominent feature of African American religion, black pastors in the South seemed more attuned to the idea of the "beloved community" announced by Martin Luther King, Jr., and forged during the struggle for civil rights. This was evident in environmental justice campaigns drawing from Biblical discourse, church-based economic development programs, interdenominational self-help projects, and above all in religiously based racial reconciliation efforts.

At the local level, black ministers joined with white ministers in biracial community groups. One example was Mission Mississippi, an organization led by the former civil rights activist Dolphus Weary. Mission Mississippi built its activities around the shared evangelical outlooks of a population from what was once the most racially polarized state in the nation, using the slogan: "The grace is greater than race." Formally uninvolved in politics, Mission Mississippi's evangelical-based prayer breakfasts and public rallies advanced the cause of a public square different from anything that had been seen before in the South. At a national level, Promise Keepers, the evangelical men's movement that captured headlines in the mid-1990s, may have seemed to many white liberals like an antifeminist nightmare, but along with a kind of soft patriarchy it embraced the goal of overcoming "the sin of racism" by bringing black and white men together in common religious cause. Among the "seven promises" to be undertaken by members of the movement, the sixth was: "A Promise Keeper is committed to reaching beyond any denominational barriers to demonstrate the power of biblical unity."[19]

Eleven o'clock on Sunday morning might still have been, as King famously said, the most segregated hour of the week, but biracial congregations could increasingly be found in metropolitan areas like Atlanta, especially in the large independent churches that drew on Pentecostal traditions. Even in rural areas, a degree of racial reconciliation could be discerned. When the phenomenon of rural church burnings arose as a public issue in the region in the mid-1990s, black and white Protestants often made new community-based alliances in rebuilding churches, and trust, across racial boundaries. In 2006, the African American members of Pleasant Sabine Baptist Church in Centerville, Alabama, received an unannounced visit from white members of Antioch Baptist Church; both churches had been destroyed by arson. "People who I thought didn't care, you know white people, they started expressing their sorrow," said one Sabine church member. "They came down and hugged us. Some of them even started crying. Even the older ones, they came and said, 'Come worship at our Church.'"[20] It is fair to say that, in the first decade of the twenty-first century, churches in the South were not only organizing sites for community activism and political campaigns, not only promoters of thisworldly prosperity, but also engines of racial reconciliation.

To be sure, there remained a lot to overcome. In 2002, Alabama experienced a remarkable attempt to mobilize a biracial social justice campaign from conservative Christian impulses when Republican Governor Bob Riley tried to persuade Alabama voters to approve by referendum a $1.2 billion tax increase to correct a state tax structure that he had concluded exploited the poor. "Jesus says one of our missions is to take care of the least among us," Riley said. Riley knew his Bible well, and voters could recall that he had been elected as a Bible-quoting religious right supporter as well as a conventional low-tax conservative Republican. A state financial crisis, as well as conscience, impelled him to propose the controversial tax increase. Riley had been converted to his tax reform proposal through the writings of Susan Pace Hamill, a University of Alabama law professor and Methodist, who drew from Christian ethics in condemning a regressive state tax structure that milked Alabama's poorest people at an 11 percent rate, compared to 4 percent for the wealthiest. "According to our Christian ethics," Riley said during his campaign for reform, "we're supposed to love God, love each other, and help take care of the poor." He insisted that it was "immoral to charge somebody making $5,000 an income tax."[21]

Riley's embrace of this neo-Social Gospel won him the support of the national Christian Coalition, now well into its post-Reed decline. As its president, Roberta Combs, put it in an *Anniston Star* op-ed, "I think this is a good plan and I think people of faith need to know about the plan." But the organization's state chapter, the Christian Coalition of Alabama (CCA) would have none of it: "Alabama does not have a tax crisis. It has a spending crisis," thundered an eight-page CCA "voter education" pamphlet distributed at Christian schools and bookstores, and at football games. "The road to a better future isn't paved with a tax increase." Riley tried to get Alabama pastors to trumpet his plan from their pulpits but in the end failed to persuade enough of them that a more equitable tax system was what Jesus would have wanted. While mainline Protestant groups did support the plan, white evangelical pastors did not, even going so far as to bring the doctrine of the spirituality of the church out of mothballs to plead that churches should stay out of politics. Needless to say, they didn't feel the same about church-based political activism when it came to moral values issues like abortion and gay rights. The kiss of death was administered by black religious leaders who, distrustful of Riley's conservative record, kept their distance from the initiative—thereby forming an odd coalition of the disengaged and distrustful with their white brethren. On September 9, Alabama voters turned down the plan by a margin of two to one.

Looking toward the future, it was critical to recall Martin Luther King, Jr.'s use of the rhetoric of southern identity in appealing to white southerners for change. Insisting that racial justice would add to "our cultural health as a region," King spoke of "our beloved Southland," a region that "has some beauty, that has been made ugly by segregation." He lauded the "intimacy of life that can be beautiful," and predicted that the nature of life in the South "will make it one of the finest sections of our country once we solve this problem of segregation."[22] If the end of segregation enabled southern blacks to embrace the region as their homeland, to see themselves as southerners no less than whites, it also created the possibility of a new regional myth in a region famous for mythologizing its past, and casting that past into the future. A perfect expression of the new myth-in-the-making was to be seen in the opening ceremony of the 1996 Olympic Games in Atlanta, created by the Trinidadian Carnival artist Peter Minshall and here described on the website of his Callalloo Company:

> The fireflies twinkle in the Southern Summer night. The full-faced Moon greets the golden Sun, to give birth to the Summer Day, and the Southern

Spirit rises upon silken wings. She dances among a landscape of Butter-flies, and ushers in a River of Southern history and culture: Old Man River with his steamboat Chariot, Belles and Gents, graceful black dancers "Wadin' in the Water," square dancing Country Girls and Boys, the flappers and musicians of the Jazz Age.

As the River's many currents blend and swirl in a rollicking Southern symphony, the atmosphere is shattered by a fierce and violent Storm. At its center is a Thunder-Bird of destruction that scatters the River, assaults the Southern Spirit, and lays waste to the field of Butterflies. In the wake of the Storm's devastation, the Southern Spirit barely lives, trembling on the brink between hope and despair. Her hope and faith prove the stronger, and take form as a grand flock of sister Spirits with bouquets of flowers upon their wings, dancing a ballet of Rebirth. They raise up the glittering Butterflies, and the entire Southern landscape explodes in a gospel chorus of joy and beauty, a celebration of life and the triumph of the human spirit: Hallelujah![23]

Even as this rehearsed the old false racist tale of elegant whites and happy darkies living in a plantation paradise destroyed by war, it opened up into the African American vision the religious promise of a biracial messianic age fit for the entire world to see, and embrace.

· 5 ·

The Southern Crossroads:
Showdown States

$\mathcal{R}$ay Waddle, who spent many years reporting on religion for the *Nashville Tennessean*, began a review of our Southern Crossroads volume with this personal reminiscence:

> Growing up in the 60s in north Louisiana, I was always noticing the angry billboards:
>
> ### GET US OUT OF THE U.N.!
>
> ### JESUS IS COMING SOON—ARE YOU READY?
>
> ### WATER FLUORIDATION . . . A COMMUNIST PLOT.
>
> These insistent messages were just a normal part of the scenery, like azaleas in bloom, icebox pies and LSU football. But the anger was puzzling. I saw it in letters to the editor, in leaflets left on the car windshield, in the scowls of TV preachers—attacks on "weak sister" liberals, blasts against secular humanism, detailed predictions of Armageddon.
>
> Why were the adults so mad? What were they afraid of? It seemed out of proportion to the facts. No one could tell me why.
>
> My part of America was always filled with gracious people, charming neighborhoods, and faithful churchgoing. But there was something else in the air—a cloud of political fierceness and aggressive Protestant argument. The very sky was a riddle of anxiety. We saw it as the staging area of a gathering apocalypse: Either Russian missiles would bear down on nearby Barksdale Air Base, or Christ himself would split the firmament in a final blaze of judgment, an ultimate furnace of truth.
>
> It didn't occur to me until I left home that our brand of confrontational culture wasn't so normal after all. It was the strange brew of a specific religious and social past, an accident of history.[1]

What we have called the Southern Crossroads—Texas, Oklahoma, Louisiana, Arkansas, and Missouri—is the southeast with a difference, a flashpoint region where the intersection of frontier ideals and Old South realities has historically produced political and religious clashes of pronounced intensity. It is intersected by at least four distinctive cultural boundaries, dividing the upland south from the Gulf coastal lowlands and Acadian Louisiana, and south from west, on a line running through Texas and Oklahoma. Three of the states joined the Confederacy; two didn't, but had strong roots in the Old South. Yet all partake of other regions, other cultures: the Midwest, the West, Mexico, the Caribbean. Altogether, the Crossroads is a place of borders and boundary lines, beginning with the Mississippi River—the "strong brown god," as T. S. Eliot called it. And where there are borders and boundaries, there are people on either side conscious of them, insisting on them, fighting for them and against them. Historically, this was a region of showdowns, where people fought intimate battles over turf, slavery, family pride and, always, religion.

In the Crossroads, the religious patterns differ from the South in subtle and not so subtle ways. Old-line Protestant churches are weaker. With calls to ministry that required no formal education and a circuit-riding clergy, Baptists and Methodists prior to the Civil War put into play a portable form of Christianity more suited to frontier conditions. As a result, a large proportion of the Presbyterian and Episcopalian families that reached the Crossroads from the east had, within a generation, became Methodists or Baptists. But even as it flattened the southeast's Protestant diversity, the Crossroads spawned new expressions of Protestantism. Restorationist groups like the Church of Christ, bent on recreating what they understood to be the life of the earliest Christians, established strong footholds, where they stood in uneasy (and sometimes openly hostile) relationship with their evangelical neighbors. Pentecostalism, emerging in the region at the turn of the twentieth century, gained its most substantial American presence there, and was bitterly contested by many Baptists and Methodists, who resented its condemnation of their lukewarmness and its siphoning of their members. But nothing set the Crossroads religiously apart from the Old South more than the substantial presence of Roman Catholicism, the first religion brought to the region by white people. Catholicism has given Louisiana, Texas, and Missouri in particular a distinctive cultural and religious flavor as well as creating strong religious tensions.

Religion is big business in the Crossroads—in more ways than one. Megachurches have become the normative religious institutions in the region. Typically these are congregations of several thousand members, led by a founder-preacher-CEO-authority figure, providing special ministries to target constituencies, and organized around intentional marketing techniques. Virtual mini-denominations unto themselves, they provide in one institution services and activities previously offered through regional or national denominational connections. Very often, they develop their own schools, mission agencies, literature, and venues of theological education. And that's to say nothing of their media ministries. Nowhere, indeed, does media outreach matter more. The region birthed two of televangelism's original icons, Oral Roberts of Tulsa and Jimmy Swaggart of Baton Rouge (Pentecostals both). In Houston, Second Baptist and Lakewood churches reach large national and international audiences by sending out their services via cable and satellite and internet. The Dallas-Fort Worth metroplex amounts to a religious broadcasting emporium, ranging from Kenneth Copeland's "prosperity gospel" ministries and T. D. Jakes' Potters' House, a televangelical empire that is reshaping African American religious life in the United States, to Baptist-evangelist-gone-charismatic James Robison's Life Today, and Edwin Young, Jr.'s Fellowship Church.

With its mighty religious fortresses, heavy spiritual throw weight, and combat readiness, the Crossroads went on the warpath in post-Vietnam America, seeking to stem the tide of barbarism by preserving "moral values" against a perceived onslaught of godless secularism, immorality, worldliness, and unbelief. Remote from both coasts, filled with cultural peculiarities and idiosyncrasies, the region nevertheless supplied many of the leaders and much of the style of the burgeoning culture wars. It is not too much to say that the Crossroads provided the country's model for religion in public life during the presidencies of Bill Clinton and George W. Bush, two of its favorite sons. To understand it, we need to look back more than a century before what Ray Waddle experienced growing up in the 1960s.

BAPTISTS WITH ATTITUDE

In the nineteenth century, nobody helped define Crossroads zealotry or did more to shape the region's distinctive approach to religion and public life than J. R. Graves. Born into a Congregationalist family in Vermont in 1820, Graves joined a Baptist church as a teenager and traveled west, eventually setting himself up in Memphis as a Baptist minister and editor. From the late 1840s until his death in 1893, he traveled the country campaigning against spiritual adversaries in what he imagined to be a war between true (Christian) religion and the forces of Romanism and rationalist infidelity. Seeing these twin evils as "working silently [for] the overthrow of our republican government and our free institutions," he predicted that "the bloodiest battleground—the Waterloo of this conflict—will be the valley of the Mississippi."[2]

Against all religious opponents, Protestant and Catholic, Graves waved the banner of Landmarkism, a historically dubious doctrine that claimed that Baptists descended through an unbroken succession of congregations practicing adult baptism back to the time of Jesus. Baptists were thus, he argued, the only true Christians. Politically, Graves promulgated a form of Christian Republicanism that saw America as "the hope of the world" and "pre-eminent among the nations of the earth." Christian citizens, he believed, were given a sacred trust to help America "exert an influence" upon the nations "in favor of Republicanism and Christianity." Yet even as he was confident of God's protection of the United States against external conquest, Graves warned against "the gradual and imperceptible undermining of the foundation upon which we rest. The glory of a nation can only be maintained by perpetuating, uncorrupted, the principles by which it was acquired."[3] Through Graves' influence, Landmarkism became a dominant force in Baptist churches throughout the Crossroads region. What is particularly important to bear in mind is its abandonment of the traditional Baptist preoccupation with keeping church and state far apart in order to protect the purity of the religious community. Crossroads Baptists had a tendency to see the world, including its political order, not as a source of pestilence and infection but as a swamp to be drained, a wilderness to be cleared, a field upon which to plant the cross. When the time came, they would be more prepared than their brethren in other parts of the country to march out of their churches and take up political arms. Then House Majority Leader Tom DeLay, a Baptist from the Houston suburb of Sugar Land, put it succinctly when he declared in 2002 that God was using him to promote "a biblical worldview" in American politics.

Crossroads Baptism was, to be sure, far from a single thing. In Arkansas, for example, many Baptist congregations declined to join the Southern Baptist Convention when, prior to the Civil War, it organized itself in opposition to antislavery Baptists in the north. As Southern Baptists became the white urbanized establishment in the state, these white Missionary Baptists preserved a measure of racial egalitarianism (connected to the presence of black Missionary Baptist congregations) as well as an economic populism that survives to this day. They sang from the old Stamps-Baxter hymnal, which featured hymns like "Footsteps of Jesus," that emphasized the need to seek the lost sheep, help the weak, and walk with the poor and lowly. Small wonder that Arkansans, to this day, have been susceptible to politicians intent on uplifting the least among us.

In the first half of the twentieth century, the Gravesian approach to civic engagement was exemplified by J. Frank Norris (1887–1952), the militant pastor of First Baptist Church in Fort Worth who became the foremost southern fundamentalist of his generation. Early in his career, Norris devoted much of his energy to attacking fellow Baptists in Texas and throughout the Southern Baptist Convention for modernism, minuscule as liberal theology was thereabouts. As editor of his own religious newspaper, the *Searchlight*, he regularly assailed Baylor University, his alma mater, as a hotbed of modernism and evolutionism, and helped establish Southwestern Baptist Seminary in Fort Worth to make up for the doctrinal laxity of Texas' premier Baptist institution of higher learning. In due course, Norris led his congregation out of the SBC altogether, forming both his own seminary (the Fundamental Baptist Bible Institute, now called Arlington Baptist College) and an organization of fundamentalist Baptist churches, the World Bible Fellowship. Besides seeking to hold fellow Baptists to the fundamentalist straight and narrow, he was a vociferous anti-Catholic, taking the position that Roman Catholics could not be real Americans. In 1926, he charged the Catholic mayor of Fort Worth with seeking to aid his church at the city's expense. When one of the mayor's supporters came to his office to try to persuade him to tone down his attacks, Norris grabbed a pistol and shot him dead. Tried for murder, he was acquitted on the grounds that he had fired in self-defense against the unarmed man.

In contrast to most fundamentalist leaders, Norris did not retreat from the public fray after the 1925 Scopes trial. Denouncing "this present godless, commercialized, pleasure gone mad, Sabbath-breaking, idol-worshipping, hellbound age," he played politics publicly and privately, endorsing national candidates and taking strong stands on the issues of the day. His anti-Catholicism led him to support Herbert Hoover over Al Smith for president in 1928; he subsequently showed a persistent proclivity for Republican candidates even while representing himself as a Democrat in the overwhelmingly Democratic Texas of his time. An opponent of both the New Deal and the labor movement, he was a vehement anti-Communist, contributing greatly to making anti-Communism a central feature of mid-twentieth century fundamentalism. The John Birch Society, the preeminent anti-Communist organization of the early Cold War period, was named after a graduate of Norris' Bible college who was killed by Chinese communists in 1945. To this day, there is a John Birch Hall on the campus of First Baptist Church, Fort Worth.

At once the autocratic leader of a huge (25,000 member) congregation,[4] head of his own institution of higher learning, governing member of many national fundamentalist organizations, and editor of his own newspaper, Norris blazed the trail for Jerry Falwell and subsequent marquee figures of the contemporary religious right. Well before the rise of the Sunbelt, he embraced a national political evangel from a regional base in the Old Confederacy—viewing himself, according to his most recent biographer, as the leader of "the southern theater in a national war on modernism." His hope was to "preserve and defend the South" from the encroachments of northern modernism, and thereby to salvage the nation as a whole. Like Graves before him, Norris saw his national mission as intimately connected to his sectarian one, thereby anticipating the "militant, individualistic, Texas brand of fundamentalism" that later in the century would come to dominate the entire SBC. Indeed, the fundamentalist takeover of the SBC in the 1980s should be seen as an essential part of Norris' legacy. This was the ecclesial counterpart to the rise to preeminence of the religious right in Republican Party politics. Nor would it have been possible without Crossroads leadership.[5]

As far back as 1963, the historian Samuel S. Hill warned of the emergence within the SBC of "a new ultraconservative power bloc" based in the western sections of the denomination's home turf. In Hill's view, this bloc was characterized by exclusivism, aggressiveness, and emotional persuasiveness. Moderates would only be able to solidify their hold on the denomination, he wrote, "if the conservative coming-to-power can be forestalled for 15 or 20 years."[6] But that was not to be. Sixteen years later, Texans Paul Pressler and Paige Patterson—backed by fundamentalist uber-pastor and Norris disciple W. A. Criswell of First Baptist Church, Dallas—launched their crusade to elect a succession of SBC presidents who were committed to an "inerrantist" interpretation of the Bible, and who would in turn appoint only inerrantists to denominational leadership positions. With the 1979 election to the SBC presidency of Adrian Rogers, pastor of Memphis's Bellevue Baptist Church, the fundamentalist forces, largely but not completely dominated by players from the Crossroads, began taking control of the denomination. In a 1988 sermon, Criswell argued that because of "the curse of liberalism today," his opponents in the SBC "called themselves moderates," but "a skunk by any other name still stinks." He insisted that "we have lost our nation to the liberals, humanists, and atheists and infidels." The United States was once known as "a Christian nation, but now we are a secular nation." By 1990 moderate Southern Baptists had been marginalized, the SBC was firmly in the fundamentalist camp, and the battle for American culture could begin in earnest.

RAMPARTS OF THE SPIRIT

From the small chapels on backcountry roads to the massive megachurches on interstate highways, Crossroads Holiness and Pentecostal Christians keep the fires of the Holy Spirit alive with special vigor. The Crossroads is where the Holiness tradition gave birth to Pentecostalism and where Pentecostalism established its strongest national presence, spreading its influence across the nation and around the globe. The fastest growing Christian movement in the world, Pentecostalism covers a movement with as many as 100 million adherents, including millions of Americans belonging to 300 different denominations, most of them tiny. Amidst the diversity, they share the conviction that conversion to Christianity needs to be followed by another life-transforming event known as baptism in the Holy Spirit—most famously represented by speaking in tongues (glossolalia). Altogether, Pentecostalism represents a powerful force in American culture—and not only because of its worship style and use of mass media.

If Christian Republicanism stripped many Crossroads Baptists of the church-state separationist gene, Holiness-Pentecostal leaders could themselves claim descent from old-time culture warriors. The roots of their religious tradition lay in Methodism—not least in the Wesleyan doctrine of sanctification, which sparked the pursuit of Christian perfection. For Methodists, the perfectionist ideal was not something to be pursued by a community of saints walled off from the secular world, but rather an impetus to change the world, in its image. The great American Protestant crusades of the nineteenth and early twentieth centuries—abolition of slavery, women's rights, the suppression of alcohol—were an outgrowth of this reform imperative. The campaign for Prohibition—what the historian Sydney Ahlstrom a generation ago called "the last great corporate work in America of legalistic evangelicalism"—received its most powerful support from the Methodist churches, which provided across-the-board institutional support and most of the militant leadership.[7]

Holiness began in the 1830s as a movement to revitalize Methodism, but did not organize itself into denominations until the 1890s, when Pentecostal impulses were themselves already stirring in the land. Swept up in the same spiritual fervor, both movements initially tended to steer clear of involvement in politics under the leadership of such figures as A. J. Tomlinson, the domineering founder of what is now called The Church of God (Cleveland, Tennessee). Writing in 1913, Tomlinson recalled that in the late 1880s he had embraced secular politics, running (and losing) a race as a populist candidate for auditor in Hamilton county, Indiana. His conversion convinced him to renounce politics; he vowed that he would never vote for anyone except Jesus. As the historian Grant Wacker has noted, "In 1908 the Church of God's General Assembly authorized its members to cast ballots—but only if they could do so with a 'clear conscience.' The record implies that very few did."[8] Nowadays, however, the signals from the top are entirely different than in Tomlinson's day. "Believers must exercise their God-given privilege and responsibility to vote," the Assemblies of God's general superintendent, Thomas E. Trask, declared in an interview published in the June 13, 2004 issue of *Pentecostal Evangel*, the denominational weekly. "I believe that we can make a difference in this nation. But it isn't going to happen by sitting on our hands." By way of example, Trask cited Assemblies of God member and U.S. Representative Marilyn Musgrave, the Colorado congresswoman who proposed a constitutional amendment to limit marriage to one man and one woman. Trask's stance on political involvement should be understood as a reemergence of the reformist impulse embedded in his tradition's perfectionist past. As he went on to say, "The church was meant to change the culture of the world. . . . [T]he responsibility for this country's welfare lies at the door of the church and at the pulpit of every minister." No nineteenth century Methodist leader could have expressed himself more clearly.

This point of view can be usefully contrasted with the more cautious, evangelistic approach to public engagement that even today continues to be articulated by Southern Baptist leadership. As "The Christian and the Social Order," a section of the SBC's Faith and Message, puts it, "Means and methods used for the improvement of society and the establishment of righteousness among men can be truly and permanently helpful only when they are rooted in the regeneration of the individual by the saving grace of God in Jesus Christ. . . . Christians should be ready to work with all men of good will in any good cause, always being careful to act in the spirit of love without compromising their loyalty to Christ and His truth." The contrast can likewise be seen in the two preeminent religious right organizations of the late twentieth century. The Moral Majority, created by Virginia Baptist Jerry Falwell, styled itself as an association of individuals of different faiths working for a common social agenda. The Christian Coalition, founded by Pentecostal Pat Robertson, not only gave itself an overtly sectarian name but also devoted much of its energy to church-based voter mobilization. Its signature program was the distribution of voter guides prior to state and national elections in tens of thousands of churches; the idea was to make churches themselves into engines of political activism.

Robertson is a native Virginian, but the Crossroads has generated more than its share of Holiness-Pentecostal culture warriors, none more prominent than James Dobson. Born in Shreveport, Louisiana, Dobson is the scion of three generations of pastors in the Church of the Nazarene, the largest of the Holiness denominations. He attended a Nazarene college in California, but rather than go into the ministry became a child psychologist, teaching pediatrics for 14 years at the University of Southern California School of Medicine. Then, reacting to the permissiveness of the 1960s, he published in 1970 a childrearing manual, *Dare to Discipline*, that sold three million copies. His own radio show came in 1977, followed by Focus on the Family, a seven-part video series that he transformed into a full-fledged family ministry and media empire. In 1991 Dobson moved the organization to Colorado Springs, helping to make the hometown of the U.S. Air Force Academy into the evangelical mecca it has become. By the late 1990s, his radio show was reaching four million listeners daily, his books had sold more than 16 million copies, and his budget was five times the Christian Coalition's. At first, he kept himself behind the scenes of partisan politics, only emerging in election years to lecture Republicans on the need to keep the conservative faith. In 1998, for example, he roiled the GOP dovecotes on Capitol Hill by threatening to bolt the party unless it gave higher legislative priority to issues like abortion. "If I go I will do everything I can to take as many people as I can with me," he said. At the turn of the millennium he was widely regarded as the most important figure on the religious right, and was soon openly engaged in political partisanship.

Dobson's ability to seamlessly meld generic conservative family counseling with a political agenda grounded in evangelical piety comes directly out of the Methodist/Holiness tradition. Yet denominational labels matter less and less in the contemporary evangelical world, so it was perhaps in the spirit of the times that Dobson did not advertise his Nazarene identity. Not that his followers seemed to care. In 1998, a cover story on Dobson in *U.S. News and World Report* portrayed as Dobson acolytes two paladins of the Christian right in Congress from the Crossroads. Then U.S. Representative Steve Largent of Oklahoma, a former star football player who served as a volunteer speaker for Focus on the Family from 1990 to 1993, credited Dobson with "sparking my interest in public policy." Missouri U.S. Representative Jim Talent, elected to the Senate in 2002, described pulling off a highway and praying along with Dobson on the radio to become a Christian. "He is the instrument through which I committed my life to Christ," Talent said. Neither, however, was a Nazarene, or (as evangelicals go) anything close to one. Largent attended Tulsa's Fellowship Bible Church, an independent evangelical congregation more Baptist than Holiness or Pentecostal. Talent belonged to the Presbyterian Church in America, a small conservative denomination that broke away from the main body of southern Presbyterianism a generation ago in order to establish an old-time Calvinism.

If, at the dawn of the twenty-first century, Dobson was the foremost exemplar of the Crossroads Holiness-Pentecostal tradition among religious right leaders, its political personification was George W. Bush's first attorney general, John Ashcroft. The son of an Assemblies of God college president and evangelist, Ashcroft grew up in the Assemblies' headquarters town of Springfield, Missouri. With the encouragement of his father, who was anxious to bring Pentecostals into the mainstream of American life, he attended Yale College on a scholarship and went to the University of Chicago for his law degree. Back in Missouri he rose through the ranks of public office—from state auditor to attorney general to congressman to governor to senator—all the while demonstrating a rigid moralism and a gift for political polarization. He expressed a sacral sense of duty upon assuming high office by having himself anointed with oil—like the ancient Israelite kings. He made it clear that he thought Congress was in the business of legislating morality; his sense that church and state were supposed to cooperate in the public weal led to the one significant piece of legislation he introduced as a senator: a section of the 1996 welfare reform act known as "charitable choice," which was designed to enable religious institutions to use federal funds to provide welfare services without hiding their spiritual lights under a bushel.

Affirmed as U.S. Attorney General on a near party-line vote, Ashcroft proved to be no less polarizing in the Bush administration than he was in Missouri. He did not stint on bringing his straight-laced piety into the Justice Department, holding morning prayer sessions and, to the merriment of the Washington press corps, erecting curtains in the department's Great Hall to screen from public view the bare breast of a statue representing the Spirit of Justice. The attacks of September 11, 2001, enabled Ashcroft to freely indulge his Manichaean worldview. As Jeffrey Toobin described it in a *New Yorker* profile of Ashcroft in 2002, "[H]e has always been serious about the binary nature of the universe, which for him is defined by right and wrong, good and evil, heaven and hell." At a notable hearing on the Patriot Act on December 6, 2001, Ashcroft made it clear that whoever was not with the administration was on the enemy side. "To those who pit Americans against immigrants and citizens against non-citizens, to those who scare peace-loving people with phantoms of lost liberty, my message is this: your tactics only aid terrorists, for they erode our national unity and diminish our resolve. They give ammunition to America's enemies, and pause to America's friends. They encourage people of good will to remain silent in the face of evil."[9]

Animated by the urgency of moral revival, unburdened with traditional shibboleths of church-state separation, and shaped by a regional culture of confrontation, the Crossroads Holiness-Pentecostal tradition would have been well-suited for cultural warfare at any time. In contemporary America, however, it also had the capacity to make moral values activism broadly palatable thanks to its historic openness to racial and gender equality. Pentecostal Christians in particular do not have to disavow the kind of racist past that bedevils much of the rest of southern evangelicalism. Their movement was biracial in its inception, and although separate black and white denominations formed early in the twentieth century, it has come naturally to them to reclaim their racially inclusive past. Indeed, there is no more multiracial and multiethnic religious community to be found in America today. It is in keeping with this reclaimed past that the Arkansas Martin Luther King, Jr., Commission gave one of its community service awards in 2004 to the white pastor of North Little Rock's First Assembly of God. Similarly, women have had leadership roles in both the Holiness and Pentecostal movements from the beginning. Today, the Assemblies of God expresses this by saying, "God has clearly communicated that neither gender is spiritually or socially superior. The Assemblies of God will continue to give women opportunities to be co-partners in the work of the Kingdom. 'God does not show favoritism.'"[10] That is a far cry from the Southern Baptist Convention's continuing insistence on restricting religious leadership to men and on upholding the patriarchal nature of the family.

Nor is Holiness-Pentecostal inclusivism restricted to race and gender. Survey Pentecostal church websites, and the lists of outreach ministries in their communities are impressive. The Sheffield Family Life Center in Kansas City, for instance, has been recognized for its work in feeding the homeless and reaching out to singles, gays, street prostitutes, prisoners, and gang members. Moreover, in their very names Pentecostal denominations such as the United Pentecostal Church International, the International Pentecostal Holiness Church, and the International Church of the Foursquare Gospel—look beyond the borders of the United States and claim a connection with their brothers and sisters across the globe. From their humble beginnings in and around the Crossroads, these people are rocking the world.

CATHOLICS AT ODDS

The ancient Catholic presence in the Crossroads created the basis for Reformation-style conflict that was missing in the southeast. Religious tensions between Anglos and Latinos in Texas and between Anglos and Cajuns in Louisiana were longstanding, and only enhanced by the arrival of European Catholic immigrants to the region in the decade before the Civil War. Southern Protestants, suspicious that Catholic allegiance to the Pope would prevail over loyalty to the Southern social order, feared a challenge to slave owning. "[T]ales of Popish plots against the nation's liberty, with immigrants acting as agents, were coupled with fantastic stories of priestly immorality and treachery," writes historian George Pozzetta. In 1854, the Catholic church at Helena, Arkansas, was burned; two years later, anti-Catholic mobs attacked convents in Galveston and New Orleans. And the Know-Nothing party rose to power. In the presidential election of 1856, the Know-Nothing candidate, Millard Fillmore, received his strongest support from southern voters. That year, even in Louisiana, with its high concentration of Catholics, the party succeeded in electing candidates and establishing newspapers such as the *New Orleans Protestant*.[11]

Once the Civil War was under way, however, hostility toward Catholics was mitigated by, among other things, the courageous behavior of nuns on the battlefields. These women, the only trained nurses among southern women, volunteered their services and opened their convents as hospitals. The acquiescence of the institutional church in slavery also helped. The survival strategy mandated by Rome for Catholic minorities was to support the existing social order of the host society; and among those things to be rendered unto Caesar was the south's "peculiar institution." As historian Randall Miller puts it, "By labeling slavery a political issue, the churchmen of the South placed it outside the Church's province. They absolved themselves of any moral responsibility to pass judgment on the social world in which they lived. The Church, rather, was obligated to support the state."[12] Not that this was solely a matter of conforming to white Protestant practices. In Louisiana, most slave owners were in fact Catholics; they would hardly have appreciated an expression of support for abolitionism from their religious leaders. Although Catholic slaveholders throughout the region were admonished both to treat their slaves well and to baptize them and bring them up as good Catholics, there was no public statement in favor of ending human bondage. Southern Catholic newspapers did their part, responding to anti-Catholic bigotry by promoting the Catholic Church's support of slavery and of the Confederate cause generally. By publishing strong endorsements of "southern rights" by bishops and prominent lay leaders, the papers influenced the laity to display loyalty to their region. Special Irish Catholic units were organized to fight on behalf of the Confederacy and Irish immigrants in general tended to assimilate willingly into plantation culture.

After the war, devastation and poverty hampered the Catholic Church's efforts to build and strengthen its institutions across the region. Many working-class white Catholics left the cities to seek employment in other states, and although their church remained committed to unity between black and white members, little effort was made to minister to the former slaves, either through evangelization or the ordination of black priests. Indeed, while many slaves in Louisiana had become nominal Catholics, they tended to join either Baptist or Methodist churches after emancipation. Among people of color, it was the lighter skinned Creoles who tended to cling to Catholicism. Meanwhile, the Catholic Church maintained a low profile in the region, as clerics and laity became increasingly conscious of their minority religious status. Combining acculturation with separation, the church created its own segregated parochial schools and social-service agencies. Meanwhile, many Catholics, drawing on Catholicism's own critique of the modern world, readily embraced the prevailing regional worldview that, in Randall Miller's words, "idealized a simpler southern past and decried the insidious secularism of industrial, urban America."[13]

In due course, some Catholic leaders did stand up against the prevailing Crossroads mores. In 1917, the church, claiming infringement of religion, protested Oklahoma's "Bone-Dry Law" that forbade importing alcohol into the state. (The in-state production of beer and wine was already banned by the state constitution.) The following year, the state Supreme Court upheld the Catholic Church's protest, thereby establishing a precedent for religious exceptions that, ironically, opened the door to Prohibition nationwide. A generation later, the bishops of St. Louis and New Orleans, the region's foremost Catholic cities, took powerful stands against Jim Crow. In 1947, seven years before the U.S. Supreme Court ruled public school segregation unconstitutional, St. Louis Archbishop Joseph E. Ritter ended segregation in his archdiocesan schools. In 1953, New Orleans Archbishop Joseph Francis Rummel deplored racism in a letter entitled "Blessed Are the Peacemakers," and then, in 1955, he mandated desegregation of Catholic schools throughout his archdiocese. When Leander Perez, the political overlord of Plaquemines Parish, resisted the order, Rummel excommunicated him.

The antisegregation voices of Ritter and Rummel were powerfully amplified by a 1958 papal statement against racism and during the 1960s the desegregation of Catholic schools and other Catholic institutions occurred more rapidly than in the rest of Crossroads society. Yet, more attuned to Perez than to Peter, many Crossroads Catholics strongly resisted this shift away from accommodation to Jim Crow. Catholic parents appeared in nationally distributed photographs screaming epithets at black youths entering New Orleans parochial schools just as white mobs would be depicted protesting the integration of Central High School in Little Rock in 1957. To this day, Crossroads Catholics continue to be pulled in different directions—by the teachings of their church, by their own varied ethnic traditions, and by the prevailing cultural norms. Among the latter is, of course, is the readiness to use religion as a weapon.

Louisiana has the largest proportion of Catholics of any state in the region, thanks to the large Cajun (Acadian) population descended from refugees who arrived from Nova Scotia in the 1760s. In recent years, the Cajuns have drifted closer to the evangelicals in the northern part of the state on moral issues, and like them have tended to become Republicans—although they do retain a residual attachment to their own ethnoreligious candidates in the Democratic Party. In a pattern common to the region, the Catholic Church has made common cause with both religious conservatives and religious liberals, depending on the issue: abortion and marriage on the one hand, poverty and the death penalty on the other. Helen Prejean, a New Orleans nun, has in recent years become the most famous crusader against the death penalty in the country, thanks in no small part to the 1995 movie *Dead Man Walking*, which was based on her best-selling book about her life.

In Texas, nearly one-third of the population are Latinos, of whom an estimated 85 percent are Catholic and constitute the principal counterweight to Anglo Republicanism and the public agenda of the religious right in the state. Since the 1970s, Latino Catholic congregations have been the engine of the most powerful grassroots political force in the country. Beginning with Community Organized for Public Service (COPS) in San Antonio, a host of organizations from the Rio Grande to Dallas have adapted the model of community organizing created in Chicago by Saul Alinsky (the Industrial Areas Foundation) to bring pressure on the powers that be, political and economic, to improve infrastructure, community services, and even statewide public school financing.[14] With moral and financial backing from the Catholic Church itself, this may be considered the most significant case of a religious left in action in America over the past generation. For its own part, the Catholic Church in Texas has expanded its ministries to meet the needs of the growing Hispanic Catholic population. Besides social services provided at the parish level, the church has actively supported undocumented workers (illegal immigrants), whether they are in need of driver's licenses or of contact with their government if arrested.

In Arkansas, an influx of Latinos (and some thousands of Vietnamese) has pushed the Catholic portion of the population toward five percent. In northwest Arkansas, for example, some of the Catholic parishes are now 75 percent Latino. The Catholic Church has responded by forming multiethnic committees to develop programs and to meet with local police to address issues of racial profiling. On policy issues, Arkansas Catholics tend to join forces with conservative Protestants in opposing abortion and the ordination of women, yet with progressives against capital punishment and in support of social services for the poor. As a small minority with few parochial schools of their own, Catholics are also working to improve public education in the state; for the most part they oppose school vouchers.

Constituting just five percent of the population, Oklahoma's small Catholic population has recognized the importance of collaboration with other religious and community groups to influence public life. Following a pattern common throughout the region, Oklahoma Catholics have worked with the Baptist General Convention on informed-consent legislation to discourage women from having abortions, and with the Oklahoma Conference of Churches (composed of 18 mainline denominations) and Amnesty International to outlaw the death penalty. The church has also worked with Central Oklahoma Turning Point, a citizen-led coalition working to improve public health. The most prominent Oklahoma Catholic of recent years has been Frank Keating, governor from 1995 to 2003. In 2002, Keating was named Chairman of the United States Conference of Catholic Bishops' National Review Board examining sex abuse by Catholic priests; however, he left the board in 2003 after Los Angeles Cardinal Roger Mahony criticized him for saying that some American bishops had acted "like La Cosa Nostra" "My remarks, which some Bishops found offensive, were deadly accurate," Keating said in his resignation letter. "I make no apology. . . . To resist Grand Jury subpoenas, to suppress the names of offending clerics, to deny, to obfuscate, to explain away; that is the model of a criminal organization, not my church."

In Missouri, German and Irish Catholics anchor the state Democratic Party in and around St. Louis and Kansas City, but are nonetheless susceptible to conservative Catholic social teachings. As in the other Crossroads states, the church divides its efforts on both sides of the conservative-liberal divide but thanks to the public stands of Archbishop Raymond Burke, the state's most important Catholic prelate, the conservative star is in the ascendant. Burke, who took office in 2003, made headlines in 2004 by declaring that he would deny communion to Democratic presidential candidate John Kerry because of his support for abortion rights. Among the new breed of outspoken conservative American Catholic prelates, Burke is the most prominent.

In sum, Catholicism in Crossroads public life does not fit neatly into the conservative political paradigm that dominates the region. Holding the conservative line on abortion and gay marriage, the church at the same time remains more committed than ever to helping the poor—especially the Hispanic immigrant population that makes up an increasing share of the faithful. These days, the distinctive character of Crossroads religion is most evident in the readiness of the Prejeans, the Keatings, the Burkes and the COPSes to get in your face, whoever you are.

SPIRITUAL WARFARE

Contemporary American religious politics was birthed in the Southern Crossroads when more than 10,000 people turned up at Reunion Arena in Dallas on August 21 and 23, 1980, for the Religious Roundtable's National

Affairs Briefing. "You'll walk away with know-how to inform and mobilize your church and community," declared a circular. "Get 'em saved; get 'em baptized; get 'em registered." In attendance were leading conservative religious leaders like Jerry Falwell and Pat Robertson, and prominent Republican politicians, most notably the GOP presidential candidate Ronald Reagan, who gave the after-dinner speech on the second day of the assemblage. Although Reagan followed the party line that this was not a partisan exercise, the disclaimers were not to be taken seriously. The event was designed to transform hitherto politically passive white evangelicals into active Republicans. And to a remarkable degree, it succeeded. By the turn of the millennium, white evangelicals had moved decisively into the Republican camp and become the source of the party's activist core. Parachurch organizations and evangelical churches themselves had emerged as important agents of political mobilization for the GOP—comparable across the Bible Belt to the role organized labor has played for the Democratic Party in the industrial heartland since the 1930s. Religion, evangelical style, became a fixture of national political rhetoric and electioneering in a way absent and unanticipated only a generation ago. And in this new religio-political landscape, the Crossroads was center stage.

According to the Akron/Pew surveys, the Crossroads is the most politically conservative region of the country—at 49.7 percent, more than five points higher than the country as a whole, and significantly higher than the next most conservative regions, the Mountain West (47.4 percent) and the South (46 percent). This is due, in part, to the high proportion of America's most conservative segment of voters: white evangelical Protestants who attend church at least once a week. But the neighboring Southern region also has a lot of frequent-attending (high-commitment) white evangelicals. In the Crossroads, the prevailing conservatism can be seen almost across the board, including among the nonreligious. Nationally, 66 percent of high-commitment white evangelicals report that they are politically conservative; in the Crossroads, it's 69 percent. (By comparison, the figure in the South is 60 percent.) Of the 10 other religious groups tracked in the Crossroads, only the region's low-commitment Catholics have a smaller proportion of conservatives than the nationwide sample. Three large groups in the region are significantly more conservative than the national average. Among high-commitment Catholics, 51.5 call themselves conservative, in comparison to the national average of 46 percent. Of the region's black Protestants, 40.6 percent say they are conservative, compared with a national rate of 35 percent. The most dramatic regional effect, however, occurs among high-commitment white mainline Protestants. In the nation at large, 51.5 percent call themselves conservative; in the Southern Crossroads the figure is 60 percent. Indeed, one of the salient regional characteristics is a far stronger alliance between high-commitment evangelicals and mainline Protestants than exists elsewhere. (By contrast, 52.4 percent of high-commitment mainliners in the South say they are conservative, just slightly above the national average.)

How does Crossroads conservatism manifest itself? On economic issues, the pull to the right is marginal, as it is on the environment. For example, 27 percent of all Crossroads voters oppose more environmental protection measures as against 26 percent in the national sample; an outright majority are pro-protection. (High-commitment white evangelicals are somewhat more likely to oppose tougher environmental enforcement, as are black Protestants.) But on welfare spending the difference with the rest of the country is clear, and so is the distinctive Crossroads alliance of high-commitment white evangelicals and mainliners. Forty percent of the evangelicals and 39 percent of mainline Protestants in the Crossroads support less welfare spending. Elsewhere in the country the proportion of high-commitment mainliners against welfare is significantly lower: 33.3 percent nationwide and, notably, 31.5 percent in the South and 29 percent in the Mountain West. White Crossroads Catholics are even more conservative on this issue: 43 percent of those who attend Mass weekly and 36 percent who do so less frequently oppose more welfare spending. (The national averages for white Catholics are 30 and 32 percent respectively.) Another area where the high-commitment white mainliners stand with their evangelical peers in the Crossroads is national health insurance: 51.5 percent oppose it, compared with 47 percent of frequently attending Crossroads evangelicals and 40 percent of high-commitment mainliners nationwide. In the South, national health care is opposed by only 34 percent of high-commitment mainliners.

Overall, no region of the country is as strongly opposed to legalized abortion as the Crossroads, with 49.9 percent of all voters saying they are pro-life, a figure slightly larger than in the South, the Mountain West, and the Midwest. (The national sample of voters shows 43.3 percent of voters taking pro-life positions.) In the Crossroads, 76.6 percent of high-commitment evangelicals are pro-life, just marginally above their national average. Low-commitment evangelicals, low-commitment Catholics, Latino Christians, and "other" Christians are all a few percentage points more pro-life in the Crossroads than their national averages. For black Protestants, high-commitment Catholics, non-Christians, and seculars the differentials are 4.3, 4, 12, and 10.6 percent respectively.

The Crossroads is also the most anti-gay-rights region of the country. Virtually every religious category in the Crossroads is more anti-gay than the national average, and many rank highest among the regions. Forty percent of high-commitment mainline Protestants in the Crossroads are anti-gay-rights, as opposed to 33 percent in the South. Among low-commitment mainliners, 27 percent are against gay rights, as compared to some regions of the country where the percentage is in the single digits. Nationwide, 50.6 percent of high-commitment evangelicals oppose gay rights, but in the Crossroads it's 57 percent. In the aggregate, gay rights are opposed by 35.1 percent of Crossroads voters; that's 6.4 percentage points above the national average. It should come as no surprise then that of the 12 states whose sodomy laws were struck down by the U.S. Supreme Court's 2003 *Lawrence v. Texas* decision, three of the four with laws prohibiting only homosexual sodomy were in the Crossroads—Missouri, Oklahoma, and Texas (the other was the neighboring state of Kansas). In the wake of *Lawrence*, the number of co-sponsors of the constitutional amendment to define marriage as "between a man and a woman" jumped to 75 members of Congress, of whom 14 came from Crossroads states. Texas led all states with eight co-sponsors, while only Arkansas—whose sodomy law had been tossed out by its own Supreme Court in 2002—failed to provide a single co-sponsor.

Looking more closely at particular religious groupings, it is possible to discern how political conservatism has gathered strength in the Crossroads. Holiness and Pentecostal Christians, who historically tended to stand aloof from politics, are joining in with gusto. If theological differences continue to separate them from other evangelicals, those evangelicals—many of whom belong to churches that have fallen under the influence of charismatic worship style—show little reluctance to make common cause with them against the forces of liberalism. The Pentecostal impact on politics can also be seen in the growing movement of many Latinos from Catholicism into Pentecostal churches. An indication of this trend in the Crossroads can be found in Arkansas' weekly Latino newspaper, *El Latino*, whose "Quien Es Quien? (Who's Who) of Hispanic Arkansas" now lists comparable numbers of Pentecostal ministers and Catholic priests. Latino Protestants are much more likely to vote Republican than Latino Catholics.

As for Crossroads Catholics, their readiness to adapt to the dominant cultural values of the region has resulted in significantly greater conservatism in the aggregate. Yet, as noted above, there are many Catholicisms in the Crossroads, with important subregional and ethnic variations. For example, in Arkansas, which has a strong public school tradition, Catholics tend to oppose school vouchers, whereas in Louisiana, with its plethora of Catholic schools and its large Catholic population, support for vouchers is high and is being spun by diocesan spokespersons as a social-justice issue. And while Latino Catholics, supporting the teaching of the church hierarchy, may be part of the regional consensus on abortion and same-sex marriage, they remain (again like the hierarchy) well to the left on issues of social welfare and economic policy. In a region where half the Catholics are Latino, this bivalence is of critical importance.

African American Protestants are also subject to the prevailing conservative winds. Many are divided over the question of including openly gay and lesbian individuals within the faith community and have adopted a "don't ask, don't tell" or avowedly exclusionary stance. The Bush administration targeted leading black pastors in the Crossroads with policies such as the "defense of marriage" designed to weaken their traditional attachment to the Democratic Party. At a time of decreased social welfare spending, the administration's faith-based initiative was attractive to many black churches, which have long seen themselves as providers of social welfare services to the communities they serve. What the political consequences of receiving such funds will be remains to be seen, but indications are that the black pastors of large megachurches like T. D. Jakes' Potter's House will not be inclined to alienate politicians who keep public funds flowing into their ministries.

How Crossroads conservatism plays out on the sectarian stage can best be seen in the current cultural struggle over homosexuality. In denominations divided on the issue, Crossroads churches have disproportionately supported the anti-gay side. The United Methodist Church, for example, has for several years seen a debate between "Reconciling" conferences and congregations—those that accept gays and lesbians as full participants in the life of the church—and "Transforming" conferences and congregations—those that offer support for homosexuals who want to leave their gay lifestyles and believe that transformation to a straight lifestyle is possible. In 1997, when at least 18 Methodist conferences addressed this issue, the Northwest Texas Conference was one of the few to call for the "healing and transformation" of gays. The following year, Northwest Texas decided simultaneously to become a Transforming and a "Confessing" conference. (The Confessing movement, while similar to the Transforming movement in its position on homosexuality, is a broader movement, which, like Good News, aims to "enable the United Methodist Church to retrieve its classical doctrinal identity."[15]) Subsequently, 45 of the Methodists' 66 conferences chose not to vote to maintain the church's official position against homosexuality ("the practice of homosexuality is incompatible with Christian teaching"), but five of the 12 conferences in the Crossroads—Missouri West, North Arkansas, and Central, North, and Northwest Texas—voted to support it. In June 2003, Arkansas Methodists passed resolutions calling on Methodist seminaries to remain faithful to traditional doctrinal standards and for the denomination to maintain its current stance on human sexuality and marriage. Later that month, after the *Lawrence* decision, the Reverend William Hinson of Houston, president of the Confessing movement, claimed that the "vast majority of United Methodist people agree that Jesus got it right, that marriage is between a man and a woman." Conceding that the Supreme Court was correct on the privacy issue, he nevertheless insisted that the church "should be a guide for the culture and not a reflector of the culture."[16]

On another front, 2,000 conservative Episcopalians from around the country showed up at Christ Church in the town of Plano north of Dallas in October 2003 to mobilize opposition to the Episcopal Church USA for confirming the appointment of an openly gay priest as bishop of New Hampshire. But while Plano had become a national center of opposition to the full acceptance of homosexuality in the Episcopal church, Crossroads Episcopalian leaders were themselves at odds on the question: The Texas and Louisiana bishops voted against Robinson's confirmation and the bishops of Arkansas, Oklahoma, and Missouri voted to confirm him. In Dallas itself, a number of Episcopalians celebrated Robinson's election, revealing Texas to be a culture war in microcosm, and not for the first time.

Though less divided than the Methodists and Episcopalians on homosexuality, Crossroads Baptists have been wounded on this battlefield as well. In March 1998 the Baptist General Convention of Texas voted to reject financial contributions from University Baptist Church in Austin and asked the church to cease publishing materials noting an affiliation with the state convention. Three years earlier the congregation had been removed from the Austin Baptist Association after ordaining a self-professed homosexual as a deacon. "You may not all agree with the way our church ministers with gays and lesbians and their families," Pastor Larry Bethune told the Convention's Executive Board. "In fact, we don't all agree at University Baptist Church but we are creating one of the few safe places for your Baptist homosexual children to work out their salvation with fear and trembling." In 1998, the church renounced its affiliation with the more liberal Cooperative Baptist Fellowship after the Fellowship approved a new policy against hiring gays or funding organizations that "condone, advocate, or affirm homosexual practice"—a policy Fellowship officials characterized as "welcoming but not affirming" of gays. Stan Hastey, director of the Washington, D.C.-based Alliance of Baptists, explained the new policy as a "made in Texas" phenomenon. "The Texas influence dominates Cooperative Baptist Fellowship life, and has from the beginning," Hastey said, adding that talks of merger between the Alliance and the Fellowship broke off years earlier because Texas leaders of the Fellowship felt "we were too far left of center on women's issues and really off the charts when it came to homosexuality."[17] Along the same lines, in 2003 the Missouri Baptist Convention withdrew funding from William Jewell College because the school had allowed the student senate to consider adding sexual orientation to the list of protections in the Student's Bill of Rights and permitted a theater student to produce portions of "The Vagina Monologues" at her senior recital. Together with its 154-year relationship with Missouri Baptists, the college lost 3 percent ($900,000) of its operating budget.

It's worth bearing in mind that in the Crossroads, unlike in some other parts of the country, it is not only the religious conservatives who fight hard. In the 1980s, even as the Lone Star State generated much of the fundamentalist energy that captured the Southern Baptist Convention, it also created some of the strongest opposition to that fundamentalism. Key churches in urban parts of Texas have either totally or partially removed themselves from the Convention, and the moderate General Baptist Convention of Texas has succeeded in maintaining control of a fourth of the board of Texas's premier Baptist university, Baylor. Likewise, the attempt to create an alternative to seminaries controlled by the SBC is centered in Texas. The ferocity on both sides of this intra-ecclesial struggle has deep roots in the historical contentiousness of Baptists in Texas and in the Crossroads generally.

SECULAR POLITICS

For all its prevailing conservatism, the Crossroads has been slower than the South to march into the GOP camp. While Oklahoma has long since been safely ensconced in the Republican red zone and Texas more recently so, Louisiana may only very lately have joined the fold and Arkansas and Missouri remain battleground states in which Democrats retain fighting chances in both statewide and presidential elections. Missourians will not soon forget the 2000 election, when John Ashcroft lost his bid for reelection to the Senate to his archrival Mel Carnahan, a month after Carnahan died in a plane crash. Carnahan's widow Jean was appointed to the seat, but lost it two years later to Dobson protégé Jim Talent, who in turn lost it in 2006 to state auditor Claire McCaskill in an election marked by bitter contention over a referendum on state funding for stem cell research that ultimately passed by a small margin. In 2003, Democrat Kathleen Babineaux Blanco won the governor's seat in a hotly contested election in which national Republican money and interest groups were giving strong support to Bobby Jindal, a son of Indian immigrants. Even in Oklahoma, surprises can happen. In 2002, a strong turnout by Cherokee voters—evangelical Protestants, for the most part, but heavily courted by the Democrats—was widely credited with defeating Dobson's other protégé, Steve Largent, in his bid to become governor.

The fact that Democratic identity has tended to remain stronger in the Crossroads among high-commitment white evangelicals (31 percent) helps explain why white Democratic politicians remain a bit thicker on the ground than in the South, where the figure is 27.6 percent. In Arkansas, for example, Democrats still outnumbered Republicans by three-to-one margins in both the state house of representatives and the state senate after the 2006 election. In the 2000 presidential election, Gov. Mike Huckabee complained that several counties had opened their polls on Sunday in order to make it easier for black churches to bus their members to the voting booths. What angered Huckabee—a sometime Southern Baptist minister who strongly advocated church involvement in politics—was simply the fact that the arrangement seemed intended to benefit Democratic candidates. In 2003, there was the months-long drama of Texas' Democratic legislators decamping to Oklahoma and New Mexico in an ultimately unsuccessful effort to prevent the GOP powers that be from redistricting congressional seats. In 2004, the delegation flipped from 17-15 Democratic to 21-11 Republican. But the GOP victory came at a high price, when Austin District Attorney Ronnie Earle indicted Tom Delay and three of his aides for campaign finance violations, eventually forcing Delay to give up his seat. In 2006, Democrats picked up two of the lost congressional seats, including Delay's. In the Crossroads, you don't go down without a fight. Yet even as the political partisans continued to duke it out, the region seemed to be on a trajectory toward becoming the most dependably Republican in the country. In the 2004 presidential election, it led all regions in voting for Bush (59.5 percent), and in 2006, it was the only region where the GOP actually increased its aggregate share of the congressional vote.

George W. Bush, of course, was the paramount Crossroads politician of his era. His personal religious journey was a typical Crossroads pilgrim's progress: from his father's Connecticut Episcopalianism to his mother's New York Presbyterianism to his wife's Texas Methodism. The story of his conversion is a classic of evangelical rescue: the walk with the famous evangelist (Billy Graham), the turning away from alcohol, the strengthening of his family life, the progress to the pinnacle of worldly success. Asked in a candidates' debate for the thinker or philosopher who had influenced him most, he answered in the spirit of Wesleyan sanctification, "Christ, because he changed my heart," and went on to explain, "When you turn your heart and your life over to Christ, when you accept Christ as the savior, it changes your heart. It changes your life. And that's what happened to me." After September 11, Bush harked back to another piece of the Crossroads past: the Christian Republicanism of J. R. Graves, complete with the conviction that the United States had been given a sacred trust to further the replacement of absolutist and clerical regimes with its own principles of government and religion. Of course, there also seemed to be something personal about Bush's determination to invade Iraq, especially since he was not above noting that Saddam Hussein had once tried to kill his father. Or maybe it was just typical Crossroads pugnacity. As he put it at a news conference on July 2, 2003, "There are some who feel like that, you know, the conditions are such that they can attack us there. My answer is bring them on."

A more improbable but equally telling Crossroads spiritual biography belongs to Bobby Jindal, who in 2007 piled up more than half the total votes in the Louisiana gubernatorial primary to become the first Indian-American governor in the nation's history. As a young man, Jindal abandoned the Hinduism of his upbringing and converted to Catholicism, associating himself strongly with the church's conservative intelligentsia. A graduate of Brown University and a Rhodes Scholar, he quickly established himself as a shining star in national GOP circles, adopting the Manichean sensibility that thrives in the region. Writing in the Catholic apologetic magazine *This Rock* in 1995, he readily adopted the culture-wars rhetoric that pitted people of faith against a secularist elite.

> The wave of political correctness, which has affected universities at every level, has also infected religious and philosophical thought. Whereas Western universities once existed to train clergymen and educate others in the fundamentals of the Christian faith, modern centers of higher learning are much more secular and skeptical toward anything remotely religious. Faith is a taboo subject among many of the educated elite; indeed, persons with strong religious convictions are often viewed with scorn and disapproval. Equating all religious beliefs with the seemingly intolerant attitude of Fundamentalists, the more ardent critics of religion are so bold as to equate faith with ignorance and disparage any attempt to support faith with reason as naive.[18]

In 1996, at the age of 24, he was appointed secretary of the Louisiana Department of Health and Hospitals, served as executive director of the National Bipartisan Commission on the Future of Medicare from 1998 to 1999, and then became the youngest-ever president of the University of Louisiana System. In 2001, newly elected President Bush appointed him Assistant Secretary of Health and Human Services for Planning and Evaluation. In 2003, he returned to Louisiana to run for governor.

The 2003 gubernatorial race may have signaled the last gasp of the traditional statewide politics in Louisiana. Blanco, the Cajun Catholic lieutenant governor prevailed by carrying the black vote, the union vote, and her native Acadiana (though she lost her hometown of Lafayette). She also picked up some normally Republican districts in north Louisiana, where white voters seemed reluctant to vote for a person of color. By 2007, however, the black vote had shrunk, thanks to Hurricane Katrina's devastating impact on the population of New Orleans, while white Protestant voters showed no more reluctance to give their votes to an Indo-Catholic conservative. This last owed something to Jindal's assiduous cultivation of Protestant churchgoers. In June of that year, John Maginnis, the shrewdest journalistic observer of Louisiana politics, noted that Sundays often found Jindal "giving testimony in Pentecostal or Baptist churches, whether large ones in Monroe, Alexandria and Shreveport or before tiny congregations, the farther back in the woods the better." Jindal told Maginnis that he felt the obligation because "there were people who witnessed to me, and I wouldn't have become a Christian if they hadn't." Jindal didn't talk politics in church, but, wrote Maginnis, "[H]e doesn't have to in order to move an audience and to forge a deep personal connection with many who felt nothing in common with him before. Few in Louisiana politics have reached out to Pentecostals as much as Jindal has since [former governor] Edwin Edwards."[19] Call it pluralism, Crossroads style.

· 6 ·

The Pacific: Fluid Identities

 he Pacific region, composed of California, Nevada, and Hawaii, looms large, because of both its immense population and its equivalent cultural significance.[1] Yet while its population is almost 10 percent of the national total, there is nothing average about it. Thanks to an extraordinary combination of peoples and faiths created by waves of internal migration and immigration, and its climate of fearless innovation, it has its own distinctive spiritual character. There, religion is an individual option, secularity is strong, and pluralism the order of the day. The Pacific region is often seen, by others and by its own denizens, as the place where the American future happens first. And during the latter decades of the twentieth century, the Pacific's distinctive approach to religion in public life—post-institutional, driven by individual seekers, wildly diverse—enjoyed a season of great national influence. Our discussion here will focus largely on California, which dominates the region with more than 90 percent of the population, and whose cultural gravity dominates Nevada, 90 percent of whose residents live within 10 miles of the California border.

Many scholars believe that the Pacific region has become "irrecoverably metropolitan" in a distinctively dispersed and multicultural way. According to this view, the region has supplanted all localisms with a culture characterized by diversity (of individual and group identities), consumption (of services, goods, and resources), mobility (of people, goods, and information), and corporate order (for state, public, and private institutions).[2] Carl Abbott, a historian of the urban west, suggests that "in the tradition of urban specialization," greater Los Angeles has come to represent "the opportunities of consumption," while the San Francisco Bay Area has come to represent "freedom in the choice of individual behavior."[3] Meanwhile, Las Vegas has

109

repositioned itself to be the next stage on from Disneyland—a theme park for every age and taste.

That is not to say that Judeo-Christian traditions have disappeared from the region's public realm. There, some regional religious groups or leaders continue to serve as balances or bridges between otherwise conflicting groups, and there has been some deference to moral arguments presented in support of or in opposition to selected public issues. But any Judeo-Christian alliance that might seem to have existed prior to World War II or in the early Cold War years has long since dissolved. The region simply lacked the kind of locally dominant religious traditions that shaped other regional cultures in the United States, such as the Baptists in the South, the Catholics in New England, or the Mormons in the Mountain West. What has been on the rise since the 1960s is "liquid modernity," the social and cultural fluidity that, in sociologist Zygmunt Bauman's view, fosters privatization by placing "the burden of pattern-weaving and the responsibility for failure . . . primarily on the individual's shoulders" while masking the power of globalizing structures.[4] It is hard—maybe impossible—for large religious groups to get traction in the region's public life.

REGIONAL DISTINCTIVES

The distinctive spiritual character of California and Nevada has been termed "Californization" by the historian Catherine L. Albanese and "Californication" by the sociologist Mark Shibley, and "advanced modernity" by others. Albanese, in an exemplary way, celebrates the "digestive power" and "wild ferment" of religion and ethnicity that has long typified California as fostering a "mysticism" of "inwardness, direct experience, and metaphysical empowerment in material life" that will most likely become "a key distinguishing characteristic of the emerging American ethnos."[5] Insofar as there is anything becoming established in the region, it is the privileging electorally of what is already the case legally, economically, and in the media: a tolerant, privatized, but widespread religiosity. In the Pacific, religion is more about an immanent style of faith satisfying the desires of the self than about transcendent faiths calling into question human ambitions, whether personal or social. As commentators point out, there has always been considerable freedom for people to believe and practice faith, or no faith, in the Pacific region. This freedom fits well with the region's optimism and openness, its individualism and mobility, and its fluid cultural life. Religion mirrors the culture with the continual upsurge of new spiritual movements, exploration of alternative beliefs, the easy flow of people into and out of congregations, and a good deal of indifference to traditional organized religion. This open spiritual environment is evident in the region's lower-than-average level of adherence to organized religion: 52.7 percent as compared to the nation's 59.5 percent in 2000, according to NARA.

The Pacific is the third least "churched" of the nation's regions, after the neighboring Pacific Northwest and Mountain West. In all three regions, from the beginning of white settlement to the present, organized religion has been a weaker force than in other parts of the nation. In the Pacific, the Gold Rush marked the beginning of a relentless stream of migration to the state from the mid-nineteenth century to the present. "[W]ith its population almost doubling every twenty years for a dozen decades," the historian Moses Rischlin observed several decades ago, "California has never had a respite to consolidate its institutions or to firm up its identity, to assert the authority of tradition or reputation."[6] Persistent, sizable immigration, in other words, is the social waterfall feeding the area's distinctive and historic fluidity. Second, the Gold Rush made indelible a widespread mystique associated with California: at the western edge of the continent, the possibilities—material and otherwise—were limited only by human will and imagination. This mystique provided an additional geographic focus for the American dream.

The persistent fluidity of society and culture in post-1846 California—a fluidity that eventually engulfed Nevada—has made the power of any religious group in the region's public life evanescent and ambiguous. Certainly California and Nevada have had distinct histories, and their respective natural, social, and cultural landscapes are not synonymous. Nevertheless, their modernization has made for a region that is fluid like America, "only more so." It is this "more so" modernity of California and Nevada that makes the region a borderland, a sociocultural place of complex and dynamic encounters and transformations. The Judeo-Christian traditions have had to accommodate themselves to historical trends in the area. Many of the people within the Pacific who are not adherents—that is, members of or regular participants in a faith community—choose nevertheless to *identify* with those communities and traditions. When asked "What is your religion, if any?" in the ARIS survey, 75 percent in the Pacific region named a religious group. This means that many people in the Pacific region affirm a "weak" religious identity as measured by institutional loyalty. That is especially the case for the large Catholic and white mainline Protestant constituencies, where 57.4 and 73.9 percent respectively are classified in the Akron/Pew surveys as low-commitment (defined as attending worship less frequently than once a week). These figures are substantially higher than the national figures of 51.7 and 64.2 percent respectively. What the figures suggest is a region characterized less by outright rejection of faith than by a secular, accommodating religious style.

This ethos amounts to an "irreligious establishment" that encompasses the faith communities themselves, creating, as one commentator says, "a religious circus in the tents of secularity."[7] In other words, even religious people enjoy their independence in making choices about belief and practice, and the ease with which they define their religious identities is in keeping with personal choices. For most of its history, California has actually been a place of rising religious adherence. In 1890, adherents made up only about one third of the population—a figure that grew slightly larger in the years of "internal" migration, when most of the state's new residents were arriving from the Midwest, South, and Southern Crossroads. In 1971, the overall religious adherence rate was 33.5 percent. But with a new and heavy flow of immigrants, now largely from Asia, Mexico, and other parts of Latin America, the adherence rate jumped to 53.8 percent in 2000.

Behind the aggregate religious statistics lies a significant dichotomy between California's southern and northern parts. Early on, a few Russian Orthodox migrants from Alaska settled in the north. Then, beginning with the Gold Rush in 1848, American migrants and some immigrants came swarming in, especially to San Francisco and its surrounding towns and hamlets. The migrants often came as unattached individuals in search of fortunes and happiness. Even in the nineteenth century, Catholics had the largest and longest established presence in the region, but close behind them came missionaries organizing Protestant churches: first Methodists, Presbyterians, Congregationalists, and Baptists, and later Lutherans, Quakers, and Disciples of Christ. Disproportionate to their numbers, Protestants in northern California were visible in temperance crusades and in trying to keep the Sabbath free of vice-ridden activities. They had a strong sense of civic responsibility, owing no doubt to a Protestant heritage of custodianship over the culture. Because of widespread public indifference and lack of support from other religious and secular groups, however, their successes were limited. In 1883, California permanently repealed the Sabbath laws, becoming the first state in the country to do so. This added to perceptions back east that the place was one of free-thinkers and infidels, if not altogether morally depraved. To no small extent, San Francisco continues to enjoy that reputation.

By 2000, the Bay Area looked quite different. In relative terms, the Catholic population had declined considerably, although at 41.9 percent it was still a strong plurality of the total religious population. Jews weighed in at 6.6 percent—more than at the earlier time. All the denominations we now call mainline Protestant had declined significantly as a proportion of the whole, often by as much as one-half. By contrast, conservative Protestantism grew by leaps and bounds in the final years of the twentieth century, and now accounted for almost 20 percent of the total. Orthodox Christians had almost tripled their slice of the pic, to 1.3 percent. Mormons constituted 2.2 percent; Eastern religions, 7.1 percent; and Muslims, 2.5 percent.

In southern California, both Catholics and Protestants were slower to organize and the region remained pervasively rural until the end of the nineteenth century. By then, large numbers of Anglo-Protestants had moved into the area—some of them southerners dispossessed by the Civil War but mostly Midwesterners. Compared to the migrants of northern California, they came as permanent settlers and either brought their families or did what they could to establish them. They were in pursuit of economic opportunity, health, a warm and comfortable place to retire; their hope was to recreate paradise. And if they didn't achieve all of the above, southern California did rapidly take on mythic significance as a place of new beginnings and fulfillment in life. In 1906, Los Angeles had a considerably higher level of reported church membership (74 percent) than San Francisco (41.7 percent) or the state generally (41.2 percent). By the 1920s, it was the most automobile-oriented city in the world; the vehicle symbolized the city's vitality and fluidity. Anglo Protestants wielded a good deal of political control over Los Angeles. But perhaps more significantly, they created a cultural climate unlike that of the state's northern tier. "As the Gold Rush had given the San Francisco region an enduring cosmopolitan tone, a place for tourists and settlers alike," wrote Elden Ernst and Douglas Firth Anderson, the "migration to Los Angeles gave that city and its metropolitan region a persistent flavor of comfortable conservatism that was open to innovation in the pursuit of the good life."[8]

During the middle and especially the later decades of the twentieth century, other populations joined southern California's Anglo-Protestants. By 2000, 61 percent of the state's Jews were living in Los Angeles County. Mexican immigration was so great that by 2000 Latinos made up more than 40 percent of the population in some southern counties—including 44.6 in Los Angeles County and 72.2 percent in Imperial County. Their presence refashioned Catholicism with ethnic festivals, personal piety as expressed in prayer and Bible study, and family-based religious activities. Latin piety did not, however, make for greater church involvement; rather, its presence meshed well with the easygoing religious environment that characterized the state. In sum, in the twentieth century southern California underwent a demographic and cultural transformation on a scale that the earlier Anglo-Protestants (not to mention the Native Americans and Mexicans) neither could have envisioned nor probably desired. Los Angeles, which began as the whitest, most Protestant big city in the United States, with its own particular vision of utopia was, by the beginning of the twenty-first century, the country's most ethnically and religiously diverse urban agglomeration.

OLD PLAYERS

Next to native peoples' traditions, Catholicism is the oldest continuing religious tradition in California. In 1769, Fr. Junípero Serra founded the first of 20 California missions under Spanish rule. Yet even before the U.S. conquest of California in 1846, Russian, French, British, and U.S. ships stopped at California ports, bringing Orthodox and Protestant Christians as well as more Catholics to settle with those already there. Religious diversity was extended further through 1850 with the arrival of adherents to Mormonism and Judaism, plus Buddhists and others from China. Nevertheless, by 1940, Roman Catholics were by far the largest religious group in California, dwarfing Protestant and Orthodox Christianity, Judaism, Mormonism, and everything else. At the century's midpoint, it was also possible to divide the state into two distinctive realms—that of the Archdiocese of San Francisco, with an activist, pro-New Deal, pro-labor tradition, and the much more conservative style of the Archdiocese of Los Angeles.

Through the 1940s and 1950s the Archbishop of San Francisco, John J. Mitty, tried to assert leadership over Catholicism in the entire state, but southern California, led by Archbishop John Cantwell of Los Angeles, resisted. Mitty, whose archdiocese tripled in membership during his long service from 1935 to 1961—was a major player in San Francisco's wartime-postwar power coalition. In the view of two historians, Mitty's leadership was a major factor in creating a Cold War labor, business, and government "coalition of the center" in San Francisco. Moreover, by the 1950s, Mitty and Sacramento Bishop Joseph T. McGucken saw that Mexican and Mexican-American migrant laborers constituted a burgeoning group with special needs. This led to Mitty's formation of the Spanish Mission Band (SMB), a small group of priests who provided not only spiritual services to the migrant laborers but also initiated credit unions, cooperative housing, and job referral services. In time the SMB priests adopted Cursillo, a Spanish-born movement, in order to foster personal commitment to Christ and his church. A young César Chávez was decisively shaped by the SMB's work. In the alternate orbit of the Archdiocese of Los Angeles, however, the Cold War era made for a theological and social conservatism that resonated with southern California's dominant Protestant tendencies. James F. McIntyre became archbishop in 1948 and in 1953 he became the first Cardinal on the West Coast. An effective administrator, he was also committed to ecclesiastical and social hierarchy and was deeply suspicious of theological or social "novelties."

But during the 1960s the cohesion of California Catholicism dissipated dramatically, as hierarchical authority was openly contested in wholly unprecedented ways and many Catholics distanced themselves from the church and its practices. Upwardly mobile, suburban baby boomers and Latino immigrants fueled demographic growth, but pulled the church in different directions. A wide range of reactions to the Second Vatican Council created tumult within the church by providing theological rationales for, and expectations of, both a reformed Catholicism and an orthodox crackdown

In San Francisco, Joseph T. McGucken, Mitty's successor, encountered the first of these symbolic struggles at the end of the 1960s, when an expensive new cathedral became a lightning rod. Debates over racism and radical politics had divided the clergy and the archdiocese in the late 1960s and in 1971 the dedication of the new cathedral was picketed by the Chicano Priests Association as the streets around the building were sealed off by police. The protesting clerics distributed a handout that quoted the Catholic labor leader César Chávez: "We don't ask for more Cathedrals, we don't ask for bigger Churches or fine gifts. We ask for the Church's presence among us. We ask for the Church to sacrifice with the people for social change, for justice, and for love of brother."[9] César Chávez represented a new development not only for Catholicism in the 1960s, but also for California's public realm: a self-conscious Latino activism.

The most dramatic moments in the 1960s crisis of Catholic unity in the public realm came in Los Angeles. For Cardinal McIntyre, Catholicism and the American dream were best served by elites in church, business, and government working together against the threat of godless communism. This elitist conservatism led to McIntyre's involvement in three controversies between 1964 and 1969 that cumulatively fractured the Catholic community's public presence. The first arose in 1964, when McIntyre's refusal to support a state law promoting fair housing practices led to a minor rebellion of his clergy and laity who wanted the church to oppose racial segregation aggressively. The second involved the shifting role of women in the church and the power of the hierarchy. In 1967, because McIntyre was unhappy with the unilateral changes that the California Sisters of the Immaculate Heart of Mary had adopted in the wake of the Second Vatican Council, he banned the order from teaching in parochial schools. The dispute became a national sensation because it involved not simply Vatican II and hierarchical authority but the role of women in the church. As Sister Anita Caspary, the superior of the Immaculate Heart Sisters, recalled in 2003, "[A]t the heart of [the] controversy, the real protagonist may have been the unchanging (and unchangeable?) male hierarchical system, and the antagonist, the female agents of change, viewed as inevitably destructive of that system."[10]

The third and final controversy came in 1969, in connection with the Chicano movement. That year, McIntyre opened a new proto-cathedral, St. Basil's Church, on Los Angeles' deluxe Wiltshire Boulevard. *Católicos por La Raza*, a new organization inspired by César Chávez, disrupted Christmas Eve Mass, fighting with riot police on surrounding streets. Seeking an equal voice for Chicanos in the archdiocese, *La Raza* also demanded public disclosure of archdiocesan finances. In the same year, strongly negative lay reaction to Pope Paul's rejection of artificial birth control and lay acceptance of legalized abortion revealed that a large percentage of Catholics were choosing not to live their lives in full accordance with the hierarchy's version of Catholic dogma and teaching. A steep decline in Mass attendance also began. Indeed, since 1972, when the state's bishops organized the California Catholic Conference (CCC) as "the official voice of the Catholic community in California's public policy arena," it has been difficult to sustain any sense that the CCC could speak for all the state's Catholics. "Official voice" seemed to mean less the bishops speaking on behalf of the faithful than the bishops speaking on their own behalf about the things they hoped to persuade their own people to accept.

More recently, other issues, most notably concerns over clerical sexual abuse of children and young people, have continued to dilute Catholic solidity in the region's civil society. But, after years of massive immigration of Catholics to the region, there have been some signs of a revival of Catholic energy. The church has emerged as one of the most prominent and active defenders of immigration in a region where immigration has been both massive and increasingly controversial. Cardinal Roger Mahony, the current Los Angeles leader, although weakened by the clerical sexual abuse scandal, played a prominent role in the 2006 immigrants' rights protests in Los Angeles and has become a national figure in the debate. Mahony's frequent evocation of the region's Mexican and Spanish past is also both historically appropriate and pastorally prudent. Bravely, given previous trouble, the cardinal also used the process of constructing a new Cathedral of Our Lady of the Angels to bridge internal divisions between workers and employers, and between Latinos and whites. The building is intended as a symbolic counterweight to the region's fluidity and multi-centered urban landscape. The contemporary public visibility yet ambiguous influence of Catholicism extends further than the landmark cathedral. The archdiocese must confront, over and over again, the problem of how to deal with prominent Catholic politicians who don't feel bound by Catholic teaching. Gov. Arnold Schwarzenegger is a pro-abortion Catholic, as was Gray Davis, the governor he supplanted. Richard J. Riordan, who served two terms as Los Angeles' mayor during the 1990s, had worked closely with Mahony on many archdiocesan projects before his election. Yet in 1998 the cardinal felt obliged to publicly rebuke Riordan for violating Catholic norms forbidding divorce and remarriage. Then twice divorced, Riordan had announced a third marriage, having received a church annulment only for the first.

If Catholicism has had to struggle with lack of cohesion since the 1960s, such has been the norm for Protestantism in the Pacific region, which from the beginning has been marked by institutional multiplicity and lively internal competition. Yet since World War II, the public role of Protestantism in the region has shifted dramatically. Mainline Protestants, who once had a much higher civic profile, have dwindled amazingly. Although they never held the establishment or quasi-establishment status here that they did in other parts of the country, the mainline denominations had deep roots, especially in and around San Francisco.

In the years following World War I, native-born, middle-class Protestants in northern California became largely resigned to their long-standing minority status in numbers and cultural power. In the Bay Area, an urban-dominated political culture that aspired to social tolerance and progressive reform—and dominated, in the eyes of local Protestants, by Catholics—was one most Protestant adherents had learned to live with and to which a few were even enthusiastic contributors. They favored, therefore, symbolic projections of their presence, like the 103-foot cross erected in a public park as a focal point for ecumenical Easter services attended by as many as 75,000 people in the 1940s. A similar cross was erected at the same time on city park land in San Diego by that city's mainliners. When built, no one foresaw legal challenges over the placement of crosses in public parks. But eventually the crosses became the topic of divisive litigation. (The Mt. Soledad case in San Diego seems on track to eventually reach the Supreme Court.) Along the way, new understandings of church-state separation and new ways of enunciating a culture of pluralism obliged mainline Protestants to disavow their earlier notions of civil religion.

Faced by the sharpening ideological struggles of the 1960s, many Protestant churches in the region have divided, dwindled, or drifted into different camps. San Francisco's lofty Glide Memorial United Methodist Church is among a number of others that have embraced radical new forms of inclusion and sought to play a prophetic role to call its community to higher norms of social justice. This church was planted in the Tenderloin district by Lizzie Glide, a Methodist philanthropist who had purchased the land, paid for the church building (1931), and left it with a sizable endowment. In 1963, the Rev. Cecil Williams, a young African American clergyman from Texas, arrived to be the director of community involvement. Three years later, he was the pastor. In 1967, he had the cross removed from the sanctuary, reminding the congregation, "We must all be the cross." Under Williams, Glide Memorial regularly came to have a full sanctuary for "celebration" services of personal testimonies, poetry, dance, and contemporary music, the latter often drawing on black traditions. The church also became known for leadership in demonstrations advocating black studies and affirmative action, for its meal program, for opening its facilities to use by groups ranging from the Hookers Convention to the American Indian Movement, for opposition to the Vietnam War, and for ministry to bring recovery to city dwellers contending with drug, alcohol, and other dependencies. Williams also organized the Council on Religion and Homosexuality in 1964. San Francisco had long been a center of relative toleration for gay men and lesbians, and Glide Memorial's congregation embraced people of all sexual orientations as well as all races and classes. Glide Memorial, committed to its prophetic stance, became a major site for grieving, comfort, and the defusing of potential civic disturbances. But it did not attract many new members.

While mainline Protestantism's new embrace of civic tolerance in a fluid society reached its leftmost limits at Glide Memorial, many mainliners tried to embrace the metropolis with less stridency. But whether in its Glide-like prophetic form or in the more priestly guise of such exercises as the Mt. Davidson Easter sunrise services, by the late 1970s the tradition found itself struggling to remain a vocal player in community life. Its aspirations were a lot bigger than the heft—symbolic, economic, administrative, or electoral—that it could bring to bear on the public square either of the Bay Area or of California generally. By the end of the twentieth century, the region's mainline Protestantism seemed to have dispersed into the sea of tolerant, personalized, California dreaming.

Judaism also has a public presence in the life of the Pacific region, one increasingly rooted in southern California and the new Jewish experience of affluence and cultural power. Before World War II, there were 130,000 Jews living in Los Angeles, with Jewish leadership in the film industry and growing numbers of Jewish clerical and garment workers provided the base for the flourishing of Jewish religious life in southern California. The elite side of this Jewish religious life was exemplified in the Wilshire Boulevard Temple, which was built in 1929 under the leadership of San Francisco-born Rabbi Edgar Magnin. Architecturally, the temple was modeled after Rome's Pantheon. Symbolically, it manifested the opulence and influence of its congregants, who included Carl Laemmle of Universal Pictures, Harry and Jack Warner of Warner Brothers, Louis B. Mayer of Metro-Goldwyn-Mayer, and William

Fox of Fox Film Company. World War II and its aftermath attracted a new wave of Jewish migrants to Los Angeles. Hollywood's Temple Israel, particularly under the leadership of Rabbi Max Nussbaum, helped focus locally a post-war Jewish political impulse that was Zionist and activist for civil rights for all. At the same time, the House Un-American Activities Committee's investigation of communism in the film industry and the ensuing blacklisting of the Hollywood Ten (1947) divided the local Jewish community over issues of Americanism and social justice and made many Jews connected to Hollywood uneasy about their associations, religious and political.

During the 1960s and 1970s, the spiritual liquidity of Los Angeles fostered further redefinitions of what it meant to be Jewish and American. Los Angeles Jews, in the words of the historian Deborah Dash Moore, "made their choices surrounded by affluence and captivated by self-fulfillment."[11] Many chose to disperse outward from ethnic neighborhoods like Boyle Heights and Fairfax. Others embraced a range of political and religious affiliations. There was still what one sociologist called a "civil Judaism," expressed through an emphasis on "the mutual responsibility of Jews, the centrality of Israel . . . and the need to challenge both the internal and external threats to Jewish survival through political activities."[12] But increasingly Jews were choosing not to affiliate with any distinctively Jewish organization. Of those who did affiliate, many came to see their religious commitment in terms of voluntary participation rather than communal obligation. The trajectory of individualized Jewish religiosity in the region can be seen in the Stephen S. Wise Temple. Established in Los Angeles by Isaiah Zeldin in 1964, by the mid-1970s the temple boasted over 1,200 members. Under Zeldin's leadership, it developed a wide range of educational programs for all ages, including summer camping, a holiday workshop series, a parenting center for infants and mothers, day school, programming for teenagers, and family-life programs for single, adoptive, remarried, and intermarried parents. "We take you from the sperm to the worm," quipped one temple official.[13]

Among the old players, low commitment mainline Protestants, Catholics, and Jews occupy crucial positions ideologically in the region's religious politics. With regard to moral liberalism, they are very similar in outlook to other Christians, secularists, and non-Christians. This amounts to a sizable ideologically liberal constituency—over 50 percent of the region's population. Because it consists of a majority of all Catholics and mainline Protestants, this sector amounts to a crucial swing vote—leaning in a liberal direction on lifestyle and cultural issues, favoring a high level of personal freedom and choice, but on occasion allying with their more conservative (and more religiously committed) Catholic and Protestant friends on bread-and-butter issues. Larger than their counterparts for the country as a whole (44.6 percent), this majority yields a disproportionate influence on public life within the region. It sets the moral and political tone.

Members of the region's kaleidoscope of new and alternative religious movements also tend to align themselves here. Many Californians continue to move beyond traditional religious affiliations, to a place somewhere between familiar traditions and thoroughgoing secularity. Many of these new or non-institutional religious movements emphasize a highly individualized spirituality and concern for personal development and human relationships. Sometimes they blend elements of many religious traditions; Asian and Native American ideas and practices are particularly popular. While some clearly wish to influence public policy—certainly those emphasizing concern for issues such as the environment and animal rights—they have generally had difficulty mobilizing and bringing their weight to bear. The de facto agreement to operate on open and tolerant principles creates a fluid, ever-shifting public role for religion that makes its influence episodic at best.

CONSERVATIVE PROTESTANTISM

The same cannot be said for the region's lively conservative Protestant scene. Protestant adherents who moved to southern California in the late nineteenth and early twentieth centuries have always seemed more troubled than their northern peers by the liquid modernity that accompanied the pursuit of the American dream. Since then, southern California has become a national center of dynamic conservative Protestantism, if in something of a bunkered, enclave mode.

The Holiness movement had local sources through the work of the Los Angeles pastor Phineas F. Bresee, a founder of the Church of the Nazarene in 1895. Pentecostalism, which stressed the supernatural gifts of the Holy Spirit, became a worldwide multiracial movement through the Los Angeles preaching of the black evangelist William J. Seymour at the Azusa Street Mission in 1906. In 1923, Sister Aimee Semple McPherson deepened the local base of Pentecostalism when she opened her 5,000-seat Angelus Temple and a few years later incorporated a new denomination, the International Church of the Foursquare Gospel. Fundamentalism—characterized by Marsden as "the response of traditionalist evangelicals who declared war on . . . modernizing trends"[14]—found important local support in Immanuel Presbyterian Church, Los Angeles. There, Lyman and Milton Stewart had the money (from Union Oil Company) and the theological inclinations to fund foreign missionaries, pay for the publication and distribution of the pamphlet series *The Fundamentals* (1910-1915), and help found the Bible Institute of Los Angeles (Biola, and later, Biola University).

American evangelicalism—a religious mass movement—has always been tied to particular religious organizations, whether denominational, interdenominational, or nondenominational, yet it has always cut across many religious institutions as well. The movement's "great" tradition, the wellspring of its identity, is an unambiguous insistence on Biblical authority (supernaturalist theological norms); conversion to Christ as Savior (personalized religious experience); disciplines of discipleship (a moralistic set of religious sensibilities); and mission to others (faith-based activism). This religious culture, perhaps not altogether paradoxically, flourished in the fluid culture of the west. For by the 1920s, conservative white southern Californian Protestants were breaking with mainline denominations to develop institutions to perpetuate their own religious values and ideals. One of the most prominent of these, Fuller Theological Seminary, came to embody much of the history of fundamentalism and allied conservative Protestantism in the state.

Charles E. Fuller was a fundamentalist convert who graduated from Biola in 1921. Well-to-do thanks to his family's involvement in the citrus industry, he was imbued with Biola's missionizing ethos. In 1930, a Bible class that he had begun had grown into an independent congregation that broadcast an evangelistic service on a local radio station. In taking to the radio, Fuller was following the lead of other Los Angeles conservative Protestants such as Sister Aimee, who had founded her own radio station in 1924, and the Rev. Robert P. "Fighting Bob" Shuler, the fundamentalist pastor of Trinity Southern Methodist Church. Fuller's earnest and irenic "Old Fashioned Revival Hour" debuted nationwide in 1937 via the Mutual Broadcast System; by 1944, some 20 million Americans were tuning in. The success of his congregation and radio ministry enabled Charles Fuller to launch Fuller Theological Seminary in Pasadena in 1947. In the spirit of its founder, the school deliberately moved away from such fundamentalist distinctives as separatism, antiintellectualism, and antimodernist militancy. As incisively explained by the historian George Marsden, it was looking to "reform fundamentalism."[15] Although this effort proved controversial, internally as well as externally, the school survived and thrived. The unchallenged leader of what is called "progressive evangelicalism," Fuller is now the largest Protestant nondenominational seminary in the United States.

Another key story evolved south of Los Angeles, as conservative Protestants helped consolidate a distinctive band of conservatism in the Orange

County suburbs. In Garden Grove, Robert H. Schuller, an Iowan sent to lead a mission for the Reformed Church in America in 1955, nurtured a new kind of congregation to meet new, middle-class, suburban needs. What became the gigantic Crystal Cathedral began in a drive-in movie theater lot. It proved to be a powerful draw in what the historian Lisa McGirr has described as the hospitable climate forged by "middle-class men and women who . . . found meaning in a set of politics that affirmed the grounding of their lives in individual success and yet critiqued the social consequences of the market by calling for a return to 'traditional' values, local control, strict morality, and strong authority."[16] It was not an accident that the year Schuller arrived to organize a congregation was also the year Disneyland opened in nearby Anaheim. Walt Disney's theme park fit Orange County, "with its mixture of nostalgia for a simple American past and its bright optimism about the future."[17] In other words, the California mystique took a decidedly neoconservative turn in postwar Orange County.

Schuller believed new forms of American life called for new forms for worship and church life. The Reformed Church was a mainline denomination with little to no cachet in the region. Further, southern California's built landscape was designed for the automobile. To reach the unchurched, Schuller took three innovative steps that led to the congregation becoming a megachurch of some 10,000 members by 1980. He decided to mute denominational ties. He built for a big, mobile, geographically dispersed congregation, eventually in a giant Crystal Cathedral, which allowed worshipers to participate indoors, outside in their cars, or via the church's televised "Hour of Power" program. Third, he innovated by combining two disparate streams of Protestant thought into what he termed "possibility thinking," yoking evangelicalism with self-help through mind-conditioning—a therapeutic gospel suited for the American dream. "It's obvious that we are not trying to impress Christians," Schuller has said about his religious site. "We're trying to make a big, beautiful impression upon the affluent nonreligious American who is riding by on this busy freeway."[18]

Fuller Seminary and the Crystal Cathedral both suggest that the booming postwar California suburbs provided a distinctive social and cultural fluidity, not only for the flourishing of Protestant evangelicalism but also for "post-denominationalism." Fuller Seminary is evangelical and nondenominational. Conservative Protestants in the region have shown their ability to tap some elements of the prevailing secular culture, while rejecting others. Calvary Chapel of Costa Mesa is another example of the flexible forms that developed alongside as well as within Protestant denominations. It represents yet another current in postwar evangelicalism—the more overtly supernaturalist and socially critical one that the sociologist Donald E. Miller has located among "new paradigm churches" centered in southern California. These churches challenge "not doctrine but the medium through which the message of Christianity is articulated."[19]

In 1965, the Rev. Charles "Chuck" Smith accepted a call to Calvary Chapel, a struggling congregation in Orange County's Costa Mesa. Although he began his pastoral work within the International Church of the Foursquare Gospel (founded by Aimee Semple McPherson in Los Angeles in the 1920s), Smith had already left it by the time he moved to Calvary Chapel. Whereas Robert Schuller targeted the unchurched middle-class families of Orange County, Chuck Smith targeted the young people drawn to the nearby beach during the 1960s and 1970s. Smith did not object to their clothing styles, and he welcomed adaptations of their music for worship services, but he insisted on personal conversion to Jesus Christ as Savior and regular Bible study in order to ground individuals in a lifestyle of responsible love to others. Smith soon had what became, in effect, a new denomination that updated informal forms of Pentecostal traditions. In 1974, Calvary Chapel built a new sanctuary that seated 2,300 people. Smith emphasized the gifts and leading of the Holy Spirit over institutional or professional order. Costa Mesa was the mother church of a host of Calvary Chapels, and Smith the father figure, but each Calvary Chapel founded by Smith's direct or indirect protégés was (and is) separately incorporated, and there was little reporting back to Smith or Costa Mesa. Moreover, another "new paradigm" neodenomination, the Vineyard Christian Fellowship, arose from Calvary Chapel after 1974. Calvary Chapel's flexible order and baby boomer-friendly ethos has distinctively reflected important aspects of late twentieth century California metropolitan society.

Calvary Chapel is an important example of postwar evangelicalism's ready growth through adaptation to California's liquid modernity. It is also a component in the conservative political bent of Orange County in particular and southern California more generally. The Calvary movement refrains from taking overt positions on contested issues in the public realm. Nevertheless, its premillennial eschatology and emphasis on traditional patriarchal family values reinforce rather than challenge conservative politics in the region.

Southern California has also produced a series of energetic figures who tie together conservative religion, conservative politics, and engagement with the popular culture. In the 1970s and 1980s, the Rev. Timothy LaHaye was perhaps the most prominent. A fundamentalist, he was—and remains—relentless in his concern for the salvation of individuals and also with what the political scientist Michael Lienesch has termed the "redeeming of America" through a "politics of moralism."[20] The urgency, for LaHaye as well as many of his supporters, is based on their dispensational premillennialism: the eschatological clock outlined in the Biblical books of Daniel and Revelation is ticking; God is on the move in our times as seen in the rise of the state of Israel; and the Second Coming of Christ, prior to a period of apocalyptic tribulation on the earth, could come at any moment. In the 1970s LaHaye emerged as one of the most prominent figures of the new religious right, supported Ronald Reagan's political career, and eventually began writing a best-selling series of novels about the end times.

Beverly LaHaye, Timothy LaHaye's wife, meanwhile led the founding in 1978 of Concerned Women for America. Around the same time, James Dobson, a psychologist and a devout Church of the Nazarene layman, resigned his staff position at the Children's Hospital in Los Angeles in order to devote his time to a ministry of teaching, writing, and broadcasting. His organization was called Focus on the Family. The LaHayes and Dobson brought a significant southern-California base to the table when the religious right jelled around the 1980 presidential elections.

Despite its public presence, this energized regional religious cluster is anything but monolithic. Privatization is as strong and deep a current among evangelicals as among mainline Protestants. Nevertheless, important elements of California evangelicalism have contributed to the shaping of a resurgent political conservatism, although with more distance imposed than is the case in places like the South and Southern Crossroads. Such elements also led to a conservative religious dominance of the California Republican Party for much of the 1980s and 1990s. Yet, the 2003 recall of Democratic Governor Gray Davis in favor of Republican Arnold Schwarzenegger—both pro-choice Catholics—suggests that the moralism of the religious right has its limits in the public arena. In a fluid, diverse regional society, faith-based values can elicit widespread support, but always in the context of a political culture of tolerant pluralism.

NEW PLAYERS

One of the most profound engines for cultural change in the region in recent decades has been the resumption of mass immigration to the United States after a forty-year pause that lasted from 1925 to 1965. Since then, California has been the focal point of a global migration of stunning size, something that is actually quite distinguishable from previous waves of migration to the state, which came largely from other parts of the United States. Now, one in every four immigrants to the United States lists California as his or her intended place of residence, according to reports by the U.S. Citizenship and Immigration Services, part of the Department of Homeland Security (formerly the U.S. Immigration and Naturalization Service). By a wide margin, California has the largest foreign-born population of any state. According to U.S. Census figures, 26 percent of California's population is foreign-born. By comparison, New York, the next most popular destination for immigrants, has a foreign-born population of about 20 percent. Hawaii (16 percent) and Nevada (15 percent), the other states of the Pacific region, rank with California, New York, and Florida as the five states in which 15 percent or more of the population are foreign born.

In 2000, California also received immigrants from 85 percent of the world's countries, making the state's population one of the most diverse in the nation. The state hosts particularly large populations of people who trace their origins to Mexico (about 8.5 million in the 2000 census), China (over 900,000), the Philippines (over 900,000), Vietnam (about 450,000), Korea (over 340,000), India (more than 300,000), and Japan (about 280,000). As a result, the public face of religion has also changed in the region. There are not only large numbers of Buddhists present for the first time in the nation's history, there are Buddhist groups from Japan, China, Korea, Vietnam, Cambodia, Thailand, Sri Lanka, and Tibet. Many Catholics come from not only Mexico and Central America but also from Vietnam and the Philippines. All of this has introduced new complexities within and between religious groups and reinforced notions about pluralistic transformation.

It has also intensified discussion about whether and how new religious and ethnic players will find their place in American life. In the Pacific region, many immigrant religious groups have found that demonstrating their "Americanness" meant greater participation in public life. Participation in civic ceremonies, public condemnation of attacks on the United States, demonstrations of patriotism, engagement in social service, lobbying for civil rights, and encouraging members to become citizens and vote have all become ways for immigrant religious groups to demonstrate that they are good Americans. Especially since the September 11 attacks of 2001, questions about loyalty have been raised regularly. American Muslims who sympathized with those who attacked U.S. targets were deemed un-American, but so were conservative Christians who condemned Islam as a false or evil religion.

Most of these post-1965 immigrants were arriving in a local culture where the religious groups that had, in prior generations, striven for sovereignty over the public culture and urged conformity with the "American way of life" were on the decline. New players—both immigrant groups and homegrown innovators—found it easier to assume a diversity of cultural outlooks and lifestyles. The region's culture raised happiness, self-fulfillment, and personal empowerment to positive religious values. Being different—"expressing oneself"—was becoming a normative way of fitting in; conformity—associated with being "square"—was decidedly out. To some degree, this was true all over the United States but it was particularly the case in the Pacific region: outsiders were "in," and insiders were "out."

How has this affected the region's religious demographics? Clearly, it has meant a growing Latin influence among Christian denominations. It has also meant growing numbers of Buddhists, Muslims, Hindus, Sikhs, Jains, and other adherents of Eastern religions, although this growth has not been as dramatic as the rise in total number of immigrants. A national survey of religious identification, the *American Religious Identification Survey* (ARIS), conducted in 2000, found that Muslims now account for approximately 0.4 percent of the region's population and members of "Asian" religions—Buddhism, Hinduism, Sikhism, etc.—collectively account for less than 3 percent. What this means is that the majority of the region's immigrants arrive as Christians. So the diversification of the region's population has had the greatest impact on Catholicism, Protestantism, and Judaism, contributing to what R. Stephen Warner has called the "de-Europeanization" of these religious families.[21]

The reform in U.S. immigration laws in 1965 coincided with a shift in attitudes among Catholic leaders in America toward diversity within the church. Until the Second Vatican Council, the Catholic Church in America laid heavy emphasis on the Americanization of immigrant Catholics. This was due to a number of circumstances, including anti-Catholic sentiment in the American public, the dominance of the Irish in the American Catholic hierarchy, and a general emphasis on cultural conformity in the American public. This Americanization policy had a detrimental effect on participation by minority Catholics in the Pacific region. Catholic leadership fretted over the poor rates of participation by Latino and Asian Catholics, especially the large numbers of Mexicans and Filipinos in these states. This was not because Mexican and Filipino Catholics were unobservant. In fact, devotionalism was relatively high among these groups. The problem was that the church did not recognize or support the vernacular piety of these Catholics.

This situation began to change after the reforms of the Second Vatican Council which, in addition to making the Mass available in vernacular languages, placed greater emphasis on personal devotion and popular piety. This new emphasis on popular devotion has, however, brought new challenges for the Catholic Church. While embracing the value of multiculturalism, the church must now negotiate the demands of increasingly diverse parishes. According to officials in the Los Angeles archdiocese, the Mass is now said in over 50 languages in the Pacific region. A shortage of priests generally, combined with an even greater shortage of priests from minority ethnic groups, has limited the church's ability to live up to its commitment to diversity. Furthermore, the parish system itself has limited the church's ability to respond adequately to the demands of different ethnic groups.

The degree to which particular Protestant denominations have been affected by immigration varies widely, as does the response of particular denominations to the demands of diversity. A few representative examples illuminate patterns to watch for. The voluntary, congregational organization of most Protestant denominations makes it possible for immigrant communities to establish independent congregations tailored to their own tastes, customs, and languages. Korean Presbyterian churches are perhaps the best known example in the Pacific region. This is a particularly interesting example because Korean Presbyterians are typically more conservative theologically and politically than their American Presbyterian counterparts in the region, and their growing presence has contributed to a conservative shift at both the regional and national level. However, the ethnic distinctiveness of Korean Presbyterian congregations has a cost, in that many second- and third-generation Korean Americans feel alienated in these congregations because they are less proficient in the Korean language and identify more with American than with Korean culture and customs. Much has been written about the success of evangelical Protestantism, and Pentecostalism in particular, among Central and South American Latinos. The fruits of these missionary endeavors are coming home to the United States among immigrants. About one-fourth of all Latinos in the country are Protestant, mostly Pentecostal.

For a variety of reasons then, the de-Europeanization of Protestant religion appears to favor conservative, evangelical, and Pentecostal churches. With few exceptions however immigrant Protestant churches have developed very little public presence. In part, this is due to theology. As noted above, for many immigrant Protestants, the church is seen as safe haven from the perils of a public culture characterized by moral license. In many of these churches, as in conservative Protestant churches generally, individual moral reform, rather than civic action, is seen as the answer to social problems. Immigrant Protestant churches have not, by and large, aligned with the politically engaged religious right.

In the region's Jewish community, immigration has added yet more diversity to the various expressions of the faith. Growth in the Pacific region's Jewish population was fueled in the 1970s and 1980s by the exodus of Jews from the Middle East and especially from Iran. Saba Soomekh reports that the economic success of Persian Jews in southern California had the unexpected effect of deterring them from civic involvement until recently. Economic and social self-sufficiency led Iranian Jews in the region to develop what she described as a "ghetto mentality," with little desire to get involved in civic life.[22]

Post-1965 patterns of immigration have also resulted in growing communities of Buddhists, Hindus, Sikhs, and Muslims in the region. Because of
the geographic proximity of the west coast to Asia, and because of the educational and economic opportunities available on the west coast, growth in these
religious traditions in America has been concentrated in the Pacific region.
Mosques, Sikh gurdwaras, and Hindu and Buddhist temples are now prominent features of the landscape. And having hardly registered in polls of religious identification for most of the twentieth century, members of these religions represented more than 3 percent of the region's population in 2000.
That number may seem small, but in a state with 34 million residents, it represents a sizable population—a million people—and numbers in a participa-
tory democracy translate into civic influence.

The ability to influence civic life varies greatly among individual groups,
of course. Research on the effect of religious pluralism on civic life in southern California, reported at a recent conference at the University of California
Santa Barbara, identified several variables that influence the social capital
(i.e., their participation in and ability to influence civic life) of particular religious groups. Clearly, the presence of economic and human capital in these
groups influences social capital. That is, groups with greater economic resources and groups whose members are highly educated and informed about
civic issues are more likely to get involved than groups that lack those resources. But just as important is the group's ability to mobilize these resources
toward collectively agreed-upon civic goals. Groups that are characterized by
internal dissent have a harder time mobilizing resources than groups that are
characterized by general consensus about civic issues. Additionally, members
of the religious group must develop some sense of the connection between
their *religious* identity and their *civic* interests. Until recently, the lack of such
a perceived connection between religious and civic interests prevented many
groups, not just Persian Jews, from getting civically involved.

With 38 percent of all Buddhists in the U.S., California hosts the nation's largest Buddhist population (although they constitute a much larger
proportion of religious adherents in Hawaii). That is hardly surprising given
the history of immigration patterns on the Pacific coast. Chinese and
Japanese Buddhists began arriving in the nineteenth century to labor in the
region's mines, railroads, farms, and fishing industry. That immigration
came to a virtual halt as a series of restrictions on the immigration and naturalization of Asians was enacted. Until 1965, when the country reopened
its borders to immigrants from the East, those Buddhist organizations that
existed in the region placed a heavy emphasis on the Americanization of
members. The Japan-based *Jodo Shinshu*, probably the largest such organization, offered members English-language classes and even organized Bud-

dhist youth associations modeled after the YMCA. The Americanization process was further promoted during World War II, when Japanese Americans living in the region were relocated or confined to internment camps. It was in one such internment camp that leaders decided to change the group's name to the Buddhist Churches of America. After 1965, the organization experienced another challenge, even as it enjoyed an influx of new-immigrant members. The organization's leadership remained very much tied to Japan, most of its priests being trained there. Furthermore, the new immigrants tended to favor the maintenance of distinctively Japanese practices in the organization, which has tended to alienate the more Americanized members. This sense of alienation, combined with an outmarriage rate of around 50 percent, has led to a real crisis of membership.

The 1965 immigration law opened up the possibility of immigration from other Asian countries as well and this has meant a significant diversification of Buddhism in the region. The Chinese and Japanese Buddhists are today joined by Buddhists from Thailand, Cambodia, Sri Lanka, Burma, Vietnam, Korea, Taiwan, and Tibet, to name but a few of the largest such groups. The tendency among these groups is to establish their own temples, although some, such as the *Wat Thai* temple in North Hollywood, have attempted to reach a broader public. The result is that virtually every variety of Buddhism in the world is now represented in California. They are joined, furthermore, by a growing number of American converts, mostly white, educated, and middle class. It is impossible to say just how many such convert Buddhists there are in the Pacific region, or nationwide for that matter. Some groups, such as the Japan-based *Soka Gakkai*, have become predominately American-convert Buddhist movements. Several major Buddhist groups see themselves as having a mission to spread the *dharma* in the United States but there is considerable disagreement among these groups over how best to do that and over how American "American Buddhism" can be while remaining authentically Buddhist.

While "Engaged Buddhism" was not invented in the Pacific region, it has certainly found a home there. In fact, one study of conversion to *Soka Gakkai* Buddhism found that, while this Buddhist organization's involvement in environmental protection and nuclear disarmament was not what initially attracted people to the religion, these activities were certainly among the reasons they stayed.[23] Socially engaged Buddhism can take many forms, but running through them all is the notion that the *dharma* can be an instrument for social change. The Buddhist Peace Fellowship, based in San Francisco, began as an attempt by Robert Aitken, Gary Snyder, and Joanna Macy to integrate Buddhist meditation practices with their social activism. Begun in the late 1970s, it is now a transnational organization that responds to social problems around the world by providing medical services, refugee relief, and by advocating nuclear disarmament.

Perhaps more than for any other religious group, the maintenance of Hinduism among immigrants from India has required considerable innovation. That is because religion is so much a part of the mainstream culture and everyday life in India. There, shrines dot the landscape, priests are readily available, monks are ubiquitous, and the institution of *samskara* (rites of passage performed over the course of the individual's life) tends to orient the individual life cycle toward sacred duties and virtuous living. This is clearly not the case in the United States. Even in California, most Hindus have to drive a long way to attend worship. Consequently, much religious activity has been moved toward the weekend and this has meant larger numbers of worshipers gathering at once, rather than individuals coming by at their leisure. Unlike temples in India therefore, U.S. temples tend to include gathering halls and kitchens, which are used for a variety of religious and cultural events. Innovation has also been spurred by the fact of the linguistic, cultural, and religious diversity of immigrants from India. Hinduism in India is a diverse conglomeration of regional cultures, each with distinctive variations of ritual, doctrine, and festival. In the United States, there are generally not a sufficient number of immigrants from a particular region in any one locality to establish separate temples, although that is beginning to change as larger numbers of Indian immigrants arrive. For the most part, the temples that have been established are more pan-Indian in spirit, housing several deities rather than only one, as would be the case in India.

Such innovations have ironically led to a concern about authenticity, which is reflected in temple architecture. The *Shree Venkatsewara Swami* Temple in the Malibu hills, for instance, was built by traditionally trained craftsmen brought from India. And plans for building new temples have become the subject of transnational conversation over the Internet. The ability to import craftsmen and traditional building materials such as marble and granite associated with particular temple sites in India is a luxury that could not be afforded by most immigrant groups. Indian immigrants have been described as perhaps the most successful immigrant group in the country, and with good reason. Many of these immigrants are highly educated professionals who immigrated to the United States in search of better career opportunities than were available in India. Since U.S. immigration laws favored highly skilled individuals and those with private financial resources, these immigrants have done exceedingly well in the United States. Although one expects, because education and professional occupation are positively associated with voting, that Hindus participate in the electoral process, they do not appear to have made a link between religious identity and civic action. This may be due to their religious beliefs. One member of the *Vedanta* Society of West Holly-wood explained an interview about Hindu involvement in interfaith activities that Hindus would not be motivated to civic activism by a desire to right an injustice because, to them, the world "*is* just."[24]

Circumstances of history have created unique challenges for Muslims in the United States. As a religious movement among urban black Ameri-cans during the civil rights movement, Islam in America developed an im-age as militantly antiestablishment. Although African American Muslims later turned toward a more orthodox understanding of Islam, the image stuck. In the minds of many Americans, that image was reinforced by political-religious movements in postcolonial societies of north Africa, the Middle East, and south Asia that began in the second half of the twentieth century and continue to the present. The unconventional but highly dra-matic tactics of some of the most militant of these movements, generally described as "terrorist," have led in the minds of many Americans to an as-sociation of Islam with violence and hatred of the United States. While most Americans associate Buddhism with the Dalai Lama, and Hinduism with Ghandi, they associate Islam with Osama bin Laden. Muslims in the United States are consequently very image-conscious and they have gone to great lengths to promote a more positive image.

In California, the Islamic Center of Southern California, the Council on American-Islamic Relations, and the Muslim American Society work not only to propagate Islam but also to establish positive public relations. The website for the Muslim American Society of Southern California, for in-stance, emphasizes such values as "brotherhood, equality, justice, mercy, com-passion, and peace"—genuine Muslim values expressed in terms drawn from the lexicon of American civil culture. The mission statement of the Council on American-Islamic Relations makes its purpose explicit: "to promote a pos-itive image of Islam and Muslims in America."[25] These organizations have well-developed public relations machinery and regularly issue press releases addressing a wide variety of local, national, and international events and is-sues. Muslim leaders are also involved in the many different interfaith associ-ations active in the Pacific region. Historical circumstances propelled Mus-lims in the region into the civic arena. When the Federal Building in Oklahoma City was bombed in 1995 and public suspicion automatically fell on Muslim radicals, American Muslims realized they had a public relations problem. Muslim organizations soon became involved in not only promoting a positive image of Islam in America, but also in advocating civil rights. More recently, civil rights activism among American Muslims has been fueled by responses to the September 11 attacks by Muslim extremists on American targets. Muslim American organizations were quick not only to condemn the attacks but also to call attention to the spate of hate crimes against people of Middle Eastern heritage in the United States.

But Muslim civic activism has not only been motivated by self-interest. Muslims in the Pacific region have interpreted the third pillar of Islam, the duty to give alms, as a civic religious duty. One particularly notable and creative expression of this is the University Muslim Medical Association Clinic in south-central Los Angeles.

The clinic was founded in 1996 in response to the medical needs of the population in this poor neighborhood and to try and improve relationships between immigrant Muslims and black Americans in the aftermath of the 1992 riots. The two UCLA students who founded the clinic initially envisioned a medical trailer that would drive through the city offering blood pressure exams and other minor services. But the students' project came to the attention of a Los Angeles city councilwoman who helped them obtain a grant from federal housing authorities to renovate an abandoned building on Florence Avenue. The city itself ponied up a grant to cover the cost of operations for the first four years.

When, in the fall of 2000, the clinic faced closure because of a funding shortage, a story by Theresa Watanabe in *The Los Angeles Times* stimulated a surge of Muslim philanthropy. Within days, Watanabe reported, donations of more than $284,000 came in, enough to keep the clinic open for another year.[26] Today, it serves thousands of patients every year and is the only free medical clinic in south-central Los Angeles. The clinic has served as a model for similar charitable efforts by Muslims across the country. Such activities are sincere but also strategic in that they attempt to counter widespread stereotypes about Islam and to promote an image of Muslims as desirable friends, neighbors, colleagues, and citizens.

On the whole, Muslims in the Pacific region have been very successful in negotiating a positive public identity. Dramatic evidence of this came in the aftermath of the attacks on U.S. targets on September 11, 2001. To be sure, there were repercussions, as hate crimes against people and religions from the Middle East increased, and the U.S. government began detaining Muslims and scrutinizing the activities of mosques and Islamic benevolent societies. However, at the same time, Americans of all different faiths were carefully scrutinizing the behavior of the U.S. government toward Muslims and perhaps their own feelings about their Muslim friends, colleagues, and neighbors. Muslims in the region responded by speaking out against violence, keeping track of hate crimes against Muslims, and forming alliances with other religious leaders to advocate for the rights of Muslims in the United States. The participation of Muslim leaders in interfaith memorials and public appearances with political officials dramatized the fact that most Muslims

in the region condemned the violence, supported U.S. efforts to combat terrorism, and grieved for those whose lives were lost. There were certainly negative consequences of the September 11 attacks for Muslims, but in some
ways events in the aftermath of those attacks demonstrated just how well-
established Muslims in the region had become.

CONCLUSION

The Pacific region is a place where the American paradox of simultaneous
deep secularity and vibrant religiosity is intensified. From its long history, but
especially since the 1960s, it has been a culture where institutional religion has
struggled to wield public influence. In a middle-class, consumption culture
that privileges what is new (even if it is sometimes little more than a repackaging of the old), pursing spiritual growth and drawing from a variety of traditions is generally looked upon as a pleasant, positive, and personal experience. Spirituality, at least in its popular versions, is defined as something to be
explored and tried out, and then finally judged subjectively as to its adequacy
or appropriateness. Many phrases are used to describe the style of religiosity
and spirituality that is so prominent in the region—privatized religion, invisible religion, spiritual seeking, religion a la carte, hybridity, mixing of the
codes, and of course the frequently cited saying that one is "spiritual but not
religious." Many people in the region can talk about their family's religious
history or even their own religious past better than they can affirm what they
themselves actually believe in the present moment. This does not mean they
have no beliefs but instead that their beliefs and doubts, convictions and cu-
riosities are all coupled together. Living faith and spirituality in a fluid environment is very much like that—at times confusing and complicated, yet at
other times quite centered and convincing. Especially for this region's large
constituencies, caught between religious extremism and a full-blown secularism, such fluidity is common.

The obligatory tolerance and individualism built into the fluid modernity of the region have made it just about impossible to imagine how any religious groups might capture a major role in the Pacific region's public life.
This may be one reason why the California solution to the challenge of religion in public life may not always be exportable to regions that do not share
its history and religious demography. And yet it is clear that many people of
faith in the region—from evangelical Protestants to devoted New Agers—
still yearn to make their deepest values and concerns the stuff of public life
and formal politics. And it is not unlikely that the future will bring new things

to the land of the new. The centrality of the immigrant experience in the region and the great debates over immigration policy might catalyze new alliances; certainly increasingly vocal Catholic advocacy of immigrants and the public mobilization of Muslims make that a possibility. And as environmental issues become more central to American politics and public life, particularly around the issue of climate change, we may see the mobilization of new religious constituencies, perhaps emerging out of the increasingly vocal "greenness" of southern California's "new evangelicals."

· 7 ·

The Pacific Northwest: The "None" Zone

There is nothing new about the prevalence of "Nones"—people who identify themselves as having no religion—in the Pacific Northwest. "The people that builded [*sic*] this empire . . . [left] the Golden Rule beyond the Rockies, and they proceeded to do others before others could do them," lamented Professor E. J. Klemme of the Washington State Normal School in Ellensburg in 1914. "In the East they were faithful church members; now they are not even church [at]tenders." According to Klemme, responsibility for that sad state of affairs lay with the geography itself: "The ascent of the Great Divide seemed too steep for church letters. The air of the Northwest seemed too rare for prayer. We have hurried forth to conquer the wilderness, but we have been conquered by it."[1]

White people came to the region looking to get rich on its natural bounty of furs, fish, timber, and gold. But the sheer immensity of the place— its snowcapped peaks, massive trees, and rushing rivers—tended to overwhelm them. In poems like "The Law of the Yukon," the transplanted Scotsman Robert W. Service[2] portrayed the northwest corner of the continent as a magnificent but pitiless land that subjected its would-be exploiters to the ultimate Darwinian test.

> In the camp at the bend of the river, with its dozen saloons aglare,
> Its gambling dens ariot, its gramophones all ablare; Crimped with the
> crimes of a city, sin-ridden and bridled with lies, In the hush of my moun-
> tained vastness, in the flush of my midnight skies. Plague-spots, yet tools
> of my purpose, so natheless I suffer them thrive, Crushing my Weak in
> their clutches, that only my Strong may survive.

Jonas Stamper, the pioneer from Kansas who moved his family to Oregon at the beginning of Ken Kesey's 1964 novel *Sometimes a Great Notion*, expressed

135

the human perspective: "[T]here was nothing, *not a thing!* about the country that made a man feel Big And Important. . . . Why, there was something about the whole blessed country that made a soul feel whipped before he got started. Back home in Kansas a man had a *hand* in things, the way the Lord *aimed* for his servants to have: if you didn't water, the crops died. If you didn't feed the stock, the stock died. As it was ordained to be. But there, in that land, it looked like our labors were for naught."[3]

To this day, the Pacific Northwest remains a vast and relatively unpopulated landscape. It represents more than one-fifth of the nation's total land base, yet it contains only 3.5 percent of the population. Among the 50 states Alaska ranks first, Oregon tenth, and Washington twentieth in size. Hence the region has far fewer people per square mile than any other region of the country (13.5 compared, for example, to 416.4 in the Middle Atlantic). But the souls that made their way out to the Pacific Northwest did not end up whipped. If they couldn't beat the wilderness, they could join it. And if the pews were never full, that didn't keep religious leaders from making themselves a powerful presence in the public life of the region.

AN INTERFAITH ESTABLISHMENT

For most of the region's history, religious institutions have been supported as emblems of social progress and for the services they provide. From the 1830s to the 1880s, mainline churches and synagogues were planted throughout the region, and Protestants and Catholics joined forces with the U.S. government to isolate and/or assimilate the indigenous Native Americans—an activity then associated (in the minds of the Protestants and Catholics) with the triumph of Christian culture. But bringing the Good News to the Indians was hardly a sufficient triumph. Between the 1880s and the 1920s, a concerted effort was required to combat "the crimes of a city"—the burgeoning culture of bars, dance halls, theaters, racetracks, and amusement parks that catered to the rootless young men and women who were flocking to the region. Religious reformers did what they could to suppress alcohol consumption, gambling, and prostitution, while mitigating the effects of these evils on women and children through a range of educational, healthcare, and social service institutions.

Recognition of the fragility of the individual sectarian enterprises brought ecumenical and interfaith cooperation to the west long before it began in other parts of the country. As early as 1860, A. M. A. Blanchet, Roman Catholic Bishop of Nesqualy, Washington, cautioned his priests against refusing to perform mixed marriages lest the Catholics choose to be married by a judge. It is similarly notable that in 1924, Protestant businessmen joined with their Catholic and Jewish counterparts to mount a campaign against a ballot initiative by the (anti-Catholic and anti-Semitic) Ku Klux Klan that would have outlawed parochial schools in Washington state. Against a hostile outside world, the religiously identified understood themselves as pioneers circling the wagons for mutual protection.

Between the Great Depression and the 1970s, mainline Protestants, Catholics, and Reform and Conservative Jews came to constitute what amounted to an interfaith religious establishment, pooling their moral and financial resources for a succession of progressive causes. And over the years interfaith cooperation for the common good has remained a more salient characteristic of religion in the Pacific Northwest than in any other region of the country. An exemplar from the first half of the twentieth century is Jewish Teamsters Union leader Dave Beck. Early in his career, Beck frequented the rectory of Immaculate Conception Church to discuss papal encyclicals on labor with Msg. Theodore Ryan, the first Washington-born Seattle diocesan priest. (In the region's strong tradition of trade unionism, important roles were also played by prominent Protestants like Methodist pastor Oscar H. McGill and Presbyterian layman James Duncan.) In 1946, Beck and wealthy Lutheran businessman Emil Sick spearheaded a fundraising drive to retire the debt on Seattle's foreclosed Episcopal cathedral, St. Mark's.

In 1960, anti-Catholic hate mail directed against the presidential candidacy of John F. Kennedy led Seattle's leading Reform rabbi, Raphael Levine of Temple De Hirsch, to propose to KOMO TV a show that would feature local Protestant, Catholic, and Jewish leaders talking about timely issues from a religious perspective. "Challenge" premiered in September with Rabbi Levine, the Catholic priest William Treacy (who became a "Challenge" regular, as well as a close friend of Levine's), and a Congregationalist minister discussing the topic, "Can We Have a Catholic President?" Subsequent programs addressed a wide range of controversial subjects, including celebration of Christmas in the public schools, open housing, and "Who crucified Jesus?" The show proved to be a hit, accumulating a weekly audience of 300,000 and lasting for 15 seasons. Levine believed that having representatives from different faith traditions speak about common problems would not only undermine religious bigotry but would make a significant impact on public discourse. The key, he thought, was to emphasize on religious unity.[4]

To this day, the default mode for religious action in the public square in the Pacific Northwest is to proceed on an interfaith basis. Just before the 2004 election, for example, Rabbi Daniel Weiner of Temple De Hirsch Sinai (renamed after a merger in 1970) and the Dean of St. Mark's, Rev. Robert

Taylor, established an organization called Faith Forward to provide religious progressives with a vehicle for expressing their opposition to the religious right. By the same token, threats to the establishment's unity are not taken lightly. In July 2007, when Pope Benedict XVI reaffirmed the Vatican's position that the Catholic Church is the only path to salvation, Steve Maynard of the *Tacoma New Tribune* reported on efforts in the Puget Sound area to make sure it did not drive a wedge between Catholics and those of other faiths. These included a meeting between the executive directors of Tacoma's Associated Ministries and the Church Council of Greater Seattle with Seattle's Catholic archbishop. "In Pierce County," wrote Maynard, "Catholics and Protestants have enjoyed a long history of working together to help people through food banks and feeding programs, [Associated Ministries' Rev. David] Alger said. They also hold joint services to worship and celebrate their Christian unity." Rev. Michael McDermott, a local Catholic priest, told Maynard that he didn't think relations between Catholics and other religious groups would be damaged by the pope's statement. "It didn't prevent McDermott and Tacoma Rabbi Bruce Kadden, the Rev. Martin Yabroff, an Episcopal priest, and Puyallup Tribal Elder Connie McCloud from joining together to pray at the opening ceremony for the new Tacoma narrows bridge July 15," Maynard noted.[5]

Civil rights for minority groups has been an ongoing establishment cause in the region since the outbreak of World War II. To its lasting credit, the Seattle Council of Churches opposed the evacuation of Japanese Americans to concentration camps and area clergy worked throughout the war for better treatment of the evacuees.[6] During the civil rights era, efforts on behalf of African Americans were not as strong or consistent as they should have been, but did indicate a growing consensus that religious congregations ought to work more vigorously on behalf of racial integration. And since the 1970s, the establishment has used ecumenical and interfaith organizations as well as paid lobbyists. In 1976, at the encouragement of Don Daughtry, a white pastor of the Beacon Avenue Church of Christ in Seattle, the Church Council of Greater Seattle formed a Task Force on Racial Justice in Education. Bringing together a broad coalition of racial and ethnic groups, as well as clergy and lay people from the various churches, the task force and the council proved essential in formulating a philosophy of integration and applying pressure to the Seattle School Board to develop a plan for integration that has since been considered a national model. A similar if less impressive effort took place in Portland. By the middle of the 1980s, the emergence of white supremacist groups in the region provided a new object of civil rights concern. In 1987, a Catholic priest named Bill Wassmuth helped organize the Northwest Coalition Against Malicious Harassment in Coeur d'Alene, Idaho as a counter to the Aryan Nations, whose compound was located in nearby Hayden Lake. Twelve years later, the coalition moved to Seattle, having merged with another organization to become the Northwest Coalition for Human Dignity. With much the same purpose, the Coalition Against Hate Crimes was started in Portland by the American Jewish Committee with the support of the Ecumenical Ministries of Oregon, an organization of mainline Protestant groups that includes both the Greek Orthodox and the Catholic Archdiocese of Portland. In 2000, the coalition brought a successful lawsuit against the Aryan Nations and at least temporarily bankrupted the organization.

Historically, the Pacific Northwest establishment has had its largest impact through its support of services for the poor, the homeless, and the traditionally vulnerable—mentally ill, imprisoned, children, and single women. Not only have major social service agencies such as Catholic Charities and Lutheran Social Services (now Lutheran Community Services) provided significant resources to address social needs throughout the region but since the 1980s the establishment has been involved in bringing bills addressing these needs before the legislatures of all three states in the region. Another example of social service activism is the Center for the Prevention of Sexual and Domestic Violence, which Rev. Marie Fortune of the United Church of Christ established in Seattle in 1977 after coming to the conclusion that religious leaders were not prepared to assist their parishioners with sexual or domestic abuse and that secular service agencies were not prepared to deal with clients' religious questions. By the 1990s the center had grown into an inter-religious organization providing education and training to address sexual and domestic violence in communities throughout the world. In the mid-1990s the Washington Association for Churches joined with the Washington State Labor Council and Washington Citizen Action to create the Washington Living Wage Coalition to raise the income levels of janitors, hospital, and other low-wage workers. In 1998, the coalition helped pass Initiative 688, a public referendum that raised the state's minimum wage and tied it to the rate of inflation. Ecumenical Ministries of Oregon has been active in the same cause, as well as on behalf of migrant workers' right to organize.

In the years following the Vietnam War, the establishment generated and supported an ongoing series of radical responses to U.S. defense and foreign policy. In 1981, the Church Council of Greater Seattle asked that congregations offer sanctuary to Central American refugees. After a dozen Christian, Unitarian, and Jewish congregations hid refugees from the Immigration and Naturalization Service, the city emerged as a leader in what became known as the Sanctuary Movement. On the nuclear weapons front, Rev. Jonathan Nelson, a Seattle Lutheran pastor, took the lead in protesting the Trident submarine, based in Bangor, Washington, as a symbol of the United

States' instigation of the arms race. In 1982, the Catholic archbishop of Seattle, Raymond Hunthausen, drew national attention when he publicly admitted that he was withholding half of his income tax in protest against government foreign policy and defense spending.

More recently, when the World Trade Organization met in Seattle from November 30 to December 3, 1999, it was met by classic interfaith action, Pacific Northwest style. Several mainline pastors and their parishioners became involved in events surrounding the meeting. While the sometimes violent protests received most media attention, in different parts of the city hundreds of religious individuals and congregations found more peaceful ways to be involved in protest. Churches opened their sanctuaries as places of refuge while halls and church classrooms were lined with tables for position papers, posters, videos, and news releases. The First United Methodist Church provided a base of operation for many of the protest activities. The protests also promoted Jubilee 2000, a worldwide religious movement to forgive the debts of the poorest nations. A march sponsored by the Washington Association of Churches (which identifies itself as "a faith-based state public policy and advocacy network"[7]) ended with the crowd linking arms around a building as a symbolic act of breaking the chains of debt, until security forces intervened. Meanwhile, a broad array of Christians, Jews, Buddhists, and Muslims joined with civil rights, environmental and labor groups to pack a sports stadium to rally for debt forgiveness.

After the attacks of 9/11, the Pacific Northwest establishment was quick to take a stand against the impending war against Iraq. By the fall of 2002 both the Washington Association of Churches and Ecumenical Ministries of Oregon had issued statements expressing "grave and profound concerns" about the prospect of initiating military engagement there, with the former calling the intent to launch a war "morally indefensible."[8] In October, the Church Council of Greater Seattle announced a protest and a crowd of between 12,000 and 30,000 marched through Seattle, one of the largest antiwar demonstrations in the country to that date. Nowhere in the country, in fact, was opposition to the war more intense. In the 2004 election, where a 24 percent plurality of Americans chose "moral values" as the issue that mattered most in their presidential vote, by far the largest portion of Pacific Northwest voters, 31 percent named Iraq as the most important issue. That was well above any other region, and twice the national percentage.

When all is said and done, however, the Pacific Northwest establishment's core focus in recent years has come to be what might be called spiritual environmentalism. Ecumenical Ministries of Oregon now makes environmentalism central to its identity, defining itself as "bringing together Oregon's diverse faith community in service to God and Creation."[9] The organization's website features a host of environmental ministries, including an Interfaith Network for Earth Concerns, Oregon Interfaith Power and Light, Watersheds and Biodiversity, and Greening Congregations and Institutions. Helping congregations in the Puget Sound area "green" themselves has been the particular focus of Earth Ministry, which was established in Seattle in 1992 "to inspire and mobilize the Christian Community to play a leadership role in building a just and sustainable future."[10] The organization's quarterly journal *Earth Letter* and its handbook, *Greening Congregations*, has given it national reach.

An important milestone in establishment environmentalism was a joint pastoral letter, "The Columbia River Watershed: Caring for Creation and the Common Good," issued in 2001 by the 12 Catholic bishops of the region (including bishops from Idaho, Montana, and British Columbia). Acknowledging the importance of the watershed for traditional economic livelihood, the letter is nonetheless an ecological manifesto, ending with the prayer, "Lord, send out your Spirit and renew the minds and hearts of the people of the region so that, being renewed, they may cooperate with your Spirit and together renew the face of the earth."[11] The following year, 377 Catholic, Protestant, and Jewish leaders in Washington state called upon the U.S. Senate to implement proposals for "energy conservation, fuel efficiency, and alternate energy development to protect God's creation and God's children." Without multiplying examples, suffice it to note that in May of 2007, having succeeded in getting all items on its environmental agenda passed by the state legislature, the Washington Association of Churches mounted a four-day Interfaith Creation Fest (with sponsorship by Muslims as well as the usual Judeo-Christian supporters designed to kick off a year of "dialogue and action, uniting the efforts of individuals, faith communities, civic organizations, businesses and government to bring healing to the earth."[12]

In contrast to the rest of the country, environmentalism is not a motherhood-and-apple-pie issue in the Pacific Northwest. There, the moral imperative of "healing the earth" points a finger of blame at the mining, fishing, and logging industries that were the traditional economic base of the region. Indeed, that imperative gets weaker once you move out of the cities and into the less populous, rural, eastern portion of the region—where Nones are thinner and evangelicals, Catholics, and Mormons are thicker on the ground. By aligning itself so clearly with the environmentalist cause, the Pacific Northwest's interfaith "Western Establishment" has put itself in the position of alienating many of the region's traditionally religious citizens. And it faces other challenges to its continuing efforts to influence the public policy and social ethos of the region. Even by its own modest standards, its institutional presence is not as strong as it once was. As in the rest of the country, tension over social and cultural issues has divided local congregations and parishes, and has created rifts between local bodies and regional and national denominational leaders. And as elsewhere, such tension has contributed to declining financial support from local bodies for ecumenical activity, national programs, and denominational infrastructure. But in a paradoxical way, the very weakness of the Pacific Northwest establishment has been a source of its strength in the public square. With its own flocks so small, it has always recognized that the only way to exert a real influence is to take on responsibility for the public at large. In staking its powerful environmental claim, it bids fair to represent the commitment not only of its own several flocks but also of many people who never darken the door of a traditional place of worship.

SPIRITUAL IF NOT RELIGIOUS

Unencumbered by institutional attachments to religion they may be, but Pacific Northwesterners should not be thought of as aspiritual. ARIS data show, for instance, that while only one-third of Pacific Northwest Nones regard their outlook as "somewhat religious" or "religious," more than two-thirds agree that "God exists" and that "God performs miracles." About half of all Nones believe that God helps them. They are, one might say, spiritually open. They encounter the sacred and cultivate spiritual lives outside conventional religious institutions. That is not to say, however, that they are spiritually undifferentiated. In this regard, it is possible to identify three types of "None religion" in the region: a constellation of New Age spiritualities including neopaganism, metaphysics, and "new spirituality" literature; the apocalyptic millennialism of a loose set of antigovernment groups such as Patriots, white supremacists, the Militia, and various kinds of survivalists; and an earth-centered spirituality that is expressed in the "secular" environmental movement (particularly the campaign to protect old-growth forests), in Native American religion, and even within official religious organizations. Taken together these movements represent the bulk of alternative spirituality, at least the kind with consequences for the public life of the region. While none of these movements is unique to this region, many of them are expressed here in their purest form, thanks to the vast geographic and cultural space available for alternative religious (or quasi-religious) expression. Their high profile in regional culture is unmatched elsewhere in the United States.

In the first years of the twenty-first century, Powell's Books in Portland reorganized its "religion" titles. Most world religions (e.g., Buddhism, Christianity, Judaism, and Islam) now have their own aisle, and there are large, distinct sections on metaphysics, holistic health ("Mind, Body and Spirit"), and earth-based religion, among other spiritual themes. The "Spirit Team" manages all this material. In individual interviews, staff at several prominent independent bookstores in the northwest attested to the popularity of new spirituality literature. Best sellers included *The Power of Now: A Guide to Spiritual Enlightenment*, by Eckhart Tolle, *The Four Agreements: A Practical Guide to Personal Freedom*, by Don Miguel Ruiz, *When Things Fall Apart: Heart Advice for Difficult Times*, by Pema Chodron, and *Mystical Dogs: Animals as Guide to Our Inner Life*, by Jean Huston. In the 1990s, the *Conversations with God* series, by Neal Donald Walsch and *The Seat of the Soul*, by Gary Zukav, were hot sellers throughout the country, including the Pacific Northwest. It is noteworthy that a number of these authors live in the region (Walsch, Zukav, and Huston all in Ashland, Oregon). Many have foundations or institutes that organize retreats and workshops featuring their work; they travel widely giving public lectures and interviews; and they maintain websites that serve as information conduits and associational hubs for spiritual seekers. These websites convey "new spirituality" ideas but also work to connect individuals of like mind in study and support groups.

Closely related to this new spiritual literature are metaphysical practices like the use of crystals for healing, psychic consultations, shamanism, and spirit channeling; all are prevalent in the region. Perhaps the most prominent metaphysical happening in the last quarter of the twentieth century in the Pacific Northwest was the emergence of Ramtha, a 35,000 year-old warrior who in 1977 "made himself known" to J. Z. Knight, then a housewife in Tacoma, Washington. In 1988, after achieving international stature, Knight established Ramtha's School of Enlightenment in Yelm, Washington. Another prominent metaphysical happening in the region was the Harmonic Convergence, an astrological event in 1987 that caused thousands of New Age practitioners to make pilgrimages to sacred sites like Mt. Shasta, just south of the Oregon border. Estimating the size and scope of these religious practices is difficult. It is increasingly easy to find open pagan communities and to interview witches willing to have their names published. Nine Houses of Gaia, a nonprofit organization promoting the interests of earth-based religions, publishes a monthly online newsletter, annually hosts The Northwest Fall Equinox Festival (in a forest near Portland), and keeps a website that posts a pagan community directory for the region. Although some aspects of a larger antiestablishment worldview can be discerned in it, the New Spirituality is fundamentally about personal transformation, about healing one's self. The hope, indeed the expectation, is that social transformation (i.e., the birth of a "new age") will come about only if individuals are spiritually reborn. In this respect, it is not different in form from the old evangelicalism.

The Aryan Nations, Christian Patriots, the Militia, assorted survivalists, and other like groups represent a loose network of antigovernment millennialists united by a strong conviction that the U.S. government is cooperating in a "New World Order" conspiracy designed to restrict the God-given liberties of American citizens (e.g., property rights, the right to bear arms, free speech). After the terrorist attacks of September 11, 2001, their websites and newsletters expressed indignation at the Bush administration's pronouncements that American citizens must be prepared to accept some limitations on their individual freedom in the fight against terrorism. Participants in these organizations believe they are not only American patriots (i.e., defenders of the U.S. Constitution) but also authentic Christians (i.e., most are theologically and culturally conservative). They expect societal collapse and are preparing largely in defensive though often creative ways to survive it. Ultimately, they are selling what it takes to make it through hard times. One of the most forceful and widely read expressions of this apocalyptic vision is *The Turner Diaries*, by William Pierce, a former physics professor at Oregon State University. First published in 1978, the book is a fictional account of rebellion against the New World Order in defense of an exclusively white and Christian nation.

While the survivalist movement is hardly confined to the Pacific Northwest, in the last quarter of the twentieth century the region became the cradle for much of its core leadership, and provided fertile ground for its growth. Why? Federal entities such as the Environmental Protection Agency, the U.S. Forest Service, and the Fish and Wildlife Service of the Department of the Interior enacted new environmental policies and enforced laws that have radically altered how people may live on the land—an affront to rural Northwesterners' fierce independence. In addition, a significant number of rural Northwesterners adhere to conservative Protestant traditions where apocalyptic and millennial themes are readily available. Finally, the emergence of a survivalist industry centered in the region has successfully exploited the millennial hopes and fears of people disoriented by economic and cultural change. Today, many of the cultural themes of the movement intersect with mainstream—albeit right-of-center—political debate. Some issues (e.g., taxation, property rights, and resisting gun control) are secular; others dovetail with the cultural agenda of the religious right (e.g., antihomosexuality, prayer in public school, and restoring America as a Christian nation).

Most widespread among the religiously unaffiliated of the Pacific Northwest, and most central to its ethos, is earth-centered spirituality—nature religion. Many of America's most prominent "nature writers" write about and/or reside in the region, and virtually all explore significant spiritual themes. In the region's canonical texts, the conviction that nature is sacred is particularly resonant. No writer illustrates this more clearly than David James Duncan, whose "confessions, Druidic rants, and reflections" have become gospel to nature lovers in the region. Duncan's *My Story as Told by Water* is a collection of autobiographical essays wrestling with the moral and spiritual implications of environmental degradation. His gospel is that because the natural world is sacred, its afflictions require a spiritual antidote. That antidote, for devotees, consists in pristine nature itself. As a prominent local environmental-activist's T-shirt put it, "May the Forest be with You."

Much contemporary environmentalism in the Pacific Northwest needs to be understood as religion, not just because it can be dogmatic and moralistic, but because its rituals and core beliefs distinguish between things sacred (wilderness) and things profane (all else, often including people). Nature religion is visible in the mission statements and policy goals of mainstream and radical environmental movement organizations, in conflicted public discourse over resource management, and in how people organize their daily lives. Northwesterners think of themselves as nature lovers and stewards of the environment, people living close to nature, and this identity has spiritual meaning. Linda Duffy, The U.S. Forest Service Ashland District Ranger, said in a public speech, "stewardship is the spiritual stream I stand in."

The watershed of this spiritual environmentalism was the crusade to preserve old-growth forests in the 1980s. The Oregon Natural Resource Council (ONRC), based in Portland, played a key role, not least by coining the term "ancient forest" and thereby replacing scientific jargon like "late-successional" and "old-growth" with something more awe-inspiring. The ONRC and such other local groups as the Native Forest Council (NFC) took the lead but were soon joined by national organizations like The Wilderness Society and Sierra Club. Together they formed powerful new coalitions like the Ancient Forest Alliance that proved adept at using federal law to halt the harvest of old-growth forests. By the early 1990s their collective efforts had won broad public support, and by 2001 the timber harvested on federal land in Oregon was about four percent of the historically high volume of 1986. The spiritual dimension of this victory is clear from a 1990 NFC pamphlet entitled "Stop the Chainsaw Massacre," which included the statement: "America's forests are priceless. They give us cold, clear water to drink. They regulate global and regional climates. They provide habitat for wildlife. And perhaps most important, in their beauty and tranquility we find spiritual enrichment and renewal."

As with any religious movement, spiritual environmentalism has its prophets and zealots. Radical forest activism in the Pacific Northwest has played a key role in drawing public attention to the ecological consequences of industrial forestry and in framing the management of public forests as an urgent problem. Radical environmentalists tend to be young, idealistic, and alienated from mainstream religious, economic, and political institutions that they find morally bankrupt. In grassroots activism, they find an alternative meaning system (neo-Marxism and some variant of "deep ecology"), symbolic rituals (forest camps and tree-sits), a compelling purpose (earth liberation; "no compromise in defense of Mother Earth!"), community (the movement), and indeed religious experience (a mindful awareness of and reverence for the beauty, power, and fragility of forest ecosystems). Forests, and forest activism, are clearly sources of religious experience for many in the environmental movement but political action is not the only context for spiritual environmentalism in the Pacific Northwest. It finds outlets in various forms of "simple living," guided by the spiritual principle that in a society with abundant material wealth, less consumption brings greater fulfillment. There has also been renewed interest in Native American myth and ritual, whereby many nonnatives disaffected from Western religion have shown a keen interest in those aspects of native spirituality that speak to how humans ought to live in relation to nature. While the Indian/environment relationship has been romanticized (i.e., the myth of the noble savage and nature as undisturbed), there is no doubt that animism and rituals of reverence structured human-environment relations in the Pacific Northwest prior to European settlement.

Two general principles undergird this variegated form of alternative spirituality: "deep ecology" and wilderness preservation. Deep ecology is a mindful exploration of human connection to natural processes; it is the basis for ritual practice designed to transform an individual's relationship with nature and thereby reform human/environment relations generally. But nothing is more central to the Pacific Northwest's nature religion than the idea of wilderness. This derives from the Romantic movement of the nineteenth century, which took what had been regarded as wasteland and reimagined it as a sublime landscape where chasms and waterfalls were places to glimpse the face of God and mountains and valleys were the cathedrals of a sacred realm.[13] For environmental groups throughout the country, the quintessential wilderness cause has been the prevention of oil drilling in the Arctic National Wildlife Refuge in Alaska (ANWR). As Robert Redford, a long-time member of the Natural Resources Defense Council, put it, "To me, the Arctic Refuge represents everything spectacular and everything endangered about America's natural heritage: a million years of ecological serenity . . . vast expanses of untouched wilderness. . . . For 20,000 years—literally hundreds of generations—the native Gwich'in people have inhabited this sacred place, following the caribou herd and leaving the awe-inspiring landscape just as they found it." Just as Alaska presents the country with its last frontier, so it represents, in Oregon and Washington, a struggle for the soul of the region. Be it noted, however, that in Alaska itself, where oil royalties flow into the pocket of every taxpayer, ANWR is viewed through a quite different lens.

Like Walsch's new spirituality movement, the nature religion expressed in contemporary environmentalism appeals largely to the middle and upper-middle class. Conservation biologists "discovered" that the loss of old-growth habitat was jeopardizing vulnerable species; lawyers pressed the issue in public policy arenas; environmental organizations recruited young, well-educated urbanites to lead the ancient forest campaign; and the movement targeted people most interested in recreational and aesthetic forests values—the professional middle class. But because the livelihood of many rural Northwesterners depended on resource extraction, the environmental movement appeared not to be in their near-term class interest.

Thus, one of the consequences of this form of alternative spirituality is tension between rural Northwesterners (remnants of the pioneer culture) and urban/suburbanites. Nature religion did not "cause" this culture clash but it has played a key role in legitimizing environmental movement politics and thus distinguishing urban (secular but spiritual) from rural (church-based) culture. Because space and resources are vast in Alaska, the frontier ethic still reigns in that state, and hence a politics favoring resource extraction. Nonetheless, spiritual environmentalists in the state—members of mainline Protestant and Catholic churches in particular—are making some headway, with the help of hard-core libertarians who have no love for oil companies from the south. In Washington, with a strong tech-based economy and a developed cosmopolitanism in the Puget Sound area, politics lean more to the left on resource issues. In Oregon, state politics break along city/country lines. Rural communities have been devastated by the economic and cultural changes of the last quarter of the twentieth century but these communities no longer dominate the state demographically. As a result, the debate over management of public land in Oregon, heavily influenced by national environmental groups, has been shifting toward the environmental sentiments of urban America.

THE EVANGELICAL COUNTERCULTURE

If the environmentalism of the religious establishment and the Nones represents the dominant spiritual culture of the Pacific Northwest, evangelicals—among whom Pentecostals seem to be the fastest growing component—are the counterculture. Contrary to the liberal image of them as millenarians whose expectations of an imminent Rapture have left them with no interest in protecting the natural world, American evangelicals are broadly supportive of environmental protection. According to the Akron/Pew surveys, nearly half of evangelicals nationwide say they are pro-protection; less than a third, antiprotection; and one-fifth, moderate. In the Pacific Northwest, however, they are significantly less environmentalist: the pro's and anti's are evenly divided at 38 percent apiece. Indeed, in no other region of the country are evangelicals less environmentally committed. But the survey numbers only tell part of story. Whereas much of the spiritual energy in the mainline and among the Nones is connected to environmentalism, evangelicals have an entirely different agenda.

For them, the region's low adherence rates have always been an opportunity for conversion, and over the past generation they have taken advantage of it. The number of evangelicals in Washington grew 32 percent between 1990 and 2000, reaching 38 percent of all religious adherents. They constitute the largest single block of adherents in Oregon and Alaska. In Washington and Oregon, their growth rates exceed the general population growth. The rates in all three states are comparable to the levels of increase in the Catholic church (the latter accounted for primarily by Hispanic Catholic migration). According to NARA, they constitute 11 percent of the adult population in the Pacific Northwest and are gaining a larger portion of the market share among those formally affiliated with religious organizations. If they are not already, they are soon likely to become the largest institutional religious family in the Pacific Northwest.

Theology is not the key to the evangelicals' growth. If it were, then such churches as the Missouri Synod Lutherans, Southern Baptists, and Seventh-day Adventists would be growing apace rather than holding steady or declining. The growth is in the independent "Christian" churches and fellowships, where aggressive and creative entrepreneurialism is the order of the day. This is not to say that evangelical theology is unimportant. It demands commitment, proclaims that the faith is absolute and ultimate, and makes clear that one must witness and show others the truth of its claims. Membership is an achieved identity—something that one must choose by one's desire to convert and become a Christian. This identity must be confirmed in a congregation, and discipleship within a small group of fellow Christians is often part of one's obligation as a member. Children are raised in a relatively demanding moral atmosphere, but under an aesthetic regime that appeals to them in the familiar idiom of popular culture. It is a potent product, offering a sectarian lifestyle and a worldview significantly at odds with the surrounding culture—especially for those with the highest levels of religious commitment.

The Akron/Pew surveys show that high-commitment evangelicals in the Pacific Northwest are a more ideologically coherent group than their opposite numbers in the country as a whole. For example, in 2000, 84 percent of them voted for George W. Bush, as opposed to 74 percent nationwide. They also are somewhat likelier to favor less welfare spending and help for minorities (though they are less hostile to gay rights). Together with their opposition to environmental protection, this underlines the portrait of a community living apart. Indeed, evangelicals coming to the Pacific Northwest from the South notice the higher levels of religious commitment there among church members; the kinds of religious norms that keep people within the fold in the Bible Belt cannot be depended to do so in the Pacific Northwest. There is also a base of political activism in the region composed of highly committed evangelicals who can be identified as members of the religious right politically and culturally.[14]

Over the past two decades, the religious right in the Pacific Northwest has in fact attempted through elective politics to reverse prevailing regional trends. It has challenged assisted suicide in Oregon, attempted to overthrow antidiscrimination ordinances on behalf of gays and lesbians, opposed affirmative action, pushed initiatives to make abortion illegal, and generally turned thumbs down on protectionist environmental policies. In all this it has been notably unsuccessful. Yet in the process Christian conservatives have gained power within the Republican Party in the region and have succeeded in electing legislators who express their views. In statewide elections and referenda, they have succeeded in polling upwards of 40 percent of the vote. In 1998, they provided the votes to override Washington Gov. Gary Locke's veto of a bill to ban gay and lesbian marriages in 1998.[15] In 2000, they helped garner 47 percent of the vote in favor of an Oregon initiative that would have prevented discussion of homosexuality in the public schools. In more than half of his interviews of evangelical pastors in the Puget Sound area, James Wellman reports that the subject of political alliances was raised and affiliations were given, all Republican. One pastor, for example, spoke about his position on the Republican Central Committee in Colorado before coming to Washington. He said he continued to be active politically and was loyal to the Republican Party, though he said he "supported men of high moral and religious character in either political party."

But the religious entrepreneurs who have built the most successful evangelical churches in the region do not come across as hard-edged ideologues. By and large, they seem to follow the California style of evangelicalism exemplified by southern California's Rick Warren: moderate in their politics, disinclined to partisan activism, and hesitant to take risks by advocating for specific public policies. A typical example of the type is Gary Gulbranson, a 50-something pastor who leads Westminster Chapel, a 3,000-member independent megachurch in Bellevue, Washington. Gulbranson embodies the entrepreneurial spirit in his commitment to theological education, foreign mission evangelism, and an aggressive focus on the moral boundaries of his community. But in an interview, he demurred from identifying himself politically. "The Christian faith is apolitical," he asserted. His task was to "challenge people to think and to vote their Christ-centered conscience." The public issues that tended to spur him to action were local. Thus, one Sunday morning in the late 1990s he noticed that a strip club had opened less than a mile from his sanctuary. "I brought this fact to the attention of my congregation, challenging them to stand up for their faith and their values in the community." Three hundred turned up at the next City Council meeting to complain. Church members also began picketing the club while lobbying for ordinances that would make it difficult for strip clubs to operate within the city limits. Four months later, Bellevue's few strip clubs were all out of business. When pushed to cite other examples of political advocacy, Gulbranson spoke mostly about his ministry to business people in Bellevue and his strong emphasis on personal and professional morality.

In a book that expands upon his Religion by Region chapter, Wellman contends that the entrepreneurial evangelicals of the Pacific Northwest constitute less a separate sectarian world in permanent confrontation with the surrounding culture than a dissenting parallel community engaged with the wider society according to its own lights. Dissent from the regional environmentalist ethic does not have to do with opposition to environmental protection so much as to the prevailing tendency to sacralize nature. As one pastor put it:

> Well, at the core of the message on environmentalism is that God created the world and he commissioned us to take care of it, and if we're not taking care of it, then we are not honoring God. So we must be taking care of the environment. And we haven't done the best job in the past. But we are not to worship the environment, and we are not to put the environment or things in the environment above the needs of humankind. Humankind comes first.[16]

By Pacific Northwest standards, this is well to the right on the ideological spectrum.

Evangelical entrepreneurs in the Pacific Northwest have seen their churches grow dramatically and have become public players in their communities. With the optimism congenital to the breed, they believe that their capacity to shape policy will grow as well, even as they recognize that they are a long way from winning over the culture as a whole. But from an outsider's perspective, there seems little likelihood that their determined fulfillment of the Great Commission will bring about an evangelical sea change in the region. While evangelicals may soon be the most numerous traditionally religious folks in the Pacific Northwest, there is little reason to think that it will cease to be the country's None Zone. The entrepreneurs should continue to have their work cut out for them for a long time to come.

A CIVIL RELIGION

According to the Italian historian Emilio Gentile, civil religion is

> the conceptual category that contains the forms of sacralization of a political system that guarantee a plurality of ideas, free competition in the exercise of power, and the ability of the governed to dismiss their governments through peaceful and constitutional methods. Civil religion therefore respects individual freedom, coexists with other ideologies, and does not impose obligatory and unconditional support for its commandments.[17]

By this definition, the spiritual environmentalism that has taken hold in the Pacific Northwest in recent years can be considered the emergent civil religion of the region (understanding that it lags behind in Alaska, where the old myth of inexhaustible natural abundance still has its devotees). This civil religion needs to be seen against the economic transformation that took place in much of the region in the 1980s and 1990s. Those whose livelihoods depended on timber, agriculture, fishing, and mining saw their economic underpinnings erode and with it their way of life. Manufacturing also declined. But those whose livelihoods were tied to the rise of Microsoft and Intel, many of them in-migrants to the region, benefited from the emergence of the new information- and service-based economy.

The transition has caused serious dislocations. In 2000, Oregon, Washington, and Alaska led the nation in rates of childhood hunger. By 2003, it became clear that the knowledge industry itself was subject to busts as well as booms; in that year, the Pacific Northwest led the nation in unemployment. Economic disruption paralleled growing confrontation with the finite character of the region's natural resources. In the summer of 2002, farmers in the Klamath Basin of southern Oregon and northern California clashed with state and federal officials over water. In 2003, Senator Ted Stevens of Alaska made clear that he took personally the Senate's defeat of the measure that would have opened the Arctic National Wildlife Refuge (ANWR) to oil drilling. Whether it be protecting temperate rain forests in the Tongass National Forest on Alaska's southeastern peninsula or Washington's Olympic National Forest, saving salmon runs, or keeping ANWR pristine, environmental protection was pitted against the need for jobs. And behind that struggle was a deeper cultural crisis in regional self-understanding. Children and grandchildren of those who viewed uncut timber as a waste faced the consequences of an inherited guiding mythos. The struggle between evangelicals and spiritual environmentalists was joined squarely over the issue of the continuing adequacy of a regional myth of abundant natural resources and economic opportunity.

Religion's public presence in the Pacific Northwest is complex and distinctive. With a minority of the population in religious institutions and those divided among many different religious communities, no single religion or denomination is sufficiently large to assure the outcome on any public issue. In this context, religious communities have had to develop alliances with other religious bodies and with those outside of religious institutions in order to influence public life. In the region's more open and fluid religious environment, these alliances have required careful nurturing, and have been influenced by broader social trends and change.

In the 1980s, activists on the religious right succeeded in organizing conservative Protestants of various denominational and nondenominational stripes around a set of cultural issues. The Oregon Christian Alliance (OCA—an affiliate of Pat Robertson's Christian Coalition) drew considerable media attention and had some success in setting the agenda for public debate over "family values." Those cultural themes did resonate with some church-going Oregonians (conservative Protestants are a relatively large piece of the state's adherent pie), but because that cultural reservoir was demographically small, the OCA won nothing significant in the long run and has largely withered away. About the same time, however, and under the radar of most news media, the old establishment began addressing a different set of moral issues—ecological and social sustainability—in interfaith coalitions that included overtly pantheistic, neopagan, and secular environmental organizations. Earth Ministry in Seattle and Interfaith Network for Earth Concern in Portland exemplified the establishment's public presence in the region not only by being nonsectarian but also because they explicitly explored the existential question at the heart of what it means to be a Northwesterner: How shall we humans live in this natural place?

The contest to redefine the culture of the fabled "State of Jefferson" exemplifies the poles of contemporary public religious debate in the region.[18] This arose out of efforts to protect the Klamath-Siskiyou region, a place the World Wildlife Fund identified as one of the world's most significant, and pitted long-time residents (who lamented the "erosion of traditional Christian values" and whose livelihood depended on using the land) in a clash against newer residents (who prize its natural beauty and recreational amenities and for whom wilderness protection is a spiritual undertaking). Conflict in the State of Jefferson came to a head with President Clinton's designation of the Cascade-Siskiyou National Monument in 2000, followed in 2001 by the Klamath Basin water crisis in which the federal government withheld irrigation water from local farmers to protect endangered fish. Similar land use and resource management issues with comparable dynamics had played out all over the Pacific Northwest in the last two decades of the twentieth century. The conflict over logging and spotted owl habitat was the pivotal event in the culture clash between the old and the new Pacific Northwest. This was followed by the "salmon crisis" and widespread debate over the breaching of four Snake River dams. Then came the restoration of whale hunting in the Puget Sound by the Makai Indians and, of course, the ongoing push for opening ANWR to oil drilling.

Environmental advocates on all these issues have made arguments for the preservation of nature that put forth scientific claims but their pleas hinge on striking a resonant moral and spiritual chord in the populace, and increasingly they have done so. These conflicts are cultural struggles about the nature of nature and what it means to live in the region. But the regional civil religion was evident in issues that seemed to have little to do with the natural environment.

In November of 1994, by a 51 percent to 49 percent margin, Oregonians passed Measure 16, the Death with Dignity Act, making the state the first political jurisdiction in the country to legalize physician-assisted suicide. A similar measure had narrowly failed in Washington in 1991. Litigation delayed enactment of the measure until February of 1997 when the Ninth Circuit Court of Appeals dismissed a suit objecting to the law. In a separate effort to block enactment, the 1997 Oregon legislature returned the measure to the ballot for reconsideration and repeal. Catholics and conservative evangelicals funded the $4 million campaign for Measure 51. A coalition of moderates, liberals, and libertarians, organized as the "Don't Let 'Em Shove Their Religion Down Your Throat Committee" spent $1 million to oppose it. The campaign portrayed religion as an obstacle to individual freedom. That portrayal, and the newly inserted element of states' rights occasioned by federal efforts to block the initiative, contributed to Oregonians' re-affirming physician-assisted suicide by a 60-40 margin.

Both the 1994 and subsequent debates over the Death with Dignity Act focused on definitions of death as a "natural process," and on what assisted suicide does to familial and civic bonds. Opponents argued that physician-assisted suicide amounted to "playing God" and so would disrupt the natural processes of death. Proponents argued that it was no more disruptive of natural processes than the extraordinary measures taken to prolong life and chided opponents for viewing death as some kind of failure. Opponents expressed repeated concern that economic motivation would lead the poor, infirm, and other marginalized people to be pressured into ending their lives. Proponents argued that the law contained safeguards to protect against that and pointed to the economic status of those who have taken advantage of the law to support their claim.

What was telling was the way individuals with degenerative diseases who supported the law portrayed physician-assisted suicide as a profoundly natural process. In a deposition posted on the Death with Dignity fund website, "Katherine L" wrote: "I know the level of participation in life—mentally, spiritually, physically, emotionally—that I believe I need to continue as a valuable and contributing member of earth's family. I feel very strongly about preserving the right to make my final, very private choice of leaving this beautiful planet in peace, with dignity." Statements from family members of those who have chosen physician-assisted suicide described it as a profoundly communal process. As the children of a mother who died in 2001 put it in a posting on the Compassion in Dying website: "We were able to gather as a family, each kiss her, and each tell her how much we loved her. She died peacefully, looking out over the Willamette River, in a room filled with love. . . . [Our mother] was proud to be an Oregonian, to live in a state less bound by convention and more open to independent and free thinking."

These statements sought to resolve individual freedom, loving social relationships, and natural beauty into a moment of unity of human and natural environment. Humanity is represented as part of a larger natural process, with physician-assisted suicide portrayed as a moment of ethical choice by a free individual acting within a loving community. However much the statements may recast the events they describe, they situate people aesthetically and even theologically within nature, and situate human life within planetary life. This vision is as distant as can be conceived from opponents' concept of assisted suicide as the act of a technologically and economically repressive society within which individuals are isolated and alienated, social bonds destroyed, and humanity assaulted because its subjection to transcendent powers is not acknowledged. The conflict on its deepest level is about the proper understanding of relationships among individuals, society, and nature.

The sentiments expressed by those supporting physician-assisted suicide locate them as part of a new religious cluster that is growing in strength, one rooted primarily in the secular but spiritual population but also incorporating members of the old religious establishment. Organized around concern for the environment understood to include natural resources, human communities, and quality of life, this cluster provides the contrasting pole to evangelicals. As the evangelical and spiritual environmental clusters grow, they have come to define the terms of public debate in the region. Because environmental and sexual politics are both about purity, the debate is over the natural relationship between the land and the souls that inhabit it. It is a debate that is likely to continue for some time. Here, it is worth noting the political polarization between evangelicals and Nones, many of whom are part of the spiritual environmentalist cluster. According to ARIS, only 14 percent of Nones in the region are Republican, as compared to 54 percent of evangelicals. By contrast, 31 percent of Nones are Democrats, as compared to 15 percent of evangelicals. Sharp definition of boundaries between these two increasingly visible religious clusters changes the religious landscape for other religious clusters in the region, pushing communities toward identifying with one pole or another—in ways that may not be congruent with their theological heritage and long-standing ethos and practice. In a word, the establishment will not have an easy time preserving the unified center that it holds so dear.

Yet the Pacific Northwest's emergent environmentalist civil religion has powerful geographic and socioeconomic as well as cultural sources. The region possesses the same vibrant and dramatic landscape it always did—geologically imposing, biologically rich, and geographically vast. It contains the world's most diverse temperate rain forests. Knowledge that forest ecosystems were being dramatically altered by industrial timber production was a disturbing revelation, one that required a moral and spiritual response. As happened to the mainline religious leaders who first came to the region, the evangelical entrepreneurs may in due course find that, when push comes to shove, the way to conquer the wilderness is to let themselves be conquered by it.

• 8 •

The Mountain West:
Sacred Landscapes in Tension

$\mathcal{D}$eserts, high plains, and above all towering mountain ranges make the Mountain West what it is. Of course, the region is more than a tourist destination populated by ranchers and miners, cowboys and Indians, living quasi-isolated lives in romantic settings. Less than one-fifth of the more than 16 million people who call this region home live on the range, in the foothills, in mountain villages, or on farms way out on the plains. The rest live in towns, suburbs, and cities where conventional patterns of American life are the rule more than the exception. The Mountain West is America's oasis region, a place of vast "empty" (i.e., unpopulated by people) spaces dotted with a few urban concentrations, often hundreds of miles apart. Yet because, throughout the region, open vistas lead the eye outward and often upward, habitation lacks the closed-in character of urban life in other parts of the country.

Here, the natural universe always seems nearby. Indeed, the landscape *is* the dominant spiritual force in the region—which helps explain why it abounds in places deemed sacred to many religious traditions.

- For Native Americans, Taos Blue Lake and Zuni Salt Lake (both in New Mexico), Canyon de Chelly (Arizona), and the Wyoming Medicine Wheel and Devil's Tower (Bear Lodge), are only a few of many sacred sites in the region.
- For Roman Catholics, the modest shrine at Chimayo (founded in 1816), one of the world's great healing sites, is widely known as "the American Lourdes."
- For the Church of Jesus Christ of Latter-day Saints and its members (the Mormons), the entire Salt Lake Valley, with all its historic connections to the establishment of Zion in the west, has a quasi-sacred character.

- Similarly, Santa Fe and Chaco Canyon in New Mexico; Sedona, Arizona; and Boulder, Colorado serve as magnets for spiritual seekers from around the globe.
- For Christians with institutional connections and those with nothing more than a generalized Christian sensibility, there is the 42-foot-high statue of Christ of the Rockies—larger than the far-better-known Christ of the Andes—that overlooks the historic Pass of the North (El Paso) between the United States and Mexico.

If geography is the touchstone of religion in the Mountain West, it also supplies secular coherence via a set of common economic and regulatory issues, including the perennial problem of water shortage, federal ownership of a huge portion of land in the region, and tourism. These issues have operated to make legislators from the region colleagues willing to work across party lines, sometimes cooperating with legislators from other western states so effectively that they are collectively known as the "Sagebrush Rebellion."

Yet when it comes to public life, the states of the Mountain West do not a single unit make. They are best thought of as forming three distinct cultural subregions, each of which reflects the different manner in which European-American culture made its way into the territory: in the south, the old Catholic heartland of Arizona and New Mexico; in the northwest, the Mormon Corridor of Utah and Idaho; and in the northeast, the "tribal" world of Colorado, Wyoming, and Montana.

CATHOLIC HEARTLAND IN TRANSITION: ARIZONA AND NEW MEXICO

The Catholic heartland was the scene of nearly the first European religious establishments in the country—the Franciscan missions in New Mexico dating from 1598 and the Jesuit missions in Arizona from about 1690. Preceding them, of course, were a range of Indian religions, of which some syncretized with Catholic Christianity while others resisted and persisted. Protestants began showing up after the Mexican-American War resulted in the transfer of the territory to U.S. control. A sprinkling of Jews arrived in the late nineteenth century, ranging in status and occupation from main street merchants and small town mayors to larger-than-life characters like Wyatt Earp's wife, Sadie Marcus, and Big Mike Goldwater of Phoenix. The surge of population growth since the 1950s has meant more Mexican Catholics, more Anglo-Catholics, more Anglo-Protestants (Baptists, evangelicals, and others), and more Nones. This subregion retains its historic religious face in the Rio Grande valley, but in Phoenix and the smaller metropolitan oases it has increasingly come to resemble southern California. The cumulative effect has been to pull the two states in religiously opposite directions, with New Mexico becoming more Catholic thanks to its growing Latino population and Arizona, driven by burgeoning metropolitan Phoenix, less.

It is on Native American bedrock that the subregion's cultural geology rests. Pueblo people were the first to arrive in the area, some in the desert and others in the valleys of the Colorado and Rio Grande rivers. But even as the Pueblo were settling in, there was an immigration of Navajo and Apache from the north and Comanche, Ute, and others from the Great Plains. Like the Pueblos, their diverse religious practices were concerned with the community's well-being and its relationship to the natural world that sustained it— but in very different ways. The encounter of the several communities on a shared landscape fostered both cultural exchange and conflict. In order to teach their children, for example, the Navajo took up the Pueblo practice of making dolls that represented the supernatural figures in their religious system. The Pueblo, a settled agricultural people, were vulnerable to the migratory and sometimes predatory ways of the newcomers.

Because there were never clear agreements about who controlled which sacred sites, intra-Indian disputes erupted regularly, and continue to this day. One of the most famous has concerned Big Mountain in northern Arizona, sacred to both Navajo and Hopi. The federal government, whose efforts to resolve the question of control began in the nineteenth century, in 1986 passed a law dividing the area between the two peoples in such a way as to require the removal of some 10,000 Navajo from Hopi land—but perhaps not surprisingly, this did not put an end to the dispute. The issue of protecting sacred sites has also involved Indians in numerous conflicts with the nonnative world. These have included decade-long efforts by the Apache to prevent the University of Arizona from building a telescope on Mt. Graham (unsuccessful) and by the Pueblo to prevent the city of Albuquerque from extending a main city street through the Petroglyph National Park (thus far successful).

The Spanish Roman Catholicism layered on top of the Indian substrate had a distinctive militancy shaped by nearly 700 years of conflict with the Moorish Islamic powers in Spain. As a state church answerable to the Spanish crown rather than the Vatican, its highest priorities were Christianization and the maintenance of social order. The Franciscan and Jesuit brothers who served the mission churches in Indian communities carried with them the project of creating new citizens for the Spanish empire. But the missionaries— located at the margins of native communities—were only able to create a distinctive kind of Catholicism in which natives learned to go to Mass, adopted

Catholic saints and holy days, but combined the whole with their own religious traditions. The most important of these was the story of the appearance of the Virgin of Guadalupe to a poor Indian at a significant Native American religious site. For centuries, she has served as a point of identity for people of mixed Spanish and native heritage in the subregion.

After the Mexican Revolution in the 1820s, Spanish Catholicism became Mexican Catholicism and control of Indian missions in Arizona and New Mexico was transferred from Spanish-born Franciscans and Jesuits to local secular clergy. Then, in the wake of the Mexican-American War of 1846–1848, the Anglos started to arrive, in waves. The first consisted of merchants and adventurers eager to profit from trade along the newly opened Santa Fe Trail. If they settled down, they often married Mexican women and converted to Catholicism. After the Civil War, a second wave of Anglo immigration brought a small mainline Protestant presence into the subregion. Protestant clergy, many of them part of a strong home missions movement, came with two goals: organizing congregations for the newly arriving Anglo population and converting the Hispanic Catholic population to English-speaking Protestantism. Unlike the Catholic missionaries who tolerated some mixing of traditions, however, they insisted on keeping a separate identity as they attempted, largely unsuccessfully, to create the kind of pan-Protestant cultural hegemony that existed in other parts of the country. While initially organizing Spanish-speaking churches, they expected the members eventually to learn to speak English and adopt Anglo cultural norms. Altogether, they only managed to convert between five and ten percent of the population. Also bent on conversion were the Latter-day Saints, who reached Arizona in 1878 with settlements in the eastern part of the state and in the Salt River valley near Mesa and Phoenix. But the biggest impact of the Anglo American occupation was to usher in a more Romanized, ultramontane Catholicism exemplified by Archbishop Jean-Baptiste Lamy in Santa Fe, and a succession of Irish and Irish American bishops in Tucson.

The most important religious development during these years was the school system established by the Presbyterians that rivaled the fledgling public school system in size and surpassed it in quality. In response, a Catholic school system was instituted in the Diocese of Santa Fe, which included Colorado as well as Arizona and New Mexico. But it was Catholic domination of the public school system itself that brought conflict between Catholics and Protestants to a head after World War II. Catholics had for decades run the public schools in many small communities in northern New Mexico and in 1948 the Protestant parents in one of them, Dixon, sued the local school board. In *Zellers v. Huff,* the New Mexico courts forbade 143 priests and nuns from ever again teaching in the public schools, and in a variety of ways mandated strict separation between church and state in primary and secondary education statewide. Catholic leaders, some of whom angrily attacked the ruling as an attack on the church itself, responded by investing heavily in parochial education across the region.[1] A half-century later, the issue of public versus parochial education remained a sore point in the state, provoking intense debate over public school vouchers.

Meanwhile, a third wave of Anglo immigration had begun with the completion of the railroads in the 1880s. Before the discovery of antibiotics, the desert climate and high altitudes provided a refuge for those with illnesses as varied as malaria and tuberculosis. Once arrived, they discovered that the Mexicans and Indians possessed healing arts beyond the ken of Western medicine. The same desert landscapes attracted writers and artists. Mary Austin and D. H. Lawrence both stayed and wrote in Taos, using themes derived from the cultural interactions of Native American, Hispanic, and Anglo cultures in that area. The Taos group of artists—Ernest Blumenschein, Bert Geer Phillips, Eanger Irving Couse, W. Herbert Dunton, and others—sought to capture the desert and mountain landscape in romantic terms, working with the quality of light, the land forms, and the cultural artifacts. Georgia O'Keeffe found in the bleached bones and bare rocks a way to illustrate the fundamental forces of life and death. Similar communities of artists flourished in Santa Fe, Sedona, and Phoenix. The arts and crafts of the Pueblo, Navajo, Pima, and Papago peoples also attracted artists and scholars. The discovery of Native American traditions and ancient folk Catholicism by Anglos coincided with an increase in attraction to supernatural phenomena in general. Not a few Anglos made their way to Indian country in Arizona and New Mexico in search of spiritual adventure.

In the 1930s, it was the search for economic survival that drew migrants, who had lost their livelihoods and their homes in the Great Depression, from the Southern Crossroads and parts of the South. They settled in the cities of Arizona and New Mexico and some found places in the new farmland created by massive irrigation projects begun in the 1920s and 1930s on the Gila, San Juan, and Rio Grande rivers. Most were Baptists, with some admixture of Holiness folks and Pentecostals. In the 1950s, concerted evangelism established Baptists as the dominant Protestant force in the subregion. Extending the Bible Belt across southern New Mexico and Arizona toward southern California, they brought into public religious debates an increasingly conservative southern evangelical voice—for example, adding to the perennial public school controversies in the subregion the fundamentalist/modernist debate over the teaching of evolution. And while they tended to oppose the Catholics on school issues after World War II, by the end of the century they had joined forces with them on vouchers.

The most recent wave of immigration might be called the Sunbelt Population Explosion. Particularly affecting Arizona, it began with retirees from the north drawn to the warm climate and workers from all over drawn to the new technology economy; never before had such a diverse population been seen in the subregion. Since the 1960s, Asian immigrants have brought the full range of Eastern religions, and not only to metropolitan Phoenix. In New Mexico, a sizable Sikh community exists in Española and a mosque calls Muslims to prayer in Abiquiu—both in an area representing the heartland of the older Spanish colonial society and the even older Pueblo cultures. These new arrivals on the religious scene have proved attractive to some Anglos, building on the longstanding subregional interest in Native American shamanism, geographical locations associated with spiritual energy, and UFOs.

What strikes a visitor to the subregion is the wide open character of its spiritual life. On the radio can be found everything from fire-and-brimstone evangelists to live Tarot card readings. Straddling the Arizona-Utah border is the fundamentalist Mormon settlement of Colorado City, while almost in Mexico stands the brilliant white mission church San Xavier del Bac, still staffed by Franciscans, still serving the *Tohono O'odham* Indian Nation for whom it was built. In Oracle, north of Tucson, the vast glass greenhouses of Biosphere 2 still shine in the sun, a $200 million tribute to a 1980s apocalyptic urge to create a self-enclosed living system lest nuclear winter wipe out Biosphere I, the earth. And on it goes—sometimes for the better and sometimes for the worse. In 1946, a Catholic order called the Servants of the Paraclete set up a house for ministering to priests from all over the world who needed help for their sexual sins. In the 1990s, it was revealed that of the hundreds who went for the cure, many had been reassigned to New Mexico parishes, where they resumed their predatory ways. The Catholic pedophile cover-up scandal hit the subregion very hard.

THE MORMON CORRIDOR: UTAH AND IDAHO

Since arriving in the Great Basin in 1847 and methodically colonizing it, the Latter-day Saints (LDS) and their church have created an extraordinarily influential presence. Not only do Mormons far outnumber members of all other religious bodies in this subregion but many of those identified as "religiously unaffiliated" need to be counted within the fold—lapsed Mormons who may not worship with "the Saints" but who continue to be loyal to the church's traditions or motivated by its worldview. Mormon dominance must be measured not only demographically but also in terms of the LDS Church's economic and political influence. In the nineteenth century, the church created a communal economy and political theocracy that to this day has left much of the land as well as the commercial and political institutions of this subregion under direct or indirect Mormon control. In contrast to other parts of the country, where religious diversity has diluted the social authority and political power of the founding religions, the Church of Jesus Christ of Latter-day Saints has retained its clout in Utah and Idaho—the Mormon Corridor. Thanks to the singular lack of religious difference and the power of a single religious institution, this is the only part of the United States that today possesses a de facto if not a de jure religious establishment.

The political consequences of Mormon dominance are not hard to discern. As of 2007, for example, all five members of Utah's Congressional delegation were Mormons. Although the lone Democrat among them was not an active member of the LDS Church, he considered himself, and his constituents considered him, a "cultural Mormon." Not since 1957 has the state had a non-Mormon governor. As of 2007, four of five justices of the state supreme court and 90 percent of its legislature were Latter-day Saints. While each of these public servants may be as independent-minded as any other religious person, there are few such other religious persons among Utah's political leaders. (That was less the case in Idaho, where only two of the four elected officials sent to Washington and one third of the members of the state legislature were Mormons.) So conservative and Republican do Mormons tend to be that in the last decade of the twentieth century the LDS Church assigned Marlin K. Jensen, a high-ranking church official, to speak publicly on the proposition that a Democrat could be a good Mormon. "We are [concerned] locally and I think there is a feeling that even nationally as a church, it's not in our best interest to be known as a one-party church," Jensen told the *Salt Lake Tribune* in an April 3, 1998, interview. "The national fortunes of the parties ebb and flow." Since then, during election season, letters from church headquarters have emphasized the importance of a two-party system.

The LDS Church makes its presence felt in politics not only indirectly through elected officials but also in direct ways. Each year in Utah, representatives of the state legislature meet formally with high-ranking church officials who are assigned to monitor political issues. "Before every general session, leadership from both parties are invited down to meet with the church's Special Affairs Committee," Utah's speaker of the house told a *Salt Lake Tribune* reporter on January 6, 2002. He added, "We've done that for as long as I've been up here." Utah's congressional delegation is no less responsive. In the early 1980s, for example, the church opposed a federal proposal to place an intercontinental missile system in Beaver County, Utah. The church's First

Presidency issued a formal statement that the MX missiles were not welcome in the state, causing a reversal in position by Utah's then-powerful Senator Jake Garn and contributing materially to the demise of the project.

More commonly, the LDS Church uses its political influence to protect its ecclesiastical programs, economic interests, and moral order. This has included a wide variety of issues, from local water rights to national tax policy to the consumption of alcohol (which is forbidden to Mormons). On February 3, 2003, according to the *Salt Lake Tribune*, church authorities and the Utah Department of Alcoholic Beverage Control (DABC) commissioners met to discuss a modest liberalization of the state's liquor laws following a federal court's rejection of the state's broad restraints on liquor advertising, including proscriptions against asking a customer if he or she wanted to order a drink or see a wine list. To the largely Mormon DABC, the new rules were "a product of seeking public comment." To restaurant owners who did not perceive themselves to be a part of the public whose comments were sought, the new laws "reflect the culture of the state. And the culture of this state is a dominant religion."[2] As might be expected, the less dominant position of the church in Idaho has made for a less powerful application of Latter-day Saint mores onto the broader population. Thus, while Utah has repeatedly rejected a state lottery, gambling was—over the determined, public opposition of LDS Church leaders—legalized in Idaho in 1989.

In theological terms, Latter-day Saints historically understood themselves to be employed in the work of preparing the world for a millennial reign when the heavenly and earthly kingdoms of God would be joined. Believers generally embraced the metaphor of kingdom to convey the scope of their project to live in a place (not just within an assembly) governed by the law of God and possessing the power to bind or give efficacy to their works on earth and in the heavenly kingdom as well. They believed there was properly no distinction between the temporal and spiritual government of the Latter-day Saints; that temporal property and labor were to be dedicated to spiritual purposes, including the good of the collective body of saints and the building up of the Kingdom of God on the earth; and that covenants made between individuals and consecrated by church ordinance were not temporal but eternal. By the 1860s, thanks to geographical distance and the nation's preoccupation with the southern insurrection, the Mormons had successfully constructed a society in the west that actualized their highest theology and governed their everyday lives, including a political system that mirrored the Mormon ecclesiastical structure and a polygamous family system.

Outsiders, however, saw the Mormons' political and economic unity as an attempt to unlawfully control individual freedom—especially the individual freedom of non-Mormons. When the discovery of local mineral deposits and the completion of the intercontinental railroad threatened to make the Mormons dependent on eastern manufactured goods and a cash economy, church leadership initiated a cooperative movement that encouraged self-sufficiency through home industry and discouraged Mormons from trading with the Gentiles, as all non-Mormons were called. Concerns about this exclusionary and anticapitalist effort was, however, outweighed by fear of the economic might of the church itself. As early as the Morrill Act of 1862, the opening salvo in antipolygamy legislation, Congress attempted to limit the amount of real estate the church could hold to $50,000, requiring forfeiture of excess amounts. The explicit goal was preventing the accumulation of wealth by "theocratic institutions inconsistent with our forms of government."

In the nineteenth century, the political dimension of Mormonism was a source of deep concern to many Americans, who believed its ecclesiastical order inhibited the free exercise of conscience and thus undermined the personal morality necessary to sustain democracy. Protestants considered the religion a "Romanish" or "popish" threat to republican government. In a nation characterized by many religious innovations, Mormonism's belief in contemporary revelation and new scripture made Latter-day Saints antinomian to a rare degree: a law unto themselves. The Mormon Zion was not merely a religious ideal but a completely realized city-state lying between the Great Plains and the California gold fields—a full-blown theocracy in the heart of a would-be enlightened republic. Eventually, a compromise between Mormons and the nation required the subordination of church marital law to federal law. But much of the church's worldview and actual power over Great Basin politics and economics, as well as Mormon social cohesion in the form of family tribalism, was left intact. And while the church's religious distinctives have changed sufficiently to permit the LDS faith to be included into America's spiritual body politic, their ideological biases remain. This helps explain many of the church's public choices as well as the reactions of its neighbors to them.

Renunciation of polygamy was the chief price the church paid for its acceptance. One cannot today be polygamous and a member of the LDS Church; excommunication is immediate for those who try. It can, however, be argued that "plural marriage," as the Latter-day Saints called their family system, remains a dimension of their sacred cosmology and supports their deeply felt sense of difference from the broader culture. Mormons continue to believe that marriage has salvific potential and functions to create familial bonds of eternal significance. This ideology underlies the LDS Church's public fight against recent initiatives to broaden the definition of marriage to include same-sex unions. At the same time, the LDS theology of marriage can drive a wedge between Mormons and their neighbors. A news poll published June

27, 2002, by the *Logan Herald Journal*, a newspaper serving a university population not far from the Idaho border, found that "70 percent of church members would object to their children marrying outside of the faith." Only eight
percent of all others polled felt this way. Obviously, since opposition to marriage outside the faith dramatically affects their social relations, this is one of
the factors making Mormons appear exclusive.

Just as problematic in a pluralistic culture is the amount of time Latter-
day Saints devote to their church callings. On the congregational and diocesan
level, church positions are all filled by laity, including positions that paid clergy
occupy in other churches. Coupled with a three-hour Sunday meeting schedule and temple attendance requirements, these commitments remove Mormons from the ordinary stream of non-Mormon social activity. For those who
do not understand the theological basis of these practices, Mormons appear at
best only superficially involved with those not of their faith and, at worst, mad-
deningly elitist. Politically, the story is equally complicated. On the one hand,
the LDS Church has clearly severed all formal ties between ecclesiastical and
political office. On the other, accepting the church's prophet-president's jurisdiction over temporal as well as spiritual matters remains part and parcel of the
Mormon faith. While some members may resent church direction in political
matters deemed moral and may exercise their agency to disagree with a given
political position of the church's leadership, open dissenters are remarkably
few. To disagree publicly becomes an issue of faith and can result in separation
from the body of the church. Indeed, tension between hierarchically defined
positions and contrary ones espoused by individual Mormons is a significant
part of the public expression of religion in the Great Basin, most especially in
Utah's Salt Lake County. Nationally, this tension has also been apparent—
most recently in the church's campaign against same-sex unions.

Finally, although the economic commonwealth that was the Utah Territory became a capitalist market with statehood, the idea that the hierarchically organized church acts on behalf of its members temporally, not just spiritually, remains a part of Mormonism's basic ideology. Today, as in the past,
church leadership continues to actively maintain its traditional property interests, developing commercial business opportunities in service to "the building of the Kingdom." Because information about the church's financial hold-
ings is not public, it is impossible to know with certainty the extent of the
church's economic power in the Mountain West. In the 1980s, one study
pointed to church ownership of "the 13 radio and TV stations, the four insurance companies, the hotel, the newspaper, the big farms . . . the real estate
companies (which control four square blocks of prime real estate in the center of Salt Lake City), the clothing mills, the book company, all the schools,
the welfare farms and industries, the big department store downtown, [and]

the investment portfolio."[3] Since this list was compiled, both the church and its host economy have boomed. In a December 9, 2001, news story, the *Salt Lake Tribune* estimated the church's assets as "exceeding $20 billion." Even if the *Economist* magazine's conservative estimate of its assets at $6 billion in February 2002 is closer to the truth, the church's total income from tithes and investments, combined with the value of its tangible property, make it comparable to the region's largest corporations in income generation and numbers of employees.

Of course, Mormonism is not the only religion in the Great Basin and the story of public religion in the Mormon Corridor also involves 150 years of minority experience on the part of those who elsewhere in the country are the majority. This is largely a story of cultural opposition. It has caused some non-Mormons to hold onto their religious identities more tightly. It has also led them to put aside their differences with other non-Mormon religions and with the unaffiliated in order to gain some measure of collective strength in the Mormon Corridor. Not until 1982, for example, did Idaho repeal its "Test Oath," originally designed to stop Mormons from voting—and, even then, the Test Oath was struck down over opposition from some 100,000 voters and 20 years after similar legislation against Chinese and Indians had been repealed. Many Idahoans continue to think that Mormons are coercive and manipulative; that they use political influence to impose their norms on others; that they use social relationships for the sole purpose of conversion; and that they judge others to be inferior. Attitudes in Utah also reflect continuing religious antagonism. On December 9, 2001, the *Salt Lake Tribune* published results of an elaborate investigation of Utah's interfaith relations that concluded that Mormons and non-Mormons were separated by a "fault line" that "haunt[s] every Utah community" on both sides of the divide. The sentiments of non-Mormons paralleled the Idaho study. Polarized by their demographic and cultural minority status, Utah's non-Mormon population often defines itself in public opposition to the Mormon majority.

Efforts to overcome this polarity constitute one of the central themes of public discourse in the Mormon Corridor. On both sides, religious leaders self-consciously pursue ecumenical efforts. The LDS leadership goes to great lengths to share the church's wealth across sectarian lines, as shown by contributions to Westminster College (once Presbyterian but now supported by a consortium of Protestants) and to the restoration of Salt Lake City's Catholic Church of the Madeline. Catholics, in turn, rewarded the LDS Church by inviting a member of its First Presidency to participate in the church's rededication. However ecumenical in spirit these efforts might be, a sense of powerlessness endures among the Mormon Corridor's other religious bodies.

For the Mormons, the Corridor is not just the site of church headquarters but a homeland. Their pioneer temples and cemeteries are sacred space and the church will expend every effort to preserve them as such. Nowhere was this more apparent than in the recent crisis over a one-block segment of Salt Lake City's Main Street. In 1998, city administrators and the LDS Church presidency announced that the portion of Main Street that runs between Mormonism's Temple Square and church headquarters would be sold to the church for $8.1 million. Consistent with the city's "Second Century Plan," the church planned to use the property for a park-like plaza that would join the two tourist centers that attract 9 million visitors each year. While pedestrians would have access through the plaza, control was ceded to the church, allowing it to forbid smoking, sunbathing, bicycling, obscene or vulgar speech, dress, conduct, and preaching or proselytizing it did not endorse.

To its critics, the plan was a conspiratorial land-grab by a church that had run roughshod over local interests to enhance its already too-public presence and to silence dissent in the area adjacent to its religious landmarks. With help from the ACLU, the First Unitarian Church of Salt Lake City (which objected to provisions limiting proselytizing to Mormons), Utahans for Fairness (who protested the church's stand on gay rights) and the Utah chapter of NOW filed suit, and in 2002 won a federal appellate court ruling that nullified the contract's restraints on use and speech on the grounds that its retention of an easement for pedestrian use created a public forum, not sacred space. "It's about time we leveled the playing field in hearing a diversity of speech and opinion," declared the Unitarian church's pastor. His victory, however, was short-lived. Two weeks later, in a story headlined "Day of Heckling on Plaza," the *Salt Lake Tribune* reported that one protestor shouted to a group of 12-year-old Mormon girls: "I'd rather be a homosexual than fornicate with you." In December, a local TV station showed evangelical Protestant missionaries passing out anti-Mormon literature and shouting through bullhorns at wedding parties posing on Temple Square. Photos in the January papers showed demonstrators bearing placards with such anti-Mormon slogans as "Jesus Saves; Joseph [Smith] Enslaves." Such reports caused even the mayor, a former ACLU attorney and avowed secularist, to reverse course. Abandoning a plan to impose constitutional limits on church regulation of the space, he agreed to sell the easement itself to the church. On June 23, 2003, the same day as the U.S. Supreme Court declined to hear the church's appeal, Salt Lake's City Council approved the sale.

Two basic facts explain the Church of Jesus Christ of Latter-day Saints' enduring power in the Mountain West. Historically, in America, there were simply too many denominations and too much competition between them for any one to dominate the others. But the Saints were driven past the edges of

America's prairie and found a place that nobody else wanted. Situated between gold mines to the west and rich plains to the east, the Great Basin sheltered Mormonism's establishment for two generations. Religious pluralism arrived too late and too anemically to vie for the cultural spoils of settlement. Competition for control came most notably from the mining industry, especially in Idaho, and from the U.S. government in Utah. But even America's economic and political power proved insufficient to fully dislodge the Mormons from their mountain kingdom, though they were required to reform it in the image and likeness of American disestablishment.

Notwithstanding its political reformation, the LDS Church's contemporary legal battles show that it remains on the edge of what is a permissible relation between American church and state. And the Mormon Church will remain on the edge for as long as it defines its president as a law-giving prophet and its mission as providing temporal order in service to the eternal. Ultimately, its claim to sacramental power fuels its economic and political activity and defines its continuing contest with the limits set for religion by American law. This means that public life in Idaho and Utah will continue to display what is, in the twenty-first century, a quite un-American degree of religious tension and intolerance.

POLARIZED TRIBES:
COLORADO, WYOMING, AND MONTANA

Geography and economics are what the states of the northeast subregion of the Mountain West have in common. Along with the Rocky Mountains, Colorado, Wyoming, and Montana all have substantial areas of plain, prairie, and basin. All have experience with extractive economies—gold, silver, and molybdenum in Colorado; gold and copper in Montana; coal, oil, and gas in Wyoming. Each has been a transportation corridor or crossroads. Each also has substantial acreage controlled by the federal government in the form of the National Park Service, the U.S. Forest Service, the Bureau of Reclamation, and the Bureau of Land Management. And they all have significant agricultural, ranching, mining, and tourist industries.

But unlike the other two subregions, they possess no religious center of gravity. To be sure, the mountains, gorges, rapidly running streams, and the meadows scattered among the mountains have a quasi-sacred power that has affected the entire religious ambiance. But when it comes to human beings, the general rule is scattered enclaves, diversity, overlaps, transformations in and contests among various religious practices; in effect, this subregion is emblematic of the Mountain West as a whole. Each state plays host to a number of religious traditions (Catholic, Protestant, and Jewish in all their forms), a plethora of additional practices and newly forming spiritual traditions, and a range of still-vital Native American religions. Although indigenous populations were dealt with quickly and often violently, each state retains important communities of Indian people whose religion, historically and in the present, stands at the very core of their being. At the same time, over half the population of this subregion is religiously unaffiliated or uncounted, ranking it second only to the Pacific Northwest as a None zone. Among the three subregions, it has the lowest percentages of evangelical Protestants and Mormons.

Mainline churches did not appear along with the first miners and settlers. The early accounts of mineral rushes and settlements suggest very little in the way of organized religion. Churches, rather, were established in Colorado, Wyoming, and Montana by way of the interlocked geographies of Indian missions, circuit riding, and transportation corridors. President Ulysses Grant's "Peace Policy" of the 1870s gave religious denominations the power to run reservation agencies. Placing Christians in church, Grant hoped, would clear out corrupt and incompetent agents. Across the west, Methodists were given 14 Indian agencies, Northern Baptists five, Congregationalists three, Episcopalians eight, and so on. Catholics, who had prior claims on 42 Indian agencies, were awarded only seven, which led them to establish their own contract school system. The policy produced competition among denominations while also building denominational commitment to certain reservations and peoples. Thanks to the labors of the missionary John Roberts, for example, Wyoming's Wind River reservation became a highly Episcopalian space. Montana's Crow reservation witnessed intense competition between Catholic and Baptist missionaries before transforming into a pluralistic spiritual setting with plenty of emphasis on refigured Crow traditions.

As elsewhere in the Mountain West, Indian missionary efforts often morphed into the founding of churches that really served nearby white settlements. In Colorado, Wyoming, and Montana, however, reservations did not structure the bulk of early church-building. Credit for that achievement goes to circuit-riding preachers. While these itinerants had made the rounds of the first gold strikes in the early 1860s, it was not until the latter part of the decade that missionary founders began to have a real impact. Seeing the west as a land of spiritual opportunity as well as sectarian competition, mobile missionaries quickly sought to establish congregations, sometimes with only minimal numbers of people. The organization of congregations and construction of sanctuaries took place above all where local or regional political power had been concentrated. In most cases, these were places connected to the outside world only by railroad lines and market relationships.

It is well not to underestimate the spiritual havoc wreaked through the partnership of missionaries and the federal government, which often turned reservations into religious ghettos. At the same time, Indian peoples' ability to make over their spiritual worlds must also not be underestimated. Both historically and at the present time, they have tended to function in terms of parallelism of belief and practice; that is, it is quite possible for the same person to attend a Christian church on Sunday, a Native American Church meeting on Monday, a traditional spiritual gathering on Tuesday, and so on. At the same time, the colonial context surrounding this religious practice gave rise to hybrid or synthetic forms. (Of these, the Native American Church, which mingles Christian understandings with the use of peyote as a sacrament, is perhaps the most prominent, with chapters on most western reservations.)

For a long time, Indian Christians—and indeed Indian clergy generally— often served as the most important interface between state and local governments and Indian people. Yet in the middle of the twentieth century, religion began to be supplanted as a force in Indian politics and social relations. The 1934 Indian Reorganization Act placed political power in the hands of tribal councils rather than Indian religious figures and new political leaders banded together in pan-Indian organizations such as the National Congress of American Indians (1944) that were needed to fight off attempts to "terminate" tribal status. At midcentury, Indian people created a "culture of politics" that displaced religious concerns in favor of pragmatic work within the apparatus of the New Deal state. Subsequently, the civil rights activism of the 1960s, made most visible in the activities of the American Indian Movement (AIM), sought to put into place a "politics of culture" in which religion figured importantly. By the 1970s, "termination" had been replaced by a new policy of self-determination, which has since provided a basis for Indian people to assert control over their own lives and resources. Key to this assertion of control has been a reclamation of traditional religious practices by Native American believers. In many cases, these persistent and newly (re)empowered ceremonies sit at the core of contemporary controversies involving native people in the states of the Rockies and the Plains.

Unlike Christianity, many Native American religious practices are not geographically transportable, but based in and on particular and specific places. Every native group has a number of sacred sites, and gaining access to them at certain times of the year has proved critical and difficult. Wyoming's Devil's Tower, for instance, has been the site of numerous struggles, court cases, and policy directives regarding access. Known as *Mato Tipila Paha* (Hill of the Bear's Lodge) by the Lakota, the volcanic outcropping is critical to ceremonies during the month of June, when believers find it a nodal point in the annual transfer of power from the Great Mystery to the earth. Yet Devil's

Tower is also a favorite rock climbing site and for many years climbers were notably insensitive to the religious practices of Indian people, yelling and hollering to one another and sometimes to people on the ground. The National Park Service proposed a climbing ban during June, and while many climbers found this a not unreasonable compromise, others protested vehemently, sometimes claiming that their own recreational activity possessed religious significance. Most struggles have been less dramatic but continue to play out in many places throughout the region, particularly where public land status gives open access to sites that Indian people would prefer to be restricted, or where private status prevents Indian people from visiting sacred sites necessary to the practice of their religion.

Within Colorado, Wyoming, and Montana, reservation geographies reflect unique religious spaces, functioning as enclaves capable of consolidating and affirming native religious practice. As communities of the culturally like-minded, they have long traditions of prescriptive social behavior and shaming practices to enforce conformity to a cultural standard uniquely different from the surrounding areas. At the same time, they serve as cosmopolitan spaces, constantly dealing with influences from the outside, including the missionary efforts of Christian evangelicals and Mormons, the hybrid influence of the Native American Church, and the passing through of curious multicultural gleaners of exotic religious practice. Because Native American people have codified treaty agreements with the United States government (and therefore formal political relations), religious issues often place them in compromised positions, with their desire for religious freedom conflicting with—and usually losing out to—other kinds of national legal and political imperatives. The "War on Drugs," it turns out, can mean bad news for Indian religious practice. So can the right of a federal agency to encourage logging, the right of a university to build a telescope on private land, the right of scientists to claim an ancient skeleton, or the right of rock climbers to ascend a piece of stone. The resulting political and legal conflicts are very much about maintaining "tradition"—in the form of religion and culture—in the midst of powerful forces for change.

Indian reservations are clearly defined spiritual enclaves in the northeast subregion but they are far from the only ones. Consider Boulder and Colorado Springs, Colorado—two cities separated by less than 100 miles but spiritually worlds apart. Early in the twentieth century, Boulder's city leaders, intuiting the end of the gold mining boom that built the city and seeing a limited future in agriculture, self-consciously sought to create a "city beautiful" by way of an imagined Athens of the West. They shifted the town's orientation away from the mines and mills and toward the Flatirons, impressive rock formations at the base of the nearby mountains. And they began—publicly and collectively—to imagine a romantic, sublime landscape, one that would be seen for the next century, often by the unchurched, as sacred and spiritual. By the 1970s, this sublime landscape would inspire a wash of spiritual seekers from the counterculture and the budding New Age movement. Buddhists arrived in force in the early 1970s, as Chogyam Trunpa Rinpoche established a monastery in the nearby hills and in 1974 the Naropa Institute (later University), which fused religious instruction with a cultural avant-garde that included poets, psychologists, composers, filmmakers, and writers. Overestimating the power of Naropa in setting Boulder's cultural tone would be difficult. Visitors like Allen Ginsberg and William Burroughs mingled with serene Buddhists and New Agers, spawning a culture that smiled on health food stores, personal improvement classes, and an easy-access religious potpourri. The sacralized landscape drew the followers of the Maharishi Mahesh Yogi (known for Transcendental Meditation), and those of the Bhagwan Shree Rajneesh, who dressed only in the oranges and yellows of sunset, and were easily confused, in some minds, with the small but visible Sikh community. Meanwhile, the mountain climbers who frequented Boulder established a pipeline to friends in Tibet and Nepal, and soon Tibetan immigrants established their own distinctive Buddhist community. Indeed, out of the 38 major Buddhist centers listed in Colorado today, more than a quarter are located in Boulder (including several devoted to various lineages of Tibetan Buddhism). New Age spiritual practices, with their multicultural mélange of spiritual traditions, thrive in the area. In 2000, the only place in the northern Rockies with a statistically visible population of Muslims was Boulder County. And there are not many places in the region where monthly Wicca meetings are advertised with such delight.

Amidst this astonishing religious diversity, mainline Protestant churches maintained their historic importance in the city. And on the campus of the University of Colorado, evangelical organizations such as Navigators, Intervarsity, and Campus Crusade plied their trade among students. In March 1990, with the help of a Campus Crusade leader and two other close friends, the university's football coach, Bill McCartney, gathered a group of 72 men at the Boulder Valley Christian Church to discuss a conference for the men of Colorado. The result was Promise Keepers, which over the next few years became the nation's quintessential evangelical men's organization. Altogether, in the 1980s and 1990s, Boulder created a new tradition of religious diversity characterized by openness and syncretism, and incarnated in a complex mixture of loose collectives, structured institutions, and organized religious communities. It had become a place of religious pluralism, built around familiar congregations, to be sure, but also out of charismatic leaders, exotic practices, individual self-actualization, and a landscape thought to evoke—or embody—the sacred. Religious refugees sought it out for its beauty, its reputation for tolerance, and its religious cosmopolitanism.

Colorado Springs had similar beginnings—a brief fling with mining around 1860 and then a turn to agriculture, ranching and, most particularly, tourism. But while Boulder was awarded the state university late in the nineteenth century, Colorado Springs (or more precisely, its near neighbor Canon City) got the state prison—a harbinger of the disciplined public sector economy to come. While tourism remained an important part of the Springs' economy, by the mid-twentieth century the city began turning increasingly to the federal pot—above all, to the headquarters of the North American Air Defense Command (its operations center built underneath nearby Cheyenne Mountain) and the United States Air Force Academy, both of which opened for business in 1958. By the 1980s, 60 percent of the economy was military-related, and the sheer demographic weight of the military presence began tilting the culture of the town away from a tourist service economy—which inevitably tends toward the tolerant—and toward a certain Cold War conservatism. Many military retirees found the town a congenial home and their presence helped consolidate a cultural climate very different from what was developing in Boulder. At first, Catholic and mainline Protestant churches were, not surprisingly, the general rule.

Faced in the early 1980s with a troubled economy, a collapsed real estate market, and the threat of post-Cold War military budget cuts, Colorado Springs' leaders cast about for new forms of economic development and decided to recruit evangelical Christian organizations. Christian groups, they decided, would pump the economy, function in post-industrial ways that did not adversely affect the beauty of the surroundings, and dovetail nicely with the conservative character of the town. In short order, the Springs became home to a number of groups with the resources and the will to intervene in national, state, and local political culture. The largest and most significant was Focus on the Family. Founded by James Dobson in southern California in 1977, the multipurpose evangelical nonprofit was recruited to Colorado Springs with the aid of a four million dollar grant from a local foundation. Its north-side headquarters was built in 1995 and within a decade had a workforce of 900 people producing radio shows, leaflets, books, television, and Internet and other media focusing on the celebration, maintenance, and defense of what it views as the "traditional" family.

Focus on the Family was soon joined by Navigators and Young Life, the International Bible Society, and the Family Research Institute, to name just a few of the nearly 100 evangelical organizations that eventually set up shop in Colorado Springs. Nationally, no city could boast such a concentration of Christian right firepower. In its way, Colorado Springs became the

Salt Lake City of evangelicalism as well as Boulder's polar opposite, at least in terms of the public and political expression of religious belief. Where the latter embodied left-liberalism, the former became the power base for a new brand of hard-edged conservative Republican politics in Colorado. From the city at the base of Pike's Peak came a torrent of words, candidates, and referendums dealing with everything from traditional hot-button issues such as abortion, homosexuality, and school prayer to term limit plans and radical tax reform measures.

How might this tale of two cities help us think about religion within the Mountain West's northeastern subregion? Both Boulder and Colorado Springs function as protected spaces with sometimes visible and coherent religious boundaries that contribute to collective senses of local identity. At the same time, however, both cities transcend their boundaries, with Boulder drawing into itself a wide array of global religious practices, and Colorado Springs aggressively reaching out to the world through political, cultural, and religious proselytizing. Colorado Springs often seems dogmatic and intolerant, willing to prescribe its own beliefs and practices as the single social standard. Boulder appears just the opposite—relativist, open to any and all kinds of diverse practice, and reluctant to impose social standards. Yet the seeming unanimity of Colorado Springs' political voices masks a modest diversity of belief and practice among evangelical organizations, often made visible in political differences. And the apparent libertarianism and tolerance of pluralist Boulder masks any number of rigid local orthodoxies. Its residents can be dogmatic and prescriptive in insisting on their particular brand of tolerance. The Mountain West in general, and in recent years the northern Rockies in particular, is often imagined as Boulder: an escape, a refuge, a possibility, a place where one might carve out a space for one's own quasi-secular, multicultural spiritual practices. On the other hand, the Mountain West and the northern Rockies have also truly been like Colorado Springs—a place of mandates, dogma, rigidity, and sometimes, intolerance.

By the 1990s, a number of changes were visible across the northern Rockies, the complex result of shifting populations and transformations in church practice. Catholic-predominated counties grew steadily in Colorado, from 28 in 1952 to 42 in 1971 to 50 in 1990. Much of that shift came at the expense of older mainline Protestantism—Episcopalians, Presbyterians, and especially Methodists—and suggested the significant demographic role of Latino immigration and labor, as well as an upsurge in conservative Protestantism. In addition, Mormon missions had created pockets of strength across the area. In Wyoming, for example, no counties were predominantly Mormon in 1971; by 1990, six were. By 2000, one could find two different patterns in Colorado. Along its eastern border ran a set of contiguous counties in which evangelical Protestant adherents made up at least 15 percent of the total population, suggesting a general movement of southern evangelicalism across the regional threshold. At the same time, a diverse set of evangelical counties spread across Colorado, Wyoming, and Montana (including Colorado Springs' El Paso County), suggesting the beginnings and even flourishing of a regional evangelical culture in the northern Rockies. Mapping the number of evangelical and other conservative Christian congregations in all three states, it is clear that Colorado's western slope and eastern plains counties have become the most conservative religious areas in the subregion.

If the Catholic clusters were likely to be defined in terms of ethnicity and the evangelical in terms of politics, class-based religious enclaves were also emerging. For while the concentrations of wealth (gathered around ski areas and vacation retreats such as Aspen, Vail, Jackson Hole, and Big Sky) have remained largely secular, in places like Crestone, Colorado, one can find economic elites (with connections to global markets and capital) retreating to the hills to find a particularly spiritual peace. Living in gated retirement subdivisions, residents are close to Zen and Tibetan Buddhist retreats, a Hindu Ashram, and a Carmelite monastery, not to mention New Age simulations, given shape in monuments like "Cresthenge" (a model of Stonehenge), a labyrinth that mimics the one at Chartres Cathedral, and even a reproduction of a ziggurat.

Politically, the culture wars have ebbed and flowed in the subregion. In 1992, Colorado became the first state to pass an amendment prohibiting localities from outlawing discrimination against homosexuals. The amendment, which originated with the Colorado Springs-based group Colorado for Family Values, brought together El Paso County's evangelical social conservatism with the libertarian cultural conservatism of the state's eastern plains and western slope residents, suggesting the power that might be wielded by such an alliance. Overturned as unconstitutional by the U.S. Supreme Court in 1995, the amendment nevertheless spawned similar efforts at state and local levels across the country. Anti-gay hate crimes such as the savage beating death of the gay college student Matthew Shepherd in Laramie in 1998 may be linked only indirectly to El Paso County religious conservatism; nonetheless the Shepherd case became the touchstone of the culture wars in the northern Rockies. The reporting surrounding Shepherd's murder took on a distinctly religious cast, as the victim, who was tied to a fence and left to die, was frequently represented in terms of crucifixion. Indeed, the attack led to a concentrated backlash against some of the activities of the religious right in the region.

In 1996, Focus on the Family's James Dobson told his five million weekly listeners that he would not vote for Robert Dole because the Republican Party was "betraying" conservative evangelical voters. He threatened that such voters would either dominate the party or leave it behind. After the election of George W. Bush in 2000, it became clear that evangelicals had never felt so much at home in a political party—and Dobson emerged as the single most important religious voice in American politics. But by 2007, he had returned to semi-outside agitator, organizing a meeting of evangelical leaders in Salt Lake City to announce that, should abortion rights supporter Rudolf Giuliani become the GOP standard bearer, the evangelical leaders would bolt the party. Colorado Springs had, in fact, played its own role in helping bring about the electoral earthquake of 2006 that returned control of Congress to the Democrats. On the eve of the election, the Rev. Ted Haggard, pastor of the 10,000-member New Life Church and head of the National Association of Evangelicals, was forced to resign after his encounters with a male prostitute were revealed in the press. It was because of Haggard's public advocacy of a state anti-gay marriage law that the prostitute had come forward and Haggard, who often mentioned his close ties to the Bush administration, became a poster boy for evangelical hypocrisy. A year later, the *Los Angeles Times* interviewed Haggard's successor at New Life on the role of politics in his congregation. "As far as me standing in the pulpit holding a voter guide, that's not going to happen," said the Rev. Brady Boyd.[4]

A NEW SWING REGION?

If a "region" in the continental United States is thought of as a bounded space in which there are enough inhabitants with roughly comparable backgrounds to create a distinctive culture, then the Mountain West was never much of a region, especially when it came to religion. To be sure, the terrible beauty of the landscape created something like a regional religious consciousness, even for the Nones who made up a large portion of the population. But there the commonality ended. Religion played a significant role in the public life of both the Great Basin and the Catholic heartland, where bona fide establishments once presided, but the Mormon and Catholic experiences in those two subregions were so different that they could be considered comparable only when set alongside the northeast subregion. There, low affiliation rates, a frontier libertarianism, and the absence of any dominant religious body made institutional religion at most a background player. More recently, however, shifts in religious demography and developments in religious politics have given evidence of greater regional coherence.

Once upon a time, much of the Mountain West voted Democratic, thanks to an anti-Eastern bias exemplified in the 1896 campaign of William

Jennings Bryan, whose famous advocacy of Free Silver was enthusiastically embraced in mining country. Although Mormons tended to vote Republican, the region's populist roots kept it in the Democratic camp through the New Deal and beyond. In the Democratic landslide of 1964, every state in the region voted for Lyndon Johnson except Arizona, home of GOP candidate Barry Goldwater. But the cultural politics of patriotism and small government that began in the Vietnam era pushed the region toward the Republicans. Beginning in 1968, not one of the Mountain West states voted Democratic in a presidential election until 1992, when Colorado, Montana, and New Mexico gave their electoral votes to Bill Clinton. Colorado and Montana returned to the Republican fold in 1996 but Arizona joined New Mexico in voting for Clinton's reelection. In 2000, New Mexico alone went—by the narrowest of margins—for Al Gore, but in 2004 switched sides to create a solid band of red from the Mexican to the Canadian border. That year, the region as a whole voted 58.7 percent to 41.3 percent for George W. Bush. Sixty years earlier, it had gone for FDR by 58.3 percent to 41.7 percent.

In congressional representation, the shift was no less dramatic and took place in much less time. Whereas half the region's members of Congress were Democrats in 1993, by 2001 the proportion had fallen to one in seven. Likewise in the Senate, the Democratic numbers dropped from four out of 14 to two. In the 1994 Republican takeover of the House of Representatives, some of the hardest-edged newcomers came from the Mountain West, including Helen Chenoweth of Idaho, Barbara Cubin of Wyoming, and J. W. Hayworth of Arizona. They would be followed into the House by the likes of Tom Tancredo and Marilyn Musgrave of Colorado and Bill Sali of Idaho. The influence of evangelicalism in the region can be the way that these regional paladins of right-wing Republicanism combined traditional, western libertarianism with "moral values" conservatism. Chenoweth, who represented Idaho's first district in the non-Mormon western and northern portions of the state, was anything but a social conservative, but she made school prayer one of her signature issues. Sali, who was elected to that seat in 2006, was himself an evangelical and staunch social conservative. Hayworth, a southern Baptist from North Carolina who came to Phoenix as a sportscaster, was a blusterer in the southern mode who combined "values" with libertarian causes. Musgrave, the favorite daughter of the Colorado Springs evangelicals, made her name as principal sponsor in Congress of anti-gay marriage legislation.

But even as values and libertarian conservatism were combining to create a potent Republican force across the region, the growth of the Hispanic Catholic population, together with greater religious diversity in some quarters, set in motion a countertrend. Indeed, it was no accident that the most vociferous opposition to immigration reform came from conservative Mountain West Republicans like Tancredo and Hayworth. In Colorado, the Democrats won control of the state senate in 2000 for the first time since the presidency of John F. Kennedy, and did the same in the state House of Representatives in 2004. That year also saw the election of the two Salazar brothers, Ken and John, to the U.S. Senate and U.S. House of Representatives respectively. Moderate Democrats from a middle-class farming family of native Spanish speakers who had lived in Colorado for generations, the Salazars could not have offered a more convincing demonstration of the growing power of Latino Catholics. Ken, who was married in our Lady of Guadalupe Church in Conejos, the oldest church in the state, was the first Hispanic in Colorado ever to hold statewide office. Two years later, the Democratic resurgence in the state continued when, with the help of an influx of Latino voters, Ed Perlmutter replaced a Republican in an open seat in the Denver suburbs. Meanwhile, in the fourth district, comprising the eastern portion of the state, Democrats came within 6,000 votes of defeating Musgrave.

Meanwhile, in Arizona, religious tensions within the Republican coalition helped elect Democrat Janet Napolitano governor in 2002. The Republican candidate, Congressman Matt Salmon, was a Mormon, and despite calls by evangelical leaders in the state to support him, the evangelical rank and file was less than enthusiastic about doing so.[5] Four years later, Arizona Democrats picked up two congressional seats, giving them half the state's total. The eighth congressional district, centering on Tucson, was an open seat created by the retirement of Jim Kolbe, a fiscal conservative but a moderate on social issues—the only openly gay Republican member of Congress. There, Gabrielle Giffords, a Jewish state senator whose signature issues were the environment and rural health care, defeated an antiimmigration conservative to capture the seat handily. In metropolitan Phoenix, Hayworth himself was defeated by Harry Mitchell, the head of the state Democratic Party. Elsewhere in the region, Montana rancher Jon Tester—who had led Democrats to take control of the state senate in 2004, eked out a victory over Republican incumbent Senator Conrad Burns; while in Wyoming, Jackson Hole Internet service entrepreneur Gary Trauner came up just 1,013 votes shy of defeating Barbara Cubin, who subsequently announced that she would not run again for the seat. Overall, Mountain West voters divided their total congressional vote in 2006 almost equally between Republican and Democratic candidates. Among the many and varied spiritual oases of the region's geography, there is, in short, reason to think that, contrary to earlier predictions of lasting Republican hegemony, the two parties will be struggling on fairly even terms for some time to come.

· 9 ·

The Midwest:
The Common Denominator?

*M*idwestern moments have come and gone in the life of the American re-public, phases when the region's frontier absorbed the expansive energy of the nation, when its voters routinely determined the outcome of presidential elec-tions, and its heavy industries and agriculture powered the nation's economy. And as the nation moves into the twenty-first century, another Midwestern moment may be upon us, as the religious cultures of more combative regions cancel one another out in the struggle to shape the nation's public life. Unlike any other region studied in this volume, the Midwest combines a tradition of tolerant religious pluralism, high rates of religious adherence, and folkways that place considerable stress on the public value of religion. The region has emerged as critical swing territory in presidential elections and, as a result, its religious culture may be entering another period of strong national influence.

There is, however, an elusive complexity about the Midwest. Many have described the region as a vast, flat space that lacks a boundary, a common cul-ture, and a defined consciousness comparable, say, to the South or New Eng-land or the Mormon Corridor. Within this great expanse in the middle of the country—11 states that make up the largest of the regions outlined in this volume—terrain and subcultures range widely. Some parts are very "north-ern," Canada-like or almost Scandinavian. Others take on characteristics of the South, especially in the states bordering the Ohio River. The western halves of the Great Plains states are geographically indistinguishable from eastern Montana, Wyoming, and Colorado. And the populated states on the region's eastern boundary are considered "back east," a half-foreign land from a perch west of Topeka.

All this might yield a pale regional malaise. But the problem is often in-verted in the Midwest, becoming the seed of confidence. As John Fenton

181

writes in *Midwest Politics*: "Unlike folks in Texas or Vermont, who identify strongly with the Lone Star State or New England, most Midwesterners think of themselves as Americans. They live in America, for the Midwest *is* America" (italics added). The widespread sense that the Midwest somehow instantiates the real America has authentic historical roots—after all, the common project in the early nineteenth century was the settlement of the region, by streams of migrants from New England, the Middle Atlantic, and the upper South. But by the end of the century, a sequence of migration bursts from various quadrants of Europe had produced an extremely complex demographic mosaic.

According to both secular indicators tracked in the U.S. Census and the measurements of religious identity in recent private surveys, the Midwest lies firmly in the middle of the pack among the regions delineated in this book. In the aggregate, its religious profile is a close approximation of the nation as a whole. About 59 percent of Midwesterners claim membership in a religious group. Of the remainder, about half identify with a specific religious tradition, but aren't members. The remaining 20 percent say they have no religious identity. Further, the market shares claimed by the largest religious groups (Catholics, evangelical Protestants, and mainline Protestants) are all very close to the national averages for these groups. But the most important criterion of Midwestern distinctiveness is that, unlike other regions of the country where religious affiliation is strong, no single group enjoys anything like the dominant role of evangelical Protestants in the South and Southern Crossroads, of Catholics in New England, or of Mormons in the Mountain West. The region is not, however, uniform. Rather, it is the product of a series of processes that have yielded, more than anywhere else, a complex patchwork.

On the first pass, it is necessary to distinguish three major geographic subregions. The first is composed of states bordering the Great Lakes: Ohio, Michigan, Illinois, Wisconsin, and northern Indiana. The populations of these states are concentrated in large and middle-sized cities. Peopled mostly by the descendants of nineteenth-century immigrants from Germany, Ireland, Scandinavia, eastern and southern Europe, these cities are the region's citadels of Catholicism. They are also home to many types of Protestants, Eastern Orthodox Christians, Jews, and recent immigrants practicing such "global" religions as Islam, Hinduism, and Buddhism. The vast rural areas of these states tend to have fewer Catholics and more Protestants of old native stock. The second geographical subregion is a zone of Lutheran dominance consisting of Minnesota, the Dakotas, and neighboring parts of Wisconsin and Iowa. Catholics are also plentiful in the eastern part of this region. Finally, there are the trans-Mississippi states of the eastern Great Plains: Iowa,

Kansas, and Nebraska. They feature fewer Lutherans and Catholics than the Dakotas and more evangelical and mainline Protestants.

A second pass shows three important patterns of religious affiliation and behavior that cut across these subregions. The first is a belt of Methodist influence stretching from central and southern Ohio and Indiana straight across to Kansas and Nebraska. This reflects the foundational role of Methodists in the nineteenth century and their continuing strength in rural areas and small towns but it also reflects the displacement of Methodist influence from the big cities of the Great Lakes and the Lutheran domain. The second pattern is the "Bible Suspender," that swath of mostly rural counties with extremely high membership rates that runs vertically down the center of the nation from western Minnesota and the Dakotas to Texas. Many religious bodies subsist within this belt but conservative and mainline Protestants are especially strong. The third important transregional pattern is the clustering of particular groups in particular spots, making much of the Midwest a mosaic of ethnoreligious microclimates. Many of these were produced by the chain migration patterns of the nineteenth century. Examples include counties in Ohio, Indiana, and Iowa dominated by Amish and Mennonite farmers; the considerable region of western Michigan where Dutch Reformed Protestants hold sway; and the patchwork of counties in many states where the descendents of German immigrants still farm, often with complex subpatterns of Catholic and Protestant affiliation. This complex pattern of local hegemonies displaced the hegemonic Methodist and Baptist presence of the region's frontier years and made it impossible for any particular group to dominate the region's civic and public culture.

The patchwork pattern has only been reinforced by more recent migrant and immigrant groups. African American Protestants, for example, are concentrated in a few major urban regions, notably Cleveland, Detroit, and Chicago. Latino immigration, Catholic and Pentecostal, is concentrated in a handful of major cities and in the meatpacking towns of the Great Plains. Muslims and practitioners of Asian religions are clustered especially in metropolitan Chicago but also in university towns. Arabs—some Muslims but mostly Christians—have established a strong presence in the Detroit area, above all in Dearborn. Jews are also clustered in the region's major cities, most heavily in the Chicago area. And although they are not the product of migration, the Indian reservations of the Dakotas, Minnesota, northern Wisconsin, and northern Michigan also create scattered concentrations of ethnoreligious particularity. The consequences of these patterns for civic and political culture in the region are considerable. To generalize, the Midwestern dispensation looks favorably on religious influence in the public culture, but usually in a much more moderate tone and style than is favored in the Southern

Crossroads or even in the South. The notion of a religiously neutral state is also deeply rooted in the regional culture—especially in its strong tradition of public education, which arose partly as a result of the need to accommodate so much historic Protestant variety. Despite the increasing religious diversity of the current era, the organized religious influence on the public culture of the Midwest still comes from two very large and still competing groups: Protestants and Catholics. The bulk of this essay will be devoted to them.

THE PROTESTANT PARADE

The variety and importance of Protestantism in the Midwest can be suggested by a brief review of Midwesterners from various Protestant backgrounds who have made a major impact on American public life. They range from William Jennings Bryan to Jane Addams to Billy Sunday to Henry Ford to Reinhold Niebuhr. Others include Thomas Dorsey, a pioneer of Gospel music; William Bell Riley, a key early twentieth century fundamentalist; Jesse Jackson; Billy Graham; Tom Osborne, the Nebraska football coach; and Hillary Clinton. It would, however, leave the wrong impression to imply that Midwestern Protestants have sought the dramatic gesture or the spectacular event. Their great contribution to national life has been faithful self-discipline of moral purpose; their great contribution to religious life, faithful development of stable churches for stable communities.

No group illustrates this more fully than the Lutherans, the largest Protestant family in the region. According to the ARIS survey, six of the seven states in the country where Lutherans counted more than 10 percent of the respondents are in the Midwest. According to NARA, about six percent of the total population in the five Midwestern states east of the Mississippi are Lutherans, and 16 percent in the six states west of the Mississippi. After setting aside the Lutherans, there are still a lot of Protestants left in the region— some 14 to 15 million. ARIS found that 7.5 percent of Midwesterners identified themselves as Methodists, more than for any other region in the United States. Additionally, several smaller Wesleyan and Holiness denominations derived from Methodism have strong pockets of adherence, especially in Ohio, Indiana, Minnesota, Kansas, and South Dakota. They are rarely flashy, but sustain in various ways the legacy of their founders, John and Charles Wesley: a deep respect for religious experience (sometimes at the expense of precise doctrine), an unusual attention to the work of the Holy Spirit, and an energetic interest in practical good works.

The other denominations of the Protestant mainline are, for the most part, well represented in the Midwest as well. Thus, while only 2.7 percent of Midwesterners reported themselves as Presbyterians, that is a higher proportion than anywhere else in the country except the Middle Atlantic and the South. The Presbyterian Church (U.S.A.), the nation's largest denomination in this religious family, is particularly well-represented in eastern Ohio, as well as in Iowa, South Dakota, Nebraska, and Kansas. Outside of New England, the historic center of Congregationalism, a higher proportion of the population in the Midwest (0.9 percent) call themselves Congregationalists than in any other region of the country. As with several of the Protestant denominations that originated on the east coast during the colonial period, the United Church of Christ retains some strength in a belt that stretches from Ohio into Illinois and then across the Mississippi into Iowa, Nebraska, South Dakota, and Kansas. Congregationalists, beginning with the Abolitionist era, have made a disproportionate impact on public life and have provided a platform for liberal Protestant activity in the region. Despite the presence of impressive Episcopalian churches in several large and midsize Midwestern cities, the Episcopal position on the ground was never particularly strong in the region. As with the Congregationalists, 0.9 percent of Midwesterners told the ARIS researchers that they were Episcopalian. With the exception of South Dakota, where there have been several successful Episcopalian missions to Native Americans, this church does not enjoy the adherence of even 1 percent of any Midwestern state's population.

The Restorationist movement arose in the early nineteenth century from efforts by leaders like Alexander Campbell and Barton W. Stone to foreswear traditional denominational labels, to follow no creed but the Bible, and to bring Christian belief and practice back to the standards of the New Testament. The movement, which was always strongest in the upper South and the lower Midwest, subsequently divided into submovements: the Christian Church (Disciples of Christ), which came most to resemble other mainline Protestant denominations; the Christian Churches, which negotiated carefully between Restorationist traditions and modern life; and the Churches of Christ, which retained most directly the localist, antidenominationalist traditions of the movement's founders.

Leading the evangelical pack, as in most parts of the country, are the white Baptists; 8.2 percent of Midwesterners identify themselves as such. But in contrast to the Methodists, the Midwest is far from their most populous region, and they don't cut the public profile they do in the South and the Southern Crossroads. The Baptist impact of public life is also muted by the fact that Baptists divide into so many separate denominations—at least six, each one of which has a strong geographical niche in the region. Similarly, the 6.3 percent of all Midwesterners who identify themselves as associated with historically African American Protestant churches is less than half the proportion reported for the South, and about two-thirds of the proportion in the Middle Atlantic and the Southern Crossroads.

In the Midwest as elsewhere, Pentecostalism is one of the most difficult movements to chart accurately because so much Pentecostal organization is propelled by local leaders, and because the more recent Charismatic movement (which brought Pentecostal practices like healing, prophesying, and speaking in tongues into other Christian traditions) is mostly an informal set of emphases (as well as contemporary worship styles featuring "praise" songs and electronic instruments). What research of different sorts testifies to is the presence of Pentecostalism in the Midwest at just about the national average. As in the country as a whole, 2.1 percent of Midwestern respondents to the ARIS survey called themselves Pentecostals or charismatics. The largest mostly white Pentecostal denomination, the Assemblies of God, has a substantial number of adherents in all 11 Midwestern states, with the highest percentages in Minnesota (1.1 percent), North Dakota (1.6 percent), and Nebraska (1.1 percent). The Church of God (Cleveland, Tennessee), which is strongest in the South, counts 228 churches in southern Ohio. Smaller Pentecostal denominations and independent Pentecostal churches are spread throughout the region. The Pentecostal influence has been pronounced on independent (nondenominational) Protestant churches, of which there have historically been more in the United States than anywhere else in the world. In the ARIS telephone poll, 9.9 percent of the Midwestern population identified themselves as "evangelical," "nondenominational," or "Christian" without any other designation. A substantial number of these people participate in the life of independent congregations of one sort or another.

Early in the twentieth century, the fundamentalist movement led to the creation of many "Bible" or "community" churches throughout the Midwest and independent churches have long been a feature of African American urban communities as well. In the last quarter century, suburban areas around the country have provided the venue for a new style of church aimed at the unchurched or lightly churched population, organized to do away with church practices unfamiliar to rising generations, presented with professional attention to music and drama, and oriented toward making the Christian message applicable to the tensions, mobility, and trials of modern American life.

The Willow Creek Community Church in South Barrington, Illinois, with up to 20,000 worshippers each week (and several branch operations in other northern Illinois cities), has been a leader in this megachurch movement. But many varieties of this same kind of church fellowship can be found in and surrounding all major cities, and sometimes in rural areas as well.

Descendants of Europe's Anabaptist movements have never been numerous in the United States but from the end of the seventeenth century (in colonial Pennsylvania) there have been significant communities in North America of Mennonites, Amish, Hutterite Brethren, and other groups influenced by the Anabaptist movement. Their commitment to pacifism has sometimes caused Mennonites and Amish to suffer during wartime but their success as farmers, and later in movement to cities and suburbs, have earned Anabaptists the respect of surrounding communities. In Holmes County, Ohio, and Lagrange County, Indiana, the Amish today make up the largest single religious body. In addition, there are significant numbers of Amish and Mennonites in central Illinois and east-central Iowa. Central Kansas is also the southern terminus of a "Mennonite Belt" that runs northward through Nebraska and South Dakota (where there are 44 Hutterite Brethren congregations promoting a communal style of life).

Like the Anabaptists, churches known as Reformed have never had an extensive presence in the United States, but as with the Anabaptists, the Midwest has been the home to significant concentrations of these Reformed Protestants. European Reformed distinctions—loyalty to the Heidelberg Catechism of the sixteenth century, unusual respect for pastors, some uneasiness with both mainline and evangelical styles of American churchmanship—remain alive in two denominations rising from Dutch immigration to the new world, the Reformed Church in America (with roots in the colonial period) and the Christian Reformed Church (which traces its ancestry to migrations of the mid-nineteenth century). These Reformed denominations are strong in western Michigan, central Iowa, and the Sioux country stretching from northwest Iowa into southeast South Dakota.

Where the Midwest comes up short by way of Protestants is among Hispanics and other ethnic groups, largely because of the relatively low rate of new immigration into the region. According to ARIS, just 1.1 percent of Midwesterners are Hispanic Protestants, the lowest percentage of any region and another 1.2 percent are Protestants in other ethnic groups. But Hispanic churches, often Pentecostal, have been growing rapidly in areas of strong migration from Mexico and Latin America—above all, in Chicago. A similar situation exists for communities with significant Korean, Cambodian, Russian, Ghanaian, and other immigrant populations, where churches are being formed at a very rapid pace.[1]

THE METHODIST TINGE

To make sense of this parade of Protestant subgroups that lie so thick but also so diffusely on Midwestern ground, it is useful to characterize them as either proprietary, ethnic, or sectarian. Proprietary churches (also known as mainline) include the Methodist, Presbyterian, Congregational, Episcopal, and Disciples churches descended from denominations that have existed for two, three, or even four centuries. Because of their historic positions, these churches are usually wealthier (or have a history of relative wealth); they usually are centrally located in cities and towns; they have their greatest appeal to the middle and upper classes; they take the value of higher education for granted; they have been moderate or conservative in political outlook (and so are longtime allies of the Republican Party); they often are the churches of civic and professional elites; they are mostly Caucasian; and they have a long history of sponsoring civic institutions like colleges, hospitals, and retirement homes.

Religiously considered, the proprietary or mainline churches are stronger on Christianity as a civilizing force, while they tend to lay less stress on the need for conversion from sin and on the exacting demands of holy living. Over the past few decades, their position as denominations trying to be comprehensive for all people has led them into long, often contentious debate over sexual issues, especially whether to ordain sexually active homosexuals for the ministry. Although these churches were not pioneers in ordaining women (Wesleyan, Holiness, and Pentecostal churches took that lead), they have been the denominations over the last half-century that have been most solicitous about promoting the equality of women in public life, including the leadership of their churches. The proprietary churches were the historic founders of religion in the Midwest but they have declined considerably in recent decades. Lutherans and also the Reformed often look like proprietary Protestants but their history as immigrant churches can lead to significant differences, whether preserving some characteristics of the established churches of Europe in places where they are in an overwhelming majority (as in many parts of Minnesota, Nebraska, Iowa, and the Dakotas) or remaining somewhat standoffish from public life when they are in a minority. Quite a few Lutherans, and even more Reformed, also emphasize religious beliefs and practices similar to those promoted in the more evangelical sectarian churches. Historically, they are the Protestants most likely to establish private schools to serve their own constituencies.

Ethnic churches are harder to describe since African American churches do not necessarily provide a template for Hispanic, Korean, or the other newer ethnic Protestants. For their part, black churches are usually located in cities; they tend to be Baptist, Methodist, or Pentecostal; they feature strong preaching and pastoral leadership; they take for granted the need to play an active role in economic affairs; and they are often sustained by a remarkably loyal corps of dedicated women. Whether they are well-financed or not (and some are), they are closer to the needs of the urban poor than are the predominately white churches. In their religious beliefs and ethical practices, black churches are usually conservative. But because of the long history of estrangement from centers of economic power, their adherents provide key votes and (less frequently) important leaders for the Democratic Party.

The sectarian Protestants are characterized by religious beliefs and practices—and sometimes by ethnic or regional (especially Southern) distinctives—that separate them to one degree or another from a majority of other Protestants or from most of their fellow American citizens. The list of such distinctives is long and diverse. The key thing is not just that these are part of church tradition but that they are maintained as vital elements in defining what it means to be a true Christian, even if holding dogmatically to that commitment offends the sensibilities of other Christians or cuts against the grain of the broader American society. Because sectarian churches define themselves by their particularistic truth claims, they have been wary about cooperating with other church bodies, including even other sectarian groups that to outsiders seem quite similar.

Considering Protestants under these broad rubrics helps make sense of their respective roles in the public life of the Midwest. The (non-Lutheran) proprietary churches do, in fact, often tend to act and think alike. A brief summary of the Protestant history of the Midwest would go like this. In the beginning were the Methodists, with Presbyterians and Baptists not too far behind, and the Congregationalists a significant presence as well. Then after the Civil War came a half-century of rapid population growth for the whole region. In that deluge were lots of Methodists, Presbyterians, and Congregationalists, but many more Catholics and Lutherans, and a full laundry list of others—Baptists, Jews, Moravians, Brethren, Mennonites, Disciples, and more. Over the course of the twentieth century, the proprietary Protestants have continued to give ground to Roman Catholics, Lutherans, sectarian Protestants, and non-Christian groups, though their earlier hegemony is still visible in many smaller communities and particular subregions. Protestants in the Midwest have come to be fairly evenly balanced between proprietary and sectarian types

For the most part, proprietary Protestants have remained more at home in rural areas, small towns, and mid-sized cities. The massive Lutheran immigration to the upper Midwest gave to that subregion a type of Protestantism that was more inward-looking than the proprietary traditions and more communal than the sectarians. The more than 100 years since the peak of these great migrations have witnessed incremental adjustments rather than dramatic change. The most reliable estimates of church adherence in 1990 showed that Lutherans had moved from strength to strength; they had become the largest Protestant presence in Wisconsin, Minnesota, Iowa, the Dakotas, and Nebraska; and had even exceeded the Catholic population in Minnesota and the Dakotas. The Baptists were the only one of the older Protestant traditions to increase their proportion of Midwestern population. They had become the largest Protestant tradition in Ohio, Michigan, Indiana, and Illinois, but because of the multitude of Baptist denominations and their largely sectarian outlook, the Baptists exerted less influence on public life than the Methodists and other proprietary churches had done in earlier eras.

Much of Michigan and Ohio, the Chicago metropolitan area of northern Illinois and northwest Indiana, southern Wisconsin, the Twin Cities, and other major cities have participated fully in the great social movements of industrialization, suburbanization, immigration, economic shift toward information technology, multicultural diversity, and extremes of wealth and poverty. Church life in these areas has fared best when congregations respond actively and intentionally to shifting social and economic realities, whether it is African American and other ethnic churches providing enclaves of support for mobile communities, or the newer seeker-sensitive churches offering much the same to mostly Caucasian audiences.

More traditional, predominately white churches have not done as well in these venues. They have, however, remained anchors of tradition in the more agricultural states west of the Mississippi and in less urban parts of the states to the east. In the second half of the twentieth century, Iowa, North Dakota, South Dakota, rural Nebraska, rural Kansas, as well as rural areas of Indiana and Illinois, have been bypassed. Population there has not risen but, in fact, in many places is draining away. In those places, the churches—whether Catholic, Lutheran, proprietary Protestant, or sectarian Protestant—have had the task of providing stability for a rapidly aging population.

Amidst the diversity, it is important to recognize the extent to which the strong Methodist foundation for Midwestern religious life has left its mark on public life, including politics. That foundation explains why Protestant life in the Midwest has been earnest, evangelical, and energetic, but not as sectarian as elsewhere in the country. Although the rise of Baptists and other similar groups in many Midwestern states is making this region more like other regions, the early Methodist history continues to distinguish the Midwest. Methodists were more individualistic than Lutherans but less so than Baptists and they bequeathed a more relaxed acceptance of organized philanthropy than the Baptists found congenial. They have been less oriented to class divisions based on wealth and status than Presbyterians or Episcopalians, less ethnically defined than Lutherans, and more likely to go with the flow of cultural change than either Lutherans or Baptists.

Of course, any claim about a lingering Methodist influence must be qualified by attending to what have become the important subregions of the

Midwest. In Ohio, Indiana, and southern Illinois, the Methodist legacy remains significant, although it has given way rapidly to Baptist and Disciples growth in recent decades. This subregion retains links to an older proprietary Protestant past because the number of Catholics and Lutherans is smaller here than anywhere else in the Midwest. In Michigan, Wisconsin, and northern Illinois, Methodist hegemony is now only a memory. Catholics and Lutherans represent the dominant religious traditions but Baptists have been expanding in Michigan, and a wide variety of evangelical, ethnic, fundamentalist, and sectarian Protestant groups sustains a lively, if not large, presence in this subregion as well. In the final subregion of Nebraska, Kansas, and Iowa, the presence of Methodism is still obvious, as is also the presence of the other proprietary denominations. Baptists, with the Southern Baptist Convention at the forefront, have been advancing rapidly in Kansas, as has the Disciples of Christ in Iowa and Kansas. Similar to the situation in Ohio, Indiana, and southern Illinois, both proprietary and sectarian Protestant churches are a major cultural presence, since Catholics and Lutherans are not as widely dispersed here as in the rest of the Midwest.

In politics, the historic strength of proprietary Protestantism has without question played an important role throughout the region. In recent years, non-Lutheran Protestants have contributed to the rise of the religious right, but with less direct impact on the winning and losing of elections than in the South and Southern Crossroads. In the 2000 presidential election, white Protestants as a whole contributed disproportionately to George W. Bush's narrow victory. Distinguishing between "mainline" and "evangelical," in a way that corresponds roughly to the "proprietary" and "sectarian" categories employed here, John Green and his associates at the University of Akron concluded that evangelical Protestants who regularly attend church (high-commitment evangelicals) accounted for 32 percent of Bush's total votes, with another 8 percent from evangelicals who do not attend church regularly (low-commitment evangelicals), 10 percent from high-commitment mainline Protestants, and 11 percent from low-commitment mainline Protestants. (By contrast, the contribution to Al Gore's total from these four groups was, respectively, 6, 7, 5, and 8 percent. For another major contrast, African American Protestant voters contributed 19 percent of Al Gore's total vote, while giving George W. Bush only 1 percent of his vote total.)[2]

To these totals Midwestern Protestants contributed their fair share. Exit polling from election day, which employed a different set of data than that used by the Green team, found that across the nation white Protestants of all sorts favored Bush over Gore by 64 percent to 34 percent (with 2 percent going to other candidates). In the Midwest, white Protestants of all sorts favored Bush over Gore by 61.5 percent to 36.5 percent (with 2 percent going to other candidates). The black Protestant vote went more strongly the other way (with the national tally favoring Gore by 92 percent to 7 percent, and in the Midwest by 94 percent to 5 percent). Since the Midwest cast about one-fourth of the votes in this election, the strong Protestant support for Bush (though slightly less than the national white Protestant average) contributed greatly to the final results.

In the last quarter century, the Republican presidential candidate has, in general, done better in the Midwest (with Wisconsin, Illinois, and Minnesota as the major exceptions) than nationwide. The strong Protestant presence certainly has played a role in these outcomes, although care is needed in attempting to specify the exact dimensions of electoral influence.

It is illuminating, however, to set this recent history into a longer historical frame. Well into the twentieth century, the Midwest was not only the most Methodist region of the country, but also, as measured by the results of presidential elections, it was just about the most consistently Republican as well. As a whole, it was more solidly Republican than the nation in its presidential votes right up to the first election of Franklin D. Roosevelt in 1932. That Republican strength in presidential elections has continued in what could now be called "the Old Methodist Midwest" (Ohio, Indiana, Iowa, North Dakota, South Dakota, Nebraska, and Kansas), by comparison both to the nation and to what can be termed "the Lutheran and Catholic Midwest" (Michigan, Wisconsin, Illinois, and Minnesota). Such generalizations are compromised in part by the strong Lutheran presence in North and South Dakota but there is a clear enough pattern to leave room for thought.

Such thought would certainly emphasize the Methodist roots for a moderately conservative Protestant ethos that has fostered a certain measure of corporate solidarity in the rural and small-town Midwest, but that has never taken hold to the same degree in cities. That ethos flourishes by nurturing a broad Protestant (and Caucasian) pluralism, but with a certain suspicion of religious and cultural groups coming from outside Protestant (and Caucasian) networks. This ethos is definitely moralistic, with an ingrained commitment to decency and public order but at the same time it only rarely looks to government for the formal enforcement of morality. Debates over Prohibition and abortion have been the major exceptions.

The moderation of such a "Methodist ethos" can also be seen in the historic Midwestern Protestant support for local public schools, with the Lutherans and Reformed the exception to this rule. Likewise, it can account for a relatively moderate tone (by comparison to the coasts and the South) in support of and opposition to labor unions, in support of and opposition to American wars of the last half century, and in support of pro-life and pro-choice positions on abortion. The moderation is less obvious west of the Mississippi on questions of agricultural policy, but that too points to the distinctive character of the region. Without pushing such speculations overmuch, it is still possible to see the results of recent presidential elections as indicating where this Methodist ethos has been maintained, and where it has faded.

Finally, it is worth wondering if the megachurches of the Midwest are not repackaging some of the old Methodist ethos into new forms for the suburbs, where they are strongest, but also in some urban and rural areas where they can also be found. Like the early Methodists, the megachurches are innovative in their efforts at reaching and sustaining adherents; they have pioneered in the production and use of a new hymnody; and their pastors have their fingers on the pulse of popular sentiment. These pastors, like most Methodist pastors through most of their history, are skilled in presenting their views on religion and other matters with a minimum of public offense. With some exceptions, the megachurches are, in political terms, less obviously liberal than the proprietary mainline and less overtly conservative than the sectarian evangelicals. It is an open question whether it will be possible soon to speak of a "megachurch ethos." If the megachurches of the Midwest continue to grow not only in absolute terms but also relative to other Protestants, such an ethos might emerge. If it does, it will reflect a most interesting development in the religious history of an American region that, more than any other, has been shaped by the orderly energy of its early Methodist pioneers.

CATHOLIC ETHNICITIES

The Midwestern Catholic world took shape during the religious battles of the nineteenth century, when Catholics responded to Protestant hostility by assuming an island mentality and concentrating on building up a religious and cultural citadel within American society. In those days, the Midwest was a region of small farming communities and wide open spaces—mission country. Lacking large institutional complexes and sizable Catholic populations, Catholicism in the region developed a spirit or style that was not so tied to the hierarchical structure and legalistic mentality of the church back east. It became and remained more open to adaptation and experimentation, notably in the area of liturgy. To this day, only 23 percent of Midwesterners are Catholic. That is considerably smaller than the Catholic slice of the pie in New England (42 percent) and the Middle Atlantic (37 percent), and somewhat less than the Pacific's 29 percent. When systematic anti-Catholic bigotry did materialize (as with the American Protective Association in the

1890s or the Ku Klux Klan in the 1920s), it tended to be strongest in the rural areas where the Catholics were least numerous.

During the burst of immigration from 1880 to 1920, the great industrial cities—Cleveland, Detroit, Chicago, and Milwaukee—became the region's great islands of Catholic life. Nowhere was this more the case than in Illinois. The Archdiocese of Chicago, which comprises Cook County and a small part of Lake County, numbers 2.4 million Catholics, two-thirds of the state's total Catholic population. Likewise, metropolitan Detroit's Catholic population of 1.5 million makes up three-quarters of Michigan's Catholic population.[3] Within these urban Catholic agglomerations, there has been great diversity. In 1900, the Catholic gospel was preached, at least some of the time, in 28 languages in Chicago. Today the number is 44. But this diversity should not be permitted to obscure the unique ethnic roots of Catholicism in the region.

The most important of these is German. While Germans settled in many regions of the country, it was to the Midwest that they came in the greatest numbers, intent on settling and farming the land. Perhaps 30 percent of them were Catholic. Today, nearly one in four Midwesterners can claim German ancestry, making them the single largest European ethnic group in the region. Ohio (2.8 million), Illinois (2.5 million) and Wisconsin (2.3 million) have the largest German-American populations. But every state in the region has a sizable proportion. This German presence sets Midwest Catholicism apart. The heartland of German Catholic influence is what historians describe as the "German Triangle"—the area anchored by Cincinnati in the east, St. Louis in the west, and Milwaukee in the north. Early on, Midwestern bishops recruited German-speaking Benedictine monks to establish monasteries in the region, which also made a difference. These monks ministered to the large numbers of German farmers who had settled in places like southern Indiana, Minnesota, and the Dakotas. The rich Benedictine liturgical tradition that the monks brought with them quickly became a marker of Midwest Catholicism, distinguishing it from the plain, stern, Irish style of liturgy that was so commonplace elsewhere in Catholic America. By the mid-twentieth century, the large urban concentrations of *das Deutschtum* (German culture, with its language and customs) had largely disappeared, although German-Americans retain a strong presence in cities like Chicago and Cincinnati and their suburbs.

In addition, rural Catholic enclaves remain. One striking example is Stearns County in Minnesota, a rural agricultural area situated in the center of the state that has been a citadel of Catholicism since the mid-nineteenth century. Fifty-eight percent of the county's population is of German ancestry and 86 percent of them are Catholic (66,563). Benedictine monks arrived in 1856 from their monastery in Latrobe, Pennsylvania. The monks took responsibility for a number of parishes in the county. In 1866 they built a monastery, St. John's Abbey, in Collegeville. This abbey, together with St. John's University, a college they had founded in 1857, became a vital center for the German Catholic community. Both institutions have flourished and remain an important locus for the Catholics of central Minnesota. Writing about the county in 1990, the historian Kathleen Conzen noted that "the descendents of German immigrants have not only preserved distinctive rural communities and cultures; they have also retained their commitment to a rural way of life to a greater extent than almost any other ancestry group—particularly Anglo-Americans—among today's rural farm population." This distinctiveness can be seen "in everything from the area's aggressive anti-abortion movement to the fiscal caution of its governmental bodies, the high persistence rates of its conservative farmers, the unusually large size of its families and the traces of traditional legalism, clericalism, and the devotionalism that still mark its spirituality."[4]

Though they never rivaled the Germans in terms of population, the Irish of the Midwest did gain considerable clout both in the church and in politics. Most settled in Illinois, Michigan, and Ohio; as for cities, Chicago was clearly the most famous Irish city in the Midwest. The Irish clergy ran the Catholic church in Chicago for much of the nineteenth and twentieth centuries. But, as their numbers declined and their Irish parishioners moved to the suburbs, the Irish clergy ceased to be the power brokers in the church. A similar scenario took place in city politics. The Irish took control in the 1930s, building a powerful machine that would rule the city into the 1970s. Richard J. Daley was the major figure in this 40-year reign of power. Elected as mayor in 1955, he ruled the city with a firm hand until his death in 1976. During his time in office the Irish held key city government, judicial, and police and fire department positions. But even before his death it was clear that the Irish control of Chicago politics was changing. This became most evident in 1983, when Harold Washington became the first African American mayor in the city's history. The Daley name returned to prominence when Daley's son, Richard M. Daley, became mayor in 1989. But his success on election day did not depend on the Irish vote. The Irish had long abandoned the city for the suburbs. The second Daley owed his tenure (elected to a fifth consecutive term in 2007) to a powerful Democratic coalition of African Americans, Latinos, and an ethnically diverse group of whites. What has happened in Chicago took place in other Midwest cities as well.

The presence of a large *Polonia*—the descendants of Polish immigrants—is also a notable feature of Midwestern Catholicism, especially in Detroit, Chicago, and Milwaukee. Polish is the third most commonly used language in the celebration of Mass, behind English and Spanish, in the region.

One of the most dramatic changes in recent years has been the immigration of thousands of Latinos to the United States, resulting in a growth of the Latino population from 22.4 million in 1990 to 35.3 million in 2000, according to the U.S. Census. This large influx has presented a special challenge for the Catholic Church, since the majority of Latinos, about 70 percent, are Catholic. To be sure, Latino Catholics have been present in the United States since colonial times. But because of the unparalleled growth of this community since 1965—as well as the initiative of both lay and clerical leaders—Latino Catholics have formed a church within a church, resembling in many ways the German Catholics of the late nineteenth century. Like the Germans, they have their own national gatherings, lobby for their own bishops, have their own parishes where they celebrate their liturgies in their own unique style, and seek to maintain their heritage. Yet, comparatively speaking, relatively few Latinos have settled in the Midwest. Only about three million Latinos have settled in the 11 states that comprise the region. More Latinos (4.2 million) live in just one California county, Los Angeles, than in the entire Midwest.

The Chicago region has attracted the lion's share of recent global immigration to the Midwest and the Chicago archdiocese now has an Asian population of 80,000, which is expected to grow by about 10 percent by 2010. A relatively new group within the Midwest Catholic mosaic, Asian Catholics are an ethnically diverse population. Because of such diversity, as well as the lack of a native clergy, they will present a formidable challenge to the church's pastoral ministry in the years ahead.

In the Midwest region there are approximately 5.8 million African Americans, about 16.7 percent of the nation's African American population. Three states in the region—Illinois, Michigan, and Ohio—account for 79 percent of the region's African American population. Nationwide, the number of African American Catholics is relatively small, an estimated 2 million, or about 3 percent of the total Catholic population. In the Midwest, the bulk of African American Catholics live in Chicago and Detroit, where they make about 4 percent of the Catholic population.

CATHOLICS IN THE PUBLIC SQUARE

The distinctiveness of Midwestern Catholicism is based on more than demography and immigrant culture. For much of the twentieth century, the region was American Catholicism's nursery for liturgical, social, and political reform. The center of this reformist tendency was the Archdiocese of

Chicago, where a zest for innovation and experimentation took hold in the late 1930s and 1940s, in many respects anticipating the spirit of reform unleashed by the Second Vatican Council of the early 1960s. A key figure in the early years was Bernard J. Sheil, an auxiliary bishop in Chicago who founded the Catholic Youth Organization (CYO) in the early 1930s. Sheil was also an activist on behalf of social justice, working closely with the emerging labor movement. He was a key supporter of a young activist, Saul Alinsky, who was attempting to organize the workers in the slaughterhouses on Chicago's south side. With Sheil's support, as well as the support of other clergy in the neighborhood, Alinsky was able to put together a neighborhood organization, the Back of the Yards Neighborhood Council. By forming a unique partnership that joined church, labor union, and community, the council was able to organize the packinghouse workers, bringing peace to a neighborhood and an industry notorious for labor unrest. Alinsky's success in Chicago launched his career as a community organizer who, for the next three decades, helped to mobilize dozens of powerless urban neighborhoods all over the nation.

In the 1950s and 1960s, the civil rights movement galvanized the nation. The nation's cities became the main arena for this struggle for full civil rights for all people regardless of their race, creed, or color. The Catholic Church in Chicago, spearheaded by a number of lay people and clergy, took a leading role in this struggle. This was highlighted in January 1963, when Chicago's Catholics hosted the first National Conference on Religion and Race, which brought together Catholics, Protestants, and Jews in an unprecedented ecumenical effort to combat racial discrimination in the United States. Once again, Chicago became the epicenter of a movement whose influence would spread well beyond the city.

The Midwest, Iowa in particular, was the center of the Catholic rural life movement that flourished in the middle decades of the twentieth century. The Catholic Charismatic Movement has also been centered in the Midwest, both at Notre Dame—in South Bend, Indiana—and in Ann Arbor, Michigan. Call to Action, one of the most active reform movements in the Catholic Church, has its headquarters in Chicago. Significantly, Catholic lay men and women are the leaders of this organization.

However, in recent years, the energy for reform that was so noticeable in the Midwest in the middle decades of the twentieth century has dissipated. Regionally, Catholicism has become more rigid, less open to the spirit of innovation, more like the church in the northeast or the Pacific. There are many reasons for this. In the wake of the Second Vatican Council (1962–1965) a zeal for renewal captured the hearts and minds of many American Catholics, fostering a climate in the church that was open to innovation. But this climate began to change by the early 1970s as the enthusiasm generated by the council waned. The activists of the 1950s and 1960s aged, losing some of the spark of their youth. In 1965, a new archbishop, John P. Cody, took control of the church in Chicago. Cody was not like his predecessors. An autocratic monarch, he succeeded in slowly but surely destroying the climate of optimism and hope generated by Vatican II. Large numbers of clergy in Chicago, many of whom had been actively involved in the changes initiated in the 1960s, left the priesthood.

During the Reagan era of the 1980s, the culture of conservatism that swept across the country during the presidency of Richard Nixon (1969–1974) became even more pronounced. Politically, Catholic suburbanites joined the shift, breaking with the ethnic urban commitment to the Democratic Party of their parents to vote Republican. Since then, white Catholics have been key swing voters in presidential elections. In its religious dimension, the rise of a more conservative stance was connected to the long papacy of Pope John Paul II, who presided over the church from 1978 to 2005. By fashioning a culture of rigid adherence to orthodox Catholic teaching John Paul did much to stifle the spirit of innovation throughout the church. The declining number of priests and women religious has also diminished the pool of potential innovators.

Perhaps the most distinctive continuing feature of the Catholic Church's effort to shape American public life has been its commitment to education. At the beginning of the twenty-first century, the Catholic parochial school system remains alive, but is much smaller than it was 50 years ago and it struggles with serious resource problems. Because of the financial demands associated with operating and maintaining parochial schools, Catholics are once again looking to the public sector for financial assistance—most importantly, to tuition voucher programs. In 1990, the first state-funded urban school voucher initiative was authorized by the Wisconsin state legislature.[5] This law allowed Milwaukee children from low-income families to attend private schools, both religious and nonreligious, using state vouchers to pay tuition. Such a radical change in the state's educational policy caused a firestorm of controversy and it was not long before the law was challenged in the courts. In 1998, the Wisconsin Supreme Court decided in a 4-2 decision that a voucher program that included religious schools was constitutional. By 2002 enrollment in Milwaukee's voucher program exceeded 10,000 students in about 100 schools, nearly 40 of which were Catholic. A similar program began in Cleveland in 1995, and was also challenged in court. In 2002, the U.S. Supreme Court, in a 5-4 decision, upheld its constitutionality. Although vouchers were in the beginning promoted by civil rights groups and conservative Republicans rather than the church, Catholics have become strong supporters. Surveys indicate that as many as 60 percent of Americans support vouchers. These same surveys show that as many as 72 percent of Catholics, together with a wide majority of born-again Christians, are "especially supportive of vouchers."[6] But it is worth noting that it is the high-commitment Catholics (those who attend church at least once a week) who favor them, rather than those who attend infrequently.

In the course of the twentieth century, Catholic Church leaders increasingly began to articulate moral and political positions they believed would benefit the welfare of American society at large. This concern for the public square took on a renewed vigor as a result of the Second Vatican Council. As one observer noted, the council "moved the Church into far greater participation in social and political affairs. The council stressed that the Church as an institution and Catholics in general had a positive obligation to involve themselves in the problems of the world."[7]

One major initiative in the post-Vatican-II era was the establishment of bishops conferences. These conferences, as well as similar instrumentalities organized at the state level, have allowed the bishops to exercise their pastoral office jointly for the welfare of their respective countries. The United States Conference of Catholic Bishops has been very active in issuing statements and lobbying on a wide range of issues, many of which relate to social justice. One of the most important pastoral letters was the 1983 letter on nuclear war. The driving force behind this letter was the Archbishop of Chicago, Joseph Bernardin, who was appointed archbishop of the most prestigious diocese in the Midwest in 1982. Known as a moderate, Bernardin envisioned himself as a major actor in the public arena, seeking to influence public policy through lobbying Congress as well as the White House and the Illinois statehouse. In a series of lectures he crafted what he described as a "consistent ethic of life," urging Americans to protect human life in the womb as well as in the face of nuclear war. In due course, he "extended his consistent ethic beyond abortion and war" to such life issues as capital punishment and poverty.[8]

Another key pastoral letter in the 1980s addressed the state of the national economy. Its principal architect was another Midwesterner, Archbishop Rembert Weakland of Milwaukee. A Benedictine monk, Weakland was elected the Abbot Primate of the Benedictine Order in 1967 at the age of 40. Ten years later, the Pope appointed him as the archbishop of Milwaukee, where he soon became identified with the more liberal wing of American Catholicism. Other dioceses even began to copy some of his "innovative policies" such as "placing women in senior positions, streamlining the bureaucracy, assuring pensions for lay employees and higher pay for teachers, establishing a program for spiritual renewal for parishes, and mandating that each parish have a lay council."[9] With Bernardin's death in 1996 and Weakland's resignation in 2002, Midwest Catholicism lost its two most charismatic leaders. No one has been able to replace either of them in terms of national prestige.

As active as church leaders are at the federal level through the United States Conference of Catholic Bishops, it is probably at the state level where the Catholic Church has the most significant influence. Every state in the Midwest has a Catholic conference that serves as the official voice of the church on matters of public policy. Though very little has been written about these conferences, they are often influential, representing the church as lobbyists in the state legislatures and keeping track of proposed legislation. In Minnesota, a typical big-state case, the conference tracks legislation dealing with issues as diverse as special education, so-called partial-birth abortion, increasing the minimum wage, prescription drug rebates, gun control, and the death penalty. In North Dakota, each year the conference publishes a report card on its achievements and its defeats. In 2003, the conference director listed the two best bills passed in the legislature: to ensure conscience protection for adoption agencies and a ban on human cloning. North Dakota's concern about the conscience clause highlights an issue of public policy that has preoccupied church leaders. Conscience clauses grant to Catholic institutions such as hospitals or social service agencies that receive federal or state funding an exemption from providing contraceptive and sterilization services that are contrary to Catholic ethical teaching.

Human life issues are paramount with state Catholic conferences. Taking their cue from the national conference of bishops, they focus on issues that both respect the dignity of the human person and serve the common good. For the most part, their agenda does reflect the opinion of most Catholics. The one area where the official church position differs considerably from the people in the pew is sexual ethics. Surveys—in the Midwest and nationwide—show that the Catholic laity is much more liberal on these issues. Abortion is a good example of this divergence of opinion. All state conferences take a strong antiabortion stance trying to halt any legislation that would enhance the status of abortion. One recent poll found that two-thirds of Catholics believe abortion should be legal. If the woman's life is in danger, the percentage of Catholics approving abortion climbs to 83 percent. If the reason for the abortion is the likelihood of a birth defect, the rate of approval declines to 51 percent. Such differences of opinion based on different situations suggest that Catholic lay attitudes about abortion are quite nuanced. But official church position on this issue does not allow for any such fine tuning. It has adopted a firm antiabortion, pro-life stance. Another issue of human life is the death penalty. The Catholic hierarchy has taken a strong antideath penalty stance. State conferences in the Midwest have also taken strong stances against the death penalty. Nonetheless, a majority of Catholics (62 percent), like most Americans, still favor it.[10]

The church is also actively lobbying on behalf of the poor. In this area there is much more agreement between the hierarchy and the Catholic laity. At the state level every state conference in the Midwest seeks to encourage legislation that will alleviate poverty. According to one national survey, the majority of Catholics, 63 percent, believes that "society has a responsibility for helping poor people get out of poverty."[11] Another poll found that three of four Catholics believed that more money should be provided for health care for poor children. Even more telling was a survey that indicated that 58 percent of Catholics believed charitable efforts toward helping the poor was essential to their faith. This came in second only to the belief that God is present in the sacraments.[12]

All of these data suggest that Catholics "have a more communitarian ethic that emphasizes solidarity, interdependence, and the common good rather than the individualism, independence, and self-help characteristic of the Protestant ethic."[13] This attitude has supported the efforts of church leaders at both the national and state level to shape public policy. Nor does the Catholic effort stop there. Every diocese has its own departments that follow the lead of the state conferences on issues of concern. An office of Catholic Charities operates in every diocese. Such offices monitor laws and ordinances that affect the welfare of the underprivileged. Some dioceses sponsor offices of peace and justice. As the Chicago archdiocese office puts it, the purpose is to promote "advocacy efforts to assist the poor and vulnerable in the Chicago area. Through education and advocacy, parishioners are encouraged to take informed action to influence pubic policy in line with the Catholic Conference of Illinois, and the U.S. Catholic Conference."[14] Thus, at all levels—national, state, regional, and local—Catholics are linked together to form a powerful political lobby that seeks to shape public policy.

MIDWESTERN TEST CASES

The complexity of the Midwest's religiocultural composition usually works to create moderate or moderately conservative public policy outcomes and to mute radical outcomes. That—and the region's occasional swings into center-left territory—puts the Midwest in an active middle spot among the nation's regions. By way of example, let us close by considering two recent episodes from opposite ends of the region: a 2006 South Dakota referendum on abortion the 2006 gubernatorial race in Ohio.

South Dakota—a very conservative state by almost every measure—was the scene of a complex struggle over abortion policy. It was nearly impossible to obtain an abortion in the state already (a single Planned Parenthood clinic provided abortion and it had to fly doctors into the state from Minnesota to perform the procedures). Pro-life strategists, including many Catholics, thought the state was a promising locale in which to create a test case that might lead the newly realigned U.S. Supreme Court to overturn *Roe v. Wade*. So, in February of 2006, the legislature passed a law designed to criminalize all abortions except those performed to save the life of the mother. It offered no explicit exceptions for rape or incest and was considered the most stringent antiabortion law in living memory. In March, Gov. Mike Rounds signed the bill, calling it "a full frontal attack on *Roe v. Wade*."[15] The bill enjoyed widespread support among both Republicans and Democrats in the legislature. But by making it a felony for a doctor to perform any abortion except to save the life of the mother, it immediately generated opposition. Rather than waiting to challenge it in court, local opponents succeeded in putting it up for referendum in the 2006 election.

Although both pro- and antiabortion camps drew much of their funding from out of state, the referendum campaign avoided much of the established rhetoric of pro-life and pro-choice and hewed to the center. Few chants of "Get your rosary off my ovary" or "Baby killers" filled the air. Led by Jan Nicolay, a former Republican state legislator and high school principal, the South Dakota Campaign for Healthy Families (which was attempting to overturn the law) acknowledged that abortion is morally problematic for many people, but emphasized what a powerful governmental restriction on individual liberty an all-out abortion ban would be. "The most extreme arguments on both sides are nowhere to be found," Monica Davey reported in the November 1 *New York Times*. "Instead, in calls from a phone bank at the ban opponents headquarters volunteers quietly tell potential voters that the law is just too narrow, failing to allow abortions in circumstances like rape or incest. The supporters of the ban meanwhile speak in gentle tones about how abortion hurts women." Both sides encourage women who have had abortions to speak publicly about their experiences, which further shaped public discussion.

Writing in the September 6 *Capital Times* of Madison, Wisconsin, Nicolay argued her key political assertion: South Dakota was not "a state defined by the religious right"; rather, its conservatism "overwhelmingly rejects government intervention into private lives."

Nicolay, it turned out, knew her Dakotans. On election day, the voters overturned the new law by a 56-44 percent margin, suggesting to many observers that criminalizing abortion was a line that even conservative states didn't want to cross. No doubt that was true but the vote also reflected the decision of a majority of the state's proprietary Protestants, along with lots of Lutherans and Catholics, to draw the line against a position connected so strongly with attempts to create a religiously based politics in the state and nation—a vote to uphold the Midwestern value of not pushing openly religious agendas too hard in the public realm. Nicolay herself flashed one telling bit of public rhetoric into her *Capital Times* op-ed when she charged that South Dakota had a legislature owned by the religious right and "a Catholic governor named Mike Rounds who was easily influenced by his bishop."

On to Ohio. Given the trends of the most recent decade—two consecutive wins by George W. Bush in the state and the rising strength of conservative Baptists, one might have expected Ohio to remain a redoubt of Republicanism. But the 2006 campaign revealed that the religious right was not the only religious force to be reckoned with in Ohio. In the race for governor, Democratic U.S. Rep. Ted Strickland demonstrated that the old moderate Methodist style had not lost its appeal in the Buckeye state. Strickland smashed Republican candidate Ken Blackwell, a darling of the religious right who always carried a Bible to campaign events, by a margin of 61 to 37 percent, carrying 72 of 88 counties. The eighth of nine children of a steelworker from rural Scioto County along the Ohio River, Strickland was an ordained Methodist minister, an unyielding proponent of the Social Gospel, and a man who had devoted a good portion of his career to combating the influence of the religious right in the Appalachian borderlands of southern and eastern Ohio.

The *Almanac of American Politics* laconically suggests that Strickland's "path to the governorship was long and there was little in his early political career to suggest he might one day end up there." Strickland ran unsuccessfully for Congress in 1976, 1978, and 1980, but won election in 1992, lost in 1994, and won again in 1996 and in the following four elections. On each occasion, he ran in the rural district that follows the broad curve of the Ohio River. In its current configuration, Ohio's Sixth Congressional District stretches more than 300 miles, from the southern suburbs of Youngstown all the way to Lawrence County, just east of metropolitan Cincinnati; for most of the way, it extends no deeper into Ohio than a single, riverfront county. In demography, culture, and outlook, the district embodies the old Butternut Ohio and looks southward.

Strickland himself fits comfortably into the culture of the place. Raised a fundamentalist Baptist, he had a conversion experience in a Methodist meeting as a teenager that led him to enroll at Asbury College, a conservative Methodist stronghold in Kentucky, and to earn a theology degree from its seminary. Ordained to the ministry, he served a church in the 1970s and worked for many years as an administrator at the Kentucky Methodist Home for Children. He then earned a Ph.D. from the University of Kentucky and worked as counselor in the Ohio prison system and as a teacher at a state college. As befits a Butternut Democrat, Strickland had a complex and moderate political message—pro-choice, opposed to gun control, and strongly populist in his economic preferences. The *Economist* described him as "something of a dream candidate: a pro-gun minister endorsed by the National Rifle Association." Yet his campaign energized many moderate and liberal religious folk in Ohio. The *New York Times* reported that two dozen Catholic nuns were volunteering on his phone bank. Over his whole career, Strickland had spoken forthrightly about his own social-justice-focused faith and jousted routinely with paladins of the religious right. But he opened his gubernatorial campaign with a series of ads on Christian radio stations and he regularly dropped the name of Jesus and Scriptural quotations into his campaign talks.

In the midst of the campaign, when opponent Blackwell charged that "Democrats believe that government is God, and God is not," Strickland instantly fired back with a quote from the Old Testament prophet Isaiah: "If you do away with the yoke of oppression, with the pointing of fingers and malicious talk, and if you spend yourselves in behalf of the hungry and satisfy the needs of the oppressed, then your light will rise in the darkness and your night will become like noonday." All of this boggled the minds of journalists and political mavens, in Ohio and elsewhere. "I don't know how long the religious rhetoric is going to play," a Youngstown State University political scientist told the *Akron Beacon Journal* on June 21, 2006. "It's very odd to argue who is closest to the Lord. It would be extraordinarily unusual to make this the central part of the campaign." Odd it may have been, but Strickland was not the only Ohio Democrat to center his campaign that year on a moderate, communally oriented style of religion. Sherrod Brown, the liberal Democratic congressman from Akron who won election to the U.S. Senate by defeating incumbent Mike DeWine, took a similar stance, arguing that his Lutheran faith compelled him to seek social justice. In 2004, Ohio had been a demonstration project for the ability of mobilized religious conservatives to carry a Republican president to victory over even an aroused Democratic electorate. By using a classic Midwestern religious message to put the GOP to rout, the Strickland and Brown campaigns offered a powerful model for national Democratic candidates of the future to follow. And by the time the 2008 election cycle rolled around, it was clear that both the Democratic National Committee and the party's principal presidential aspirants had taken the lesson to heart.

Having served as the fulcrum of national politics in successive presidential elections, the Midwest shows every sign of remaining a good barometer of the national mood, and perhaps even providing the model for religion in American public life in the twenty-first century. Sometimes the common denominator is just what is required.

· 10 ·

Retelling the National Story

*T*he preceding chapters have given some indication of how religion in the public life of the regions relates to the story of religion in the public life of the nation as a whole. Here we pull the fragments together, incorporating region into the national narrative as it has unwound since World War II, which ushered in a new era of religious pluralism.[1] First, however, we must briefly consider the prior place of religion in American public life. From the beginning of the republic there has been a need to deal with the country's religious diversity, not only legally but also by way of informal rules and intellectual constructs, in order to create a decent civil society. In the pursuit of collective interests, electoral politics has often been the means by which Americans have expressed their communal religious identities—both in conflict with each other and through common cause. There have also been, from time to time, major episodes in the life of the nation where religion, in one form or another, has played a powerful role.

THE RISE AND FALL OF PAN-PROTESTANTISM

The framers of the Constitution addressed the challenge of religious diversity in the population of the new republic by banning religious tests for office and (via the First Amendment) ordering Congress to "make no law respecting an establishment of religion or prohibiting the free exercise thereof." Influenced by the values of the Enlightenment, they sought to ensure that American citizenship was in no way impaired by a person's religious commitments. Luther Martin, a Maryland delegate who was not in agreement with that point of view, sent home a letter from Philadelphia grousing that the ban on religious tests for office had been voted through by a large majority with little discussion, even though "there were some members so unfashionable as to think, that a belief of the existence of a Deity, and of a state of future rewards and punishments would be some security for the good conduct of our rulers, and that, in a Christian country, it would be at least decent to hold out some distinction between the professors of Christianity and downright infidelity or paganism."[2] The more fashionable view was expressed by George Washington in 1790 in his famous letter to the Jews of Rhode Island:

> The citizens of the United States of America have a right to applaud themselves for having given to mankind examples on an enlarged and liberal policy—a policy worthy of imitation. ALL possess alike liberty of conscience, and immunities of citizenship. It is now no more that toleration is spoken of, as if it was by the indulgence of one class of people that another enjoyed the exercise of their inherent natural rights.[3]

The constitutional guarantees of the religious rights of all citizens only went so far, however. The language of the First Amendment, which emerged from a congressional conference committee set up to reconcile the House and Senate versions of the Bill of Rights, was designed to accommodate differing views among the states regarding the public place of religion. The House delegation was led by James Madison, the Constitution's most important drafter, who a few years earlier had led the campaign to establish strict separation of church and state in Virginia. Madison was on record in favor of constitutionally banning state as well as federal religious establishments, including any tangible government support for religious institutions. But appointed with him to the House delegation was Roger Sherman of Connecticut—a staunch Congregationalist devoted to maintaining his state's religious Standing Order, which privileged Congregationalism. The Senate conferees included Madison's ally Charles Carroll, a Maryland Roman Catholic who had made his first public mark attacking his state's support of Anglican clergy. But the leader on the Senate side was another Connecticut man, Oliver Ellsworth, shortly to become the nation's second Chief Justice and, like Sherman, a pillar of Congregationalism.

Ellsworth's views on church and state are evident in a report he wrote for the Connecticut General Assembly in 1802 opposing a petition from Connecticut Baptists to get rid of the state's Congregationalist Standing Order. It read, in part:

> This opinion . . . is founded on the principle . . . that every member of society should, in some way, contribute to the support of religious institutions. In illustration of this principle, it may be observed, that the primary objects of government are the peace, order, and prosperity of society. . . . To

the promotion of these objects, particularly in a republican government, good morals are essential. Institutions for the promotion of good morals are therefore objects of legislative provision and support; and among these, in the opinion of the committee, religious institutions are eminently useful and important. . . .

The right of the legislature to oblige each individual of the community to contribute towards the support of schools for the instruction of children, or of courts of justice for the protection of rights, is not questioned; nor is any individual allowed to refuse his contribution, because he has no children to be instructed, no injuries to be redressed, or because he conscientiously believes those institutions useless. On the same principle of general utility, in the opinion of the committee, the legislature may aid the maintenance of that religion whose benign influence on morals is universally acknowledged. It may be added that the principle has been long recognized, and is too intimately connected with the peace, order, and happiness of the state to be abandoned.[4]

In taking this position, Ellsworth spoke for the New England way (not including Rhode Island). That region had been settled by Calvinist dissenters committed to establishing communities based on a common faith, and the ideal was hard to give up, even in attenuated form. New Englanders were entitled to regard the First Amendment as a victory because, by forbidding Congress to make any law "respecting" a religious establishment, it permitted them to keep their religious quasi-establishments. Indeed, Thomas Jefferson wrote his famous line about the importance of creating a "wall of separation between church and state" the same year as the Ellsworth report, in response to a letter from a group of Baptists in Danbury, Connecticut; but both he and the Baptists acknowledged that the federal government had no power to overturn state law in this regard. Connecticut held on to its Congregationalist Standing Order until 1818, while Massachusetts maintained its requirement that all citizens belong to a church until 1833. Yet if Ellsworth's argument for direct government support of religion eventually failed even in New England, his belief in the civic need for religion came to be widely shared.

By the mid-1790s, the fashion for keeping religion well away from the affairs of state was beginning to change. In 1795, for example, one of the commencement orations at Dickinson College in Pennsylvania was entitled, "The Necessity of Religion for the Support of the Civil Government."[5] And then there were these famous sentences from Washington's Farewell Address, published in September of 1796:

Of all the dispositions and habits which lead to political prosperity, Religion and morality are indispensable supports. In vain would that man claim the tribute of Patriotism, who should labour to subvert these great

Pillars of human happiness, these firmest props of the duties of Men & citizens. The mere Politician, equally with the pious man ought to respect and to cherish them.[6]

What had happened to bring about the change of perspective? In three words: The French Revolution. When Washington asked, again in the Farewell Address, who could "look with indifference upon attempts to shake the foundation of the fabric" of free government, the foundation he had in mind was religion, and the attempts were those of Jacobin France.[7] A few years later, in her history of the American Revolution, Mercy Warren took great pains to demonstrate that the "skepticism and the late appearance of a total disregard to religious observances in France" had in no way resulted from "the democratic struggles of the nation."[8] Having done away with religion as a legal buttress to the state, Americans of the revolutionary generation felt they may have sowed the whirlwind, and not only in the streets of Paris.

By the 1810s, Christianity as a general proposition had come to be widely regarded as a necessary undergirding of the American thing. The "general Principles, on which the Fathers achieved Independence," John Adams wrote to Thomas Jefferson in 1813, were "the general Principles of Christianity" and "the general Principles of English and American Liberty."[9] The legal historian Sarah Gordon has traced what she calls "the de facto establishment of 'general' Christianity" and how it became embedded in nineteenth century jurisprudence.[10] Beginning with *People v. Ruggles* in New York in 1811, American courts undertook to uphold religion in order to support the civil order, in this case finding individuals guilty of blasphemy on the theory that Christianity was protected by the common law inherited from England—and that protecting the local religion had always been deemed essential to the law. As the Supreme Court of Pennsylvania put it in the 1824 *Updegraph* case, "Christianity, general Christianity, is, and always has been, a part of the common law of *Pennsylvania*; Christianity, without the spiritual artillery of *European* countries . . . not Christianity with an established church, and tithes, and spiritual courts; but Christianity with liberty of conscience to all men." The point can be underscored by way of an 1833 sermon by the Rev. Jasper Adams of Charleston, South Carolina, that was widely circulated and commented upon. "[W]hile all others enjoy full protection in the profession of their opinions and practice," wrote Adams, "Christianity is the established religion of the nation, its institutions and usages are sustained by legal sanctions, and many of them are incorporated with the fundamental law of the country."[11]

What General Christianity meant was Protestant Christianity—not the Protestantism of any particular sect but a pan-Protestantism that encompassed the diverse religious commitments, real or nominal, of the large majority of Americans in the early years of the republic. As an ideology, there was something to be said for it. This was the era of the spiritual efflorescence known as the Second Great Awakening, when revivalist Protestantism established itself as the dominant religious form in a population rolling westward to the Mississippi and beyond. Warring and competing sects there were, including many newly invented ones, but most marched under an optimistic, enthusiastic Protestant banner. The degree to which it covered up profound differences of worldview only became evident during the Civil War, which (among other things) set two profoundly different conceptions of the religious order against each other. The contest between Southern and Northern religious ideologies, both based in evangelical Protestantism, is the most powerful argument there is for taking region into account as a basis for competing religious worldviews in American history.

Quite aside from the sectional Protestant divide, by the Civil War pan-Protestantism had begun to shift from an ideological umbrella covering most Americans to a shield wielded against a tide of non-Protestant immigrants, beginning with the Irish Catholics fleeing the Potato Famine of the 1840s. From the Know-Nothing party through state legal battles over the use of the King James Bible in the public schools to Prohibition and the defeat of Democratic presidential candidate Al Smith in 1928, Roman Catholicism was kept at bay from the Christianity that was Adams' established religion of the nation. That non-Protestant religious groupings, including Jews, enjoyed "full protection in the profession of their opinions and practice" was only true up to a point, as the suppression of Mormon polygamy made clear.[12] The last hurrah of pan-Protestantism in American society was Prohibition—the culmination of decades of agitation against alcohol by a broad phalanx of Protestant reformers that, in the end, amounted to a campaign against Roman Catholic influence on the culture.

But even apart from the restrictions imposed upon those groups that departed from conventional American mores, it was the case that, through World War II, non-Protestants remained outside the de facto American religious establishment, relegated to the tier of those who were supposed to know their place. In the regions of the northeast and Midwest, the division was expressed in voting behavior. White Protestants were for the most part Republicans; the Episcopal Church was, so the quip went, the Republican Party at prayer. Catholics and, increasingly, Jews and African American Protestants, found their home in the Democratic Party. (Because of the legacy of the Civil War, white Protestants in the South maintained a solid Democratic allegiance, nationally as well as regionally, until the national party's support for civil rights weakened their ties to the heirs of Jefferson and Jackson.) Thus it was that the New Deal coalition that bestrode American political life in the middle of the twentieth century gave the lie to pan-Protestantism as a national religious ideology.

POSTWAR DISPENSATIONS

As late as 1931, U.S. Supreme Court Justice George Sutherland could write, in the majority opinion of *United State v. Macintosh*, "We are a Christian people." By the end of World War II, that had become too narrow a term to use in American public discourse. As we have seen, the Middle Atlantic was the source of the new ideological construct for the postwar era: Americans were now a Judeo-Christian people. The "Judeo-Christian" locution had been deployed on the eve of World War II by liberals as a rhetorical means of protecting Jews in a world where virulent anti-Semitism was rife and where Fascists and their sympathizers had adopted "Christian" as an identifying term. Now, in the postwar world, "Judeo-Christian" served to designate the common religious commitment of Americans against the "atheistic Communists" on the other side of the Cold War. Thus did the president of the Military Chaplains Association of the United States, Daniel Poling, address his organization's annual convention in 1952 with the words, "We meet at a time when the Judeo-Christian faith is challenged as never before in all the years since Abraham left Ur of the Chaldees." Or, as J. B. Matthews, executive director of Senator Joseph McCarthy's Permanent Sub-Committee on Investigations, put it the following year, the Communist conspiracy was aiming "at the total obliteration of Judeo-Christian civilization."[13]

What stood behind the Judeo-Christian rhetoric was, or seemed at the time to be, a population categorized by the title of Will Herberg's book: *Protestant-Catholic-Jew*. Although Herberg himself acknowledged that there were some who didn't fall into one of the categories—the Eastern Orthodox, for example—they did not, in his view, amount to much: "America today may be conceived, as it is indeed conceived by most Americans, as one great community divided in three big sub-communities religiously defined, all equally American in their identification with the 'American Way of Life.'"[14] Did most Americans actually conceive of their country in that way? Certainly there were large parts of the United States where the tripartite schema bore little or no relationship to the situation on the ground. The fact that *Protestant-Catholic-Jew* came to define religious pluralism in the postwar period testifies to the willingness of the rest of the country to acquiesce to Middle Atlantic religious preeminence. The ecumenical movement headed by the mainline

Protestant-dominated National Council of Churches was at the height of its powers, ensconced in its new headquarters on the upper west side of Manhattan. Across town, St. Patrick's amounted to the Vatican of American Catholicism. And nowhere in the country were Jews so plentiful or their influence stronger than in Gotham.

Yet insularity and prejudice were still important features of the religious scene in postwar America. American Protestantism, especially in its upper reaches, retained considerable barriers against entry, from restrictive covenants in housing subdivisions to formal and informal exclusions from boardrooms and clubs. Catholicism was still closely tied to the urban immigrant experience, and in the years prior to the Second Vatican Council maintained much of the defensive posture against the modern world that it had embraced in the nineteenth century. As for the Jews, even as they streamed for the suburbs, they remained a people apart. So the Middle Atlantic model of distinct ethnoreligious communities minding their own business in reasonable harmony with each other was plausible and even compelling. In the 1950s, what it provided was an appealing image of the several separate but equal tribes of American religion pulling together against the common Communist foe.

But the 1960 presidential election demanded something more thoroughgoing in the way of effacing the history of pan-Protestant cultural hegemony. Notwithstanding the Catholic Church's demonstration of its Americanism by vigorous anti-Communism, the ghost of anti-Catholic prejudice had still not been laid and John F. Kennedy knew what he was up against when he became the Democratic Party's standard-bearer. In his most famous pronouncement of the campaign, he told the assembled Protestant ministers of Houston, "I believe in an America where the separation of church and state is absolute—where no Catholic prelate would tell the President (should he be Catholic) how to act, and no Protestant minister would tell his parishioners for whom to vote." Yet these were not only the words of a Roman Catholic who needed to put Protestant fears to rest or, for that matter, of an urbane, rather religiously indifferent man who just wanted to get on with the business of becoming president. They were words that expressed the hard-won New England view that religion should be kept clear of the political fray, that the civic order functions best when religion is confined to the private sphere of individuals and faith communities.

It might be a coincidence that Thomas Jefferson advanced his notion of a wall of separation in a letter to Baptists in Connecticut, but New England is where the wall has proven most congenial and robust to the present day—as witness the discomfort of New England politicians like Howard Dean and John Kerry in discussing their religious views during the 2004 election cycle.

In a recent study of JFK and Catholicism, Thomas J. Carty suggests that Kennedy's religion should never have been any kind of political issue, and that religion is best kept out of politics altogether except perhaps when it comes to some quiet lobbying behind the scenes by the ecclesiastical powers that be. That this perspective emanated from Carty's own roots in New England Catholicism is clear from the book's Acknowledgments: "My maternal grandfather, James B. Murphy, discouraged me from discussing religion and politics in public," Carty begins, and concludes by expressing the hope that his young daughter "listens when I tell her not to discuss religion and politics in public!"[15]

In the country at large, the ideology of church-state separationism in fact reached its high-water mark during the Kennedy era. It was emblemized in the Supreme Court's decisions banning prayer and Bible reading in the public schools—*Engle v. Vitale* (1962) and *Abington Township v. Schempp* (1963). The manifesto for the era was *The Secular City* by Harvey Cox, a young assistant professor of theology and culture at Andover Newton Theological School (soon to make his way to the Harvard Divinity School). Written in the elegiac afterglow of the Kennedy presidency, the book celebrated JFK as the avatar of the pragmatic urban reformer. The desacralization of public life, in Cox's view a splendid thing, did not mean that individuals had to let their religious commitments go by the board. On the contrary, these commitments enjoyed ever more protection—as in the Supreme Court's 1963 decision in *Sherbert v. Verner* (1963) guaranteeing state unemployment benefits to a Seventh Day Adventist who lost her job because she refused to work on her Sabbath. It was the private conscience over the religious collective that was privileged under the New England dispensation. One could be forgiven for seeing this as a harking back to the spiritual individualism of the nineteenth century New England Transcendentalists.

But even amidst the ascendency of the New England way, religion as collective public action was gathering strength more forcibly than had been felt in American domestic politics since the war for Prohibition. The gathering strength of the civil rights movement, led by black Southern clergy, brought to bear on the nation's most pressing problem the African American vision of a new South, a new America, that could redeem the promise of liberty for all. In due course, Martin Luther King, Jr.'s famous enunciation of that millennial vision, his "I have a Dream Speech" from the Lincoln Memorial, became a constituent part of the national civil religion. That this was a religiously inclusive vision in the postwar sense is clear from King's next best-known utterance, the *Letter from the Birmingham Jail*, which was provoked by a public statement from eight Alabama clergymen who were themselves Protestant, Catholic, and Jewish. The tri-faith clergy criticized King's latest campaign against segregation as "unwise and untimely"; King responded that rather than defend the status quo, what was needed was the prophetic witness common to all three traditions. The South, he wrote, would one day know that those who had demonstrated at lunch counters "were in reality standing up for what is best in the American dream and for the most sacred values in our Judaeo-Christian heritage."[16]

It was a different species of millennialism that awaited the country at the end of the decade—one that emerged from the fluid spiritual environment of the Pacific. Hippie culture was spawned in San Francisco and a glance at the important figures and writings of that era shows how important California was to the moment. Intellectual gurus of the time included Norman O. Brown at the University of California at Santa Cruz (*Life Against Death*), Theodore Roszak of the California State University at Hayward (*The Making of the Counter Culture*), San Francisco Buddhist beat poet Gary Snyder, and Los Angeles-based author Carlos Castaneda (*The Teachings of Don Juan*), to name a few. The most famous, or notorious, centers for spiritual learning were likewise California-based, including Synanon in Santa Monica and the Esalen Institute in Big Sur. By the 1970s, a sense that New Age spirituality was the order of the day had begun to sink into American culture at large. Spreading out from the Pacific, its influence filtered almost imperceptibly over the entire map of American religion, creating the sense that the United States was now peopled by an increasingly deinstitutionalized aggregation of seekers, spiritual but not religious, suiting their individual needs by mixing and matching traditions in the great cafeteria of faith. After a postwar pluralism of distinct communities, a New Frontier pluralism of individual faith commitments in a secular public square, and a collective prophetic religion on the march, the Pacific's New Age postulated a pluralism of the self that subsisted within all Americans, each of whom contained spiritual multitudes.

The image of American religion cut loose from traditional institutional moorings was shaped in the 1970s by the national preoccupation with cults. Attachment to these New Religious Movements (as the religion scholars called them) was hardly restricted to the environs of California; the efflorescence of communal religious life could be found across rural and urban America. What the phenomenon seemed to express, however, was the spiritual rootlessness and the liberation from moral restraints emblemized by the Pacific region. And long after the era of sex, drugs, and rock 'n' roll had passed, the Pacific construal of contemporary American religion continued to hold sway. It was part and parcel of a constructed portrait of an America where people were free to create their own "lifestyles." It stood for "the Sixties"—a cultural watershed that continued to resonate in the nation's public culture into the twenty-first century.

The emergence of the religious right at the end of the 1970s was, in an important sense, a regional response to the Pacific New Age. Inspired by the activist example of black Southern church leaders, white Southern evangelicals took up arms against changes in the national culture that seemed to threaten their way of life. While the banning of school prayer and the allowance of abortion may not have conjured up images of California, the preeminent lifestyle issue in the culture wars—"the gay lifestyle"—seemed to have its epicenter in San Francisco. More broadly, the culture war that cast its shadow over American society from the 1970s into the new millennium centered on the goal of preserving "traditional family values" against the values that seemed to emanate from the hot tubs and gay bars, the ashrams and gaming palaces of the Pacific. It was not in his native north Louisiana but in southern California that James Dobson wrote the childrearing manual, *Dare to Discipline*, that sounded the clarion against permissive parenting in 1970.

The regional counterstroke to "the Sixties" embodied some tension between the harmonial vision of community characteristic of the South and the showdown culture of the Southern Crossroads. It began, in a sense, with Jimmy Carter, whose born-again identity, shocking as it was to the secular media elite, drew a wide spectrum of evangelical support in the 1976 campaign, ranging from Pat Robertson to Jesse Jackson. Coming along in the wake of Watergate, Carter sought to be a transformative figure of national reconciliation, but by the end of his term, conservative white evangelicals turned their backs on him, and in 1980 embraced culture war as their preferred politics. In August of that year, the two kinds of regional response were also on view when, during the birthing of the national religious right at the National Affairs Briefing in Dallas, Bailey Smith, pastor of First Baptist Church in Del City, Oklahoma, and the newly elected president of the Southern Baptist Convention, let drop the remark that "God does not hear the prayer of a Jew." Amidst a firestorm of controversy, it was left to Virginia's Jerry Falwell to patch things up with the Jewish community. At a meeting with Marc Tannenbaum, director of Interreligious Affairs for the American Jewish Committee in New York, Falwell devised a statement asserting that God "loves everyone alike" and "hears the cry of any sincere person who calls on Him"—and summoning Americans of all faiths "to rise above every effort to polarize us in our efforts to return this nation to a commitment to the moral principles on which America was built." Smith, by contrast, stuck to his theological guns, receiving a standing ovation from the Conference of Southern Baptist Evangelists the following June when he declared, "If the Bible says it, it is true, and you should tell it," and noting that while he loved the Jewish people, "unless they repent and get born again, they are in trouble."[17]

Falwell's Moral Majority, which headlined the religious right through the 1980s, sought to create at least the appearance of spiritual inclusivity. And into the 1990s, this ideal could be found at the national level in organizations like Promise Keepers—albeit the soft patriarchy and commitment to racial reconciliation of that movement was often misinterpreted outside the evangelical world as a disguise for political activism. The misinterpretation was understandable because the decade witnessed the accession of harder-edged culture-warriors. Emblematic of the transition was the passing of the baton for organizational preeminence from the Moral Majority to Pat Robertson's Christian Coalition. To be sure, Robertson and Ralph Reed, the Coalition's moving personalities, were both from the South (Virginia and Georgia, respectively), as was Newt Gingrich, Republican of Georgia, who became speaker after the GOP captured control of the House of Representatives in the 1994 election. But, increasingly, power within the movement passed to Louisiana native James Dobson and, in Congress, to Texas' Tom DeLay, who became majority whip after the 1994 takeover and was the driving force behind the impeachment of President Clinton in 1998. The impeachment had all the trappings of a Southern Crossroads morality play featuring special prosecutor Kenneth Starr, a Restorationist (Church of Christ) Savonarola out of west Texas, in hot pursuit of Bill Clinton, the kind of Arkansas Baptist who knocks up your sister and still your momma's sweet on him. In the sequel, the reins of the national government passed to the likes of the Southern Crossroads' John Ashcroft, Tom DeLay, Dick Cheney, and above them all, George W. Bush.

As his presidential administration opened, Bush, who famously named Christ as his favorite philosopher, seemed attached to the kind of social philosophy that animated evangelical reformers of the nineteenth century: Bring individuals to Christ, change their hearts, and society will change with them. Indeed, the only policy Bush seemed to have a personal stake in when he assumed office was his faith-based initiative, which aimed to make it possible for religious organizations to obtain public money to provide social services without hiding their spiritual light under a bushel. But presidential discourse drew heavily on the confrontational style of the Crossroads generally and, in particular, expressed a latter-day version of J. R. Graves' Christian republicanism, which had sought to transform society by any means necessary. While many of Bush's supporters on the religious right looked askance at the government entanglements this seemed to invite, the president was unperturbed. Like his forebears in the perfectionist tradition, he seemed to believe that the state could only profit from the ministrations of the church, and that neither was a threat to the other. It was after the September 11 attacks, however, that

Gravesian republicanism fully reemerged, as the president repeatedly declared his intention of bringing God's gift of liberty to the unfree peoples of the world. Of course, there also seemed to be something personal about his determination to invade Iraq, since he was not above noting that Saddam Hussein had once tried to kill his father. As he put it with typical Crossroads pugnacity at a news conference on July 2, 2003, "There are some who feel like that, you know, the conditions are such that they can attack us there. My answer is bring them on."

Among the broader cultural consequences of 9/11 was a turning away from the sense that "do your own thing" religion, Pacific style, had become normative in American society. The emblem of this shift was "the American Taliban," John Walker Lindh. Born in Washington, D.C., in 1981, Lindh was the middle child of three in an apparently unremarkable American family. His father worked as a lawyer for the U.S. Department of Justice while his mother was a home healthcare aide. The family moved to Marin County north of San Francisco in 1991, where Lindh went to an independent high school for self-directed learners before converting to Islam and dropping out at 16. He joined a mosque in San Francisco and changed his name to Suleyman al-Lindh and then to Suleyman al-Faris. The conversion came as a shock to his parents but being religiously diverse themselves—father Catholic, mother a converted Buddhist—they soon accepted his choice. Late in 1998, he traveled to Yemen to study at the Yemeni Language Institute for a year, returned to Yemen in February of 2000, and later that year went to Pakistan. There he enrolled in a fundamentalist *madrasa*, or religious school, from which he proceeded to Afghanistan, training with al Qaeda and fighting with the Taliban against the Indians in Kashmir.

As eager as Americans were to condemn Lindh, they also sought an explanation for his choices—and found it in the Marin County lifestyle. One of the first CNN reports about him, aired on December 3, mentioned his teenage home as "a liberal area . . . where residents would be more likely to bear Birkenstocks than bear arms." Shelby Steele wrote in the December 10, 2002, *Wall Street Journal* that Marin's "post-'60s cultural liberalism" allowed a place where "traditional American history, culture and religion are without any special authority." Jeff Jacoby of the *Boston Globe* charged on December 16 that, "if [Lindh's parents] had been less concerned with flaunting their open-mindedness and more concerned with developing their son's moral judgment, he wouldn't be where he is today. His road to treason and *jihad* didn't begin in Afghanistan. It began in Marin County, with parents who never said 'no.'" Even former President George H. W. Bush was "so offended by John Lindh" that he called him a "misguided Marin County hot-tubber," the Associated Press reported January 25. The same day, Peter Fimrite of the

San Francisco Chronicle proclaimed, "[T]he courtroom of public opinion has already reached a verdict on Marin County."[18]

In the wake of 9/11, the Southern Crossroads style came into its own, with religious conservatives leading the way. It was, to a degree, a return to the era of the Cold War, with atheistic communism now replaced by militant Islam—or Islamofascism, as some of the tougher-minded ideologues preferred to call it. To its credit, the administration took an early stand against treating all Muslims as the enemy, President Bush famously referring to Islam as a "religion of peace" and regularly welcoming Muslim leaders to the White House. So while some stridently anti-Islamic voices were to be heard, and some ratcheting up of hostility to Islam registered in the polls, Americans by and large declined to construe the "War on Terror" as an out-and-out war of religion. The real divide was domestic and there the image of the American spiritual cafeteria gave way to a portrait of a society bifurcated into "people of faith"—Christians and Jews and others too—and those without faith or much of it. The bifurcation took on a strongly partisan cast, with the GOP styled as the party of the religious and the Democrats as the party of the secular. Survey data did in fact indicate a marked preference on the part of more religiously observant Americans for Republicans, and no less of a preference among the least religious for the Democrats. This tendency had begun to manifest itself as far back as the 1970s but it did not become pronounced until the 1990s. By the 2000 election, exit polls showed that 60 percent of frequent worship attenders (those who said they attended worship once a week or more) were voting Republican in presidential and congressional contests. The significance of the religious divide was recognizably geographical—driven home by the ubiquitous red state/blue state maps that supplied visual evidence of the ancient division of the country into churchgoing (rural) heartland and secular (urban) coasts. By the 2004 election cycle, the "God gap" had become conventional wisdom, thanks to widespread media attention.[19]

REGION AND NATIONAL VOTING

In November of 2004, as is customary in the wake of a national election, journalists rushed onto the field of battle while the smoke was still clearing to search out the meaning of it all. What greeted them was a national exit poll showing that, by a small plurality, "moral values" was "the one issue that mattered most" to Americans voting for president. This datum seemed to fit the red state/blue state maps, suggesting that once again the country had narrowly picked the conservative side in a geographically organized culture war.

"Take an afternoon off for recriminations, a morning for whining, then race through the Kubler-Ross stages of grief and get back to work," wrote *Boston Globe* syndicated columnist Ellen Goodman on November 6. "Job No. 1: moral values." After an initial avalanche of like-minded commentary emphasizing the crucial impact of moral-values voters, however, the small size of their actual plurality began to register. The best measure of the exit poll data shows that 23.7 percent of voters selected moral values as their most important issue, just ahead of the 21.1 percent who selected "the economy and jobs"; who in turn barely beat out the 20.3 percent who named "terrorism"; who were themselves not far in front of the 15.7 percent who pointed to "Iraq." The remaining 19.2 percent gave priority to other economic concerns—health care, taxes, and education.[20]

Almost immediately, a cascade of revisionist punditry declared moral values to be a bogus explanation of the reelection of President Bush. Whatever the two words meant—and couldn't they mean different things to different people?—the exit poll numbers showed that the American electorate in 2004 had diverse issue priorities. Religious conservatives, so the new interpretation went, played a less central role in Bush's victory than first advertised—and perhaps a very modest one. As *Washington Post* columnist E. J. Dionne put it on November 9, "John Kerry was not defeated by the religious right. He was beaten by moderates who went—reluctantly in many cases—for President Bush." Although the revisionist line had something to be said for it, like the original interpretation it erred in seeking a single phenomenon to explain, across the board, the presidential result. In order to make proper sense of the survey, what was required was a regional analysis, for Americans in some regions selected moral values in much higher proportions than those in other places. And what this analysis showed was that moral values voters were more important to the president's victory than the national totals implied.

As table 1 shows, President Bush and his Democratic challenger, Senator John Kerry, each won four regions of the country. Bush carried the Southern Crossroads, Mountain West, and South handily and just squeaked by in the Midwest. Meanwhile, Kerry won big in the Pacific, Middle Atlantic, and New England, and prevailed narrowly in the Pacific Northwest.

The second column of table 1 shows that one-quarter or more of the electorate in each of the Bush regions cited moral values as the issue that mattered most, outstripping the aggregate national figure. By contrast, less than one-quarter did in each of the Kerry regions.[21] Simply put, moral values came in first place in all four of Bush's regions, and in none of Kerry's. Nationally, more than four out of five moral values voters cast their ballots for the president, a pattern with only modest variation by region. These voters accounted

Table 1.   Region, the Bush vote, and Moral Values Voters

Region	Bush Vote	% Moral Values Voters	% Bush Vote from Moral Values	% Total Vote from Bush Moral Values Voters
Bush Won				
Southern Crossroads	61.5	27.2	39.5	25.6
Mountain West	58.1	35.4	45.9	27.8
South	55.9	25.2	39.7	21.8
Midwest	51.2	25.7	42.0	21.8
National	**51.1**	**23.7**	**37.4**	**19.2**
Kerry Won				
Pacific Northwest	48.1	19.1	29.9	13.5
Pacific	45.4	19.8	27.6	12.6
Middle Atlantic	44.2	16.7	27.9	11.5
New England	41.4	22.5	35.5	15.3

for 37 percent of total Bush support nationwide (third column in table 1) but this proportion varied geographically to a significant degree. In the Bush regions, moral values voters made up two-fifths or more of the president's backers, while in the Kerry regions, they provided less than two-fifths—and in three out of four cases, less than one-third. In other words, the president won where his voters cared most about moral values. The final column in table 1 reports Bush's moral values voters as a percentage of the total vote cast in each region (and not just as a proportion of the Bush vote). This *absolute value* of the president's moral values constituency amounted to more than one-fifth of the vote in the South and Midwest, and more than one-quarter in the Southern Crossroads and Mountain West. But it was much smaller in the Kerry states, ranging from one-sixth to less than one-eighth of the total vote cast.

These are not trivial figures. The 21.8 percent of the vote cast by Bush moral values voters in the Midwest was *ten times* larger than the president's winning margin in that region (about two percent). Just as importantly, this constituency was also larger than his margin of victory in his three strongest regions. By contrast, the Bush moral values constituency was smaller than Kerry's margin of victory in *his* three strongest regions. Only in the Pacific Northwest did this constituency outstrip Kerry's margin—but not by quite enough to put Bush over the top. In sum, the moral values vote was critical to the outcome in every part of the country except for the New England, Middle Atlantic, and Pacific regions.

It is important to recognize that terrorism and the economy, the two issues that rivaled moral values in importance nationally, did not vary nearly as much geographically. Even though economic conditions and the apparent threat from terrorists varied a good deal from region to region, "security moms" were about as likely to vote for Bush in Los Angeles as in Atlanta, and "factory dads" backed Kerry at about the same rate in Pittsburgh and Milwaukee. The one other issue that varied significantly from region to region was Iraq, where the geographic pattern was the opposite of moral values. In the Bush regions, an average of 12 percent named Iraq as the most important issue, while in the Kerry regions the average was 22 percent, led by a large 31 percent in the Pacific Northwest. In nearly inverse proportion to the Bush moral values voters, Iraq voters gave about three-quarters of their ballots to Kerry. So in terms of issues, the picture of the 2004 election was this: terrorism and the economy provided each presidential candidate with a strong and roughly equal voter base across the nation but it was the interplay of moral values and Iraq that made the difference. In all the regions won by Bush, moral values trumped Iraq by margins of 2-to-1 or more, while in the Kerry regions the two issues were closely balanced, except for the Pacific Northwest, where Iraq held a 3-to-2 margin over moral values.

What explains the regional variation in issues priorities? When it came to moral values, religious identity was the primary factor. The first four columns in table 2 report the percentage of the Bush moral values voters in the three largest Christian traditions and in all the other religious groups combined. Nationally, white evangelicals provided 48 percent of the Bush moral values vote, Catholics 19 percent, and mainline Protestants 15 percent (and the other groups the remaining 18 percent). Evangelicals were the backbone of the Bush moral values vote in all regions, with Latter-day Saints (found in the "other" column here) making a significant contribution in the Mountain West and Pacific, and Catholics doing the same in the Middle Atlantic and New England. The final column in table 2 looks at those who say they attend worship regularly—once a week or more—regardless of religious affiliation. Nationally, 71 percent of the Bush moral values voters were regular attenders. These figures were comparable or greater for the Bush regions, and lower for the Kerry regions, but still substantially above 50 percent. Altogether, nearly three times as many selected moral values (35 percent) as selected Iraq (12 percent). Among only those who said they attend worship more than once a week, the numbers were 42 percent and 10 percent, respectively. This basic pattern held across all regions. In short, whatever moral questions were raised by the Iraq war in the 2004 campaign—including, perhaps, the abuse of prisoners—they did not register strongly with the most religious segment of the American electorate.

Table 2.   Region and the Sources of the Bush Moral Values Vote

Region	Evangelicals	Catholics	Mainline Protestants	All Others	Regular Attendees
Bush Won					
Southern Crossroads	51%	14%	15%	20%	71%
Mountain West	33%	8%	5%	54%	82%
South	55%	16%	15%	14%	77%
Midwest	49%	24%	19%	8%	70%
National	**48%**	**19%**	**15%**	**18%**	**71%**
Kerry Won					
Pacific Northwest	55%	3%	12%	30%	71%
Pacific	38%	14%	13%	35%	64%
Middle Atlantic	39%	33%	13%	15%	65%
New England	48%	21%	17%	14%	58%

Table 3 is concerned with the electoral bottom line: the number of Bush moral values voters provided by these religious categories as a percentage of the total vote on a region-by-region basis. In the Bush regions, the contribution from evangelicals averaged 11 percent, while in the Kerry regions it averaged six percent. This roughly 2-to-1 ratio applied among mainliners (average of 3.2 percent versus 1.8 percent) and "others" (average of 6.3 percent to 3.1 percent). Only the Catholic moral values voters didn't fit the pattern. They supplied about as large a proportion of the Bush moral values vote as they did in New England and the Middle Atlantic. They made the biggest contribution in the Midwest (5.1 percent) and virtually none at all in the Pacific Northwest (0.2 percent). In the South and Southern Crossroads they supplied about as large a proportion of the Bush moral values vote as they did in New England and the Middle Atlantic. Looking across the board at regular worship attenders of all religious stripes who selected moral values, these constituted 13.7 percent of the national vote. But in all the Bush regions together, the average contribution was 18.2 percent, while in all the Kerry regions it was 8.5 percent. The bottom line is that the Bush moral values constituency had its biggest impact in those parts of the country where there are the most evangelicals and the largest number of regular attenders (many of whom were, of course, evangelicals).

Altogether, evangelicals were twice as likely as their share of the population to select moral values on the exit poll, and it is not hard to understand why. For years, the evangelical subculture had used both words to characterize its public concerns; "moral" (as in Moral Majority) had been a shibboleth

Table 3. Region and Religion: Bush Moral Values Voters as % of Total Vote

Region	Evangelicals	Catholics	Mainline Attendees	All Others	% Total Voters	Regular Attendees	Less than Regular Attendees
Bush Won							
Southern Crosswords	13.1	3.5	3.9	5.1	25.6	18.2	7.4
Mountain West	9.1	2.3	1.5	14.9	27.8	22.1	5.7
South	12.5	3.5	3.4	3.2	22.6	17.3	5.3
Midwest	10.5	5.1	4.1	2.0	21.8	15.2	6.6
National	**9.2**	**3.6**	**2.9**	**3.5**	**19.2**	**13.7**	**5.5**
Kerry Won							
Pacific Northwest	7.3	0.2	1.6	4.4	13.5	9.6	3.9
Pacific	4.8	1.7	1.6	4.5	12.6	7.9	4.7
Middle Atlantic	4.5	3.8	1.5	1.7	11.5	7.6	3.9
New England	7.4	3.2	2.6	2.1	15.3	8.8	6.5

of the religious right ever since it emerged on the national scene. During the 2004 campaign, the Southern Baptist Convention created a web page that stated the message in no uncertain terms: "What are your core values as we approach Election Day 2004? Would your list include Jobs? The Economy? Health-Care? Education? National Security? As important as those issues are, think about what your core values should be as a follower of Jesus." By contrast, nonevangelical religious communities were far less tied to moral values rhetoric and thus even the most religiously committed among them were less likely to choose that expression as their most important issue on the exit poll. But regional culture mattered: Nonevangelicals were more likely to choose moral values in the Bush regions than in the Kerry regions. As Moral Majority founder Jerry Falwell had originally hoped, the coalition of the moral did extend beyond evangelicals, but more in the evangelical heartland than elsewhere.

Two years later, the American polity seemed to have turned a corner. In the 2006 midterm elections, the preference of frequent worship attenders for the GOP declined for the first time in two decades, shrinking from 20 percentage points, where it had held in congressional voting in 2000, 2002, and 2004, to under 13. No less tellingly, the less observant—those who said they attended worship anywhere from a few times a month to not at all—flocked to support Democratic congressional candidates. Their preference for Democrats doubled twice, from six percentage points in 2002 to over 13 in 2004 and then to more than 25 in 2006—a gap larger than the GOP preference among frequent attenders had ever been. The net result of these two vote differentials was increased polarization of the electorate along religious lines. This could be seen most clearly by comparing the votes of frequent and less frequent attenders for the *same* party over the three elections. Measured this way, the religion gap grew from 13.2 to 16 to 19 percentage points—with most of the growth attributable to the increased preference for Democrats on the part of the less observant. No better index of this trend was the behavior of the most secular segment of the voting public, the religiously unaffiliated, whose preference for Democratic congressional candidates jumped from 61 percent in 2002 to 70.9 percent in 2004 to 75.3 percent in 2006. Overall, the political bottom line for 2006 was that the Republicans acquired a bigger problem with less religious voters than the Democrats had with more religious ones—a sharp reversal of fortunes from 2004.

The shift in partisan fortunes can be seen in regional voting patterns. In 2004, each party carried the same four regions in the aggregate congressional vote as it did in the presidential vote. But two years later, the Democrats carried six regions and came within four-tenths of a percentage point of carrying a seventh—the Mountain West. The only region that went solidly for the

GOP was the Southern Crossroads, where Republican congressional candidates actually increased their proportion of the vote over 2004. As recently as 2002, congressional voting in the Crossroads had broken slightly in favor of the Democrats, by a margin of 50.2 percent to 49.8 percent. Then, in 2004, the Democratic congressional vote total dropped to 42.4 percent and, in 2006, to 40.3 percent. Why?

The explanation may have something to do with the extent to which Crossroads voters persisted in casting their ballots on the basis of social issues. By a small margin, more respondents in the Crossroads cited "values" as "extremely important" to their vote in 2006 than in any other region—as compared to 2004, where the Crossroads fell well behind the Mountain West in the proportion of voters identifying moral values as the most important issue. Beyond that, it is possible that the 2006 vote reflected a stubborn defense of President Bush in his native Texas, where more than half the region's population lives. Meanwhile, Hurricane Katrina, having depleted New Orleans of a significant portion of its black population, shrunk Democratic totals in Louisiana. Politically, the Southern Crossroads (or much of it) appeared to be realigning with the Republicans at a time when the rest of the country was going in the opposite direction. In the wider world of ideology and worldview, the Crossroads—the country's most heavily churched region—had ceased to be the leading edge of the national culture. Throughout George W. Bush's first term, annual Gallup surveys found that there were more Americans who thought organized religion should have greater influence in the nation than who thought it should have less. From 2005 through 2007, however, it had been the other way around. As George W. Bush prepared to ride off into the sunset, the country seemed prepared for a new religious dispensation.[22]

WHAT'S NEXT?

The 2006 election shifted the country's religious politics in two ways. It unsettled the Republican Party's quarter-century long embrace of an ever more religious public square while at the same time impelling the Democratic Party to make a priority of demonstrating its spiritual bona fides to the electorate. A harbinger of the former came in the person of David Kuo, sometime deputy director of the White House Office of Faith-Based and Community Initiatives, whose tell-all book, *Tempting Faith*, created a stir just prior to the election. In a *New York Times* op-ed, November 16, 2006, Kuo harked back to the old Southern emphasis on the "spirituality of the church" by quoting some lines of John W. Whitehead of the Rutherford Institute, a conservative Christian organization based in Charlottesville, Virginia. "Modern Christianity, having lost sight of Christ's teachings, has been co-opted by legalism, materialism and politics," Whitehead wrote on the Institute's website. "Simply put, it has lost its spirituality. Whereas Christianity was once synonymous with charity, compassion and love for one's neighbor, today it is more often equated with partisan politics, antihomosexual rhetoric and affluent megachurches."

What sent the GOP into a tizzy, however, was the way religion threatened to upset its prospects in the next presidential campaign. The candidate who emerged as the evangelical champion, former Arkansas governor Mike Huckabee, was, thanks to his Missionary Baptist roots, something of an economic populist who sent the party's economic conservatives around the bend.[23] Far more acceptable to them was Mitt Romney, but his Mormonism proved difficult to stomach for the evangelicals, who for years had been encouraged to believe in the desirability of a "Christian" president. It began to dawn on GOP leaders that the party's de facto religious test for office might have a downside. The new mantra of leading Republican figures, clerical and lay, was that the country was electing "a president, not a pastor."

For its part, the Democratic Party did not miss the significance of the religiously inflected campaigns of its victorious candidates for governor and senator in Ohio, which resolved disagreements about the wisdom of putting faith to work on the stump. The Democratic National Committee staffed up with people who knew their way around a prayer book, and looked for places to encourage faith-based candidacies. One such was the 2007 Mississippi gubernatorial race, in which a pious Southern Baptist named John Arthur Eaves, Jr., gave the GOP incumbent, former D.C. lobbyist Haley Barbour, a run for his money by promising to throw the moneychangers out of the Temple. The CEO for the Democratic National Convention was Leah Daughtry, an ordained Pentecostal minister who presided over a "faith council" whose job it was to reach out to a wide range of religious leaders. Party chair Howard Dean himself made a point of meeting privately with clergy on his travels around the country—including even the likes of Richard Land, chief politico for the Southern Baptist Convention. "In the past, we've come off as dismissive to evangelicals," Dean told *Newsweek* in an October 1, 2007, interview. "But our party has become much more comfortable talking about faith and values."

If, as it had in the past, the nation were to look to regional models in constructing a new religious regime, there were several untried options that seemed to meet the needs of the time. In an increasingly diverse and religiously polarized nation, the three subregions and numerous widely separated enclaves of the Mountain West offered Americans an archipelago of spiritual diversity. In Colorado alone, there was the shamanic yin of Boulder to the evangelical yang of Colorado Springs. The southern tier was pulling apart, with New Mexico cleaving to its Catholic roots and Arizona, led by Phoenix, trending toward southern California-style diversity. As ever, the Mormon corridor of Utah and southern Idaho maintained its distinctive ethos, even as Montana and Wyoming maintained to their historical, substantially unchurched, identities.

Widely diversified, embracing everything from a live-and-let-live sensibility to hegemonic designs on the culture as a whole, the Mountain West let each spiritual community stake out whatever turf it could claim and hold. Contests to expand one's territory, often conceived in sacred terms, there would be. But writ large for the nation as a whole, the region advanced the concept of a country of widely disparate values and ideals, coexisting more by necessity than commitment to a common cause. Its secular shibboleth was federalism, an ideological construct that had gathered force in the 1990s as a pet project of Supreme Court Justice (and Arizona native) Sandra Day O'Connor. To be sure, federalism retreated after the attacks of 9/11 and undivided Republican government made a more unified American project the order of the day. But with the return of divided government in Washington, there was a possibility that state and regional self-determination might resume their upward course, making the religious pluralism of the Mountain West an increasingly attractive option for a nation growing more religiously disparate—and, perhaps, more polarized.

Another option was suggested by the Pacific Northwest. With the ascension of global warming to a prominent place on the national policy agenda, that region's environmentalist civil religion offered a spiritual ethos of widening appeal. In a country where powerful, centralized religious leadership seemed unlikely to return, why not embrace the Northwest's longstanding commitment to the idea that religious leaders need to combine forces across sectarian lines in order to make anything happen? If interfaith action were due for a national revival, then the region's ability to bring together those lacking formal religious ties with its own establishment (of Catholics and mainline Protestants and much of the Jewish community) provided a model that might advance the cause of a progressive public agenda. In such a context, conservative evangelicals would become, in the nation as they were in the Pacific Northwest, the recognized counterculture, hewing to their dominant commitment to the saving of souls.

Yet in the repertoire of regions, perhaps the most likely source of a new religious regime lay in the Midwest. That would signify the closest thing to a return to the Middle Atlantic style that characterized the postwar period— but with a less "ethnic" emphasis on ascribed identity, a greater place for the evangelical voice that had returned with such vigor in American society, and a greater emphasis on the common good, on the values of community. The Midwest's Methodist DNA, emphasizing personal spiritual discipline (as the more conservative evangelical denominations do) and social reform (as the rest of the liberal mainline denominations do), was well-calibrated to a society that seemed anxious to combine moderately conservative views on social issues like abortion, school prayer, pornography, and the "traditional family" with moderately liberal views on economic issues such as social welfare spending and health care. Hillary Clinton, the Midwestern Methodist, might have been quoting an African proverb when she wrote that it took a village to raise a child, but the values it expressed were very much home grown. To be sure, she was a hybrid character, politically the product of the Southern Crossroads, where she learned the tough ropes as the wife of the governor of Arkansas, and the Middle Atlantic, where she learned to ring the ethnoreligious changes as twice-elected senator. Likewise, Illinois Senator Barack Obama's determination to run for the 2008 Democratic nomination on a platform of bringing people together was very much in keeping with his Midwestern identity—though his own spiritual journey began in the fluid Pacific state of Hawaii, and seemed finally to arrive in the South of Martin Luther King, Jr.

Such hybridity is not out of place, however, because the Midwest is where the country comes together now. It is the place with the largest political deviations—from deep red states like Kansas and Nebraska to the deep-blue state of Illinois to the swingiest of swing states—Ohio, Michigan, Wisconsin, and Iowa. Although it is far from the most religiously diverse region, it is the one where the country's main religious players all have strong hands to play. Evangelical Protestants are a powerful and growing presence but nowhere does the Protestant mainline retain so much of its historic strength and influence. For their part, Catholics are as well-represented there as they are in the country as a whole and Jews are big players in the region's big metropolitan areas. Nor does it seem entirely accidental that the first Muslim member of Congress should come from the Midwest. In 2006, Keith Ellison, who converted to Islam as a 19-year-old in his native Detroit, won in the fifth district of Minnesota (Minneapolis and St. Paul) on a strong antiwar platform. "We were able to bring in Muslims, Christians, Jews, Buddhists," Ellison said after the election. "We brought in everybody." If there is to be a new style of religious pluralism in America, there is something to be said for having it emerge from the Midwest.

Appendix

$\mathcal{I}$n order to provide the best possible empirical basis for understanding the place of religion in each of the regions of the United States, the Religion by Region project contracted to obtain data from three sources: the *North American Religion Atlas* (NARA); the 2001 *American Religious Identification Survey* (ARIS); and the 1992, 1996, and 2000 *National Surveys of Religion and Politics* (NSRP).

NARA. For the project, the Polis Center of Indiana University-Purdue University at Indianapolis created an interactive Web site that made it possible to map general demographic and religious data at the national, regional, state-by-state, and county-by-county level. The demographic data were taken from the 2000 U.S. Census. The primary source for the religious data (congregations, members, and adherents) was the 2000 *Religious Congregations and Membership Survey* (RCMC) compiled by the Glenmary Research Center. Because a number of religious groups did not participate in the 2000 RCMS—including most historically African American Protestant denominations—this dataset was supplemented with data from other sources for adherents only. The latter included projections from 1990 RCMC reports, ARIS, and several custom estimates. For a fuller methodological account, go to www.religionatlas.org.

ARIS. *The American Religious Identification Survey* (ARIS 2001), carried out under the auspices of the Graduate Center of the City University of New York by Barry A. Kosmin, Egon Mayer, and Ariela Keysar, replicates the methodology of the *National Survey of Religious Identification* (NSRI 1990). As in 1990, the ARIS sample is based on a series of national random digit dialing

(RDD) surveys, utilizing ICR, International Communication Research Group in Media, Pennsylvania, national telephone omnibus services. In all, 50,284 U.S. households were successfully interviewed. Within a household, an adult respondent was chosen using the "last birthday method" of random selection. One of the distinguishing features of both ARIS 2001 and NSRI 1990 is that respondents were asked to describe themselves in terms of religion with an open-ended question: "What is your religion, if any?" ARIS 2001 enhanced the topics covered by adding questions concerning religious beliefs and membership as well as religious switching and religious identification of spouses/partners. The ARIS findings have a high level of statistical significance for most large religious groups and key geographical units, such as states. ARIS 2001's detailed methodology can be found in the report on the *American Religious Identification Survey* 2001 at www.trincoll.edu/Academics/AcademicResources/values/ISSSC/research/ARIS+2001.htm.

NSRP. The *National Surveys of Religion and Politics* were conducted in 1992, 1996, and 2000 at the Bliss Center at the University of Akron under the direction of John C. Green, supported by grants from the Pew Charitable Trusts.

Together, these three surveys include more than 14,000 cases. Eight items were asked in all three surveys (partisanship, ideology, abortion, gay rights, help for minorities, environmental protection, welfare spending, and national health insurance). The responses on these items were pooled for all three years to produce enough cases for an analysis by region. These data must be viewed with some caution because they represent opinion over an entire decade rather than at one point in time. A more detailed account of how these data were compiled may be obtained from the Bliss Institute at www.uakron.edu/bliss.

Notes

PREFACE

1. Jerald C. Brauer, "Religion and Regionalism in America," *Church History* 54, No. 3 (September 1985): 371.

CHAPTER 1

1. For an account of the sources of data used in this volume, see Appendix. For purposes of clarity, "members" or "adherents" refer to people who are actual members of a religious body; those who identify with a religious tradition but are not necessarily members are called "identifiers."

2. The size of this group is obtained by subtracting the number of members of religious bodies from the total population—which means that it includes some people who belong to a religious body whose membership has not, for whatever reason, been tallied.

3. This is an estimate obtained by combining historically white Baptist groups, the historically African American denominations, the Wesleyan/Holiness/Pentecostal groups, and "Other Conservative Christians." The figures for the other regions are 19 percent (Middle Atlantic), 22 percent (Mountain West) 23 percent (Pacific), and 26.6 percent (Midwest).

4. Alaska (like Hawaii) was not included in the ARIS survey, which asked the question, "What is your religion, if any?."

CHAPTER 2

1. Jameson J. Franklin, ed. Narratives of New Netherland, 1609–1664 (New York: 1909), 123–125.

2. Patrick Henry, "'And I Don't Care What It Is': The Tradition-History of a Civil Religion Proof-Text," *Journal of the American Academy of Religion* 49.1 (1981): 41.

3. Will Herberg, *Protestant-Catholic-Jew* (Garden City, NY: Doubleday, 1960 [1955]), 23.

4. Nathan Glazer and Daniel Patrick Moynihan, *Beyond the Melting Pot: The Negroes, Puerto Ricans, Jews, Italians, and Irish of New York City*, second edition (Cambridge: MIT Press, 1970), viii–ix.

5. Andrew Hacker, "Liberal Democracy and Social Control," *American Political Science Review* 51.4 (1957): 1011.

6. Glazer and Moynihan, *Beyond the Melting Pot*, xxxi.

7. Gary Stem, "The Lutheran Minister Suspended for 9/11 Service," *The Journal News*, July 10, 2002 (www.thejournalnews.com/newsroom/071002/10lutheran.html); and Todd Hertz, "Benke Suspended for 'Syncretism' after 9/11 Event," *Christianity Today*, July 29, 2002 (www.christianitytoday.com/ct/2002/129/31.0.html).

8. William Piotrowski, "The Diallo Killings: Sharpton *Ecumenistes*," *Religion in the News* 2.2 (Summer 1999).

9. *Village Voice*, April 6, 1999. Conceived "ethnically," the protests did not seem to represent a "religion story" to New York newspapers, not one of which assigned a religion reporter to cover them. In a subsequent conversation, Gustav Niebuhr, then a religion reporter for the *New York Times*, said it had never occurred to him to write about the Diallo affair.

10. Thomas W. Spalding, "Catholic Church in Maryland," in Michael Glazier and Thomas J. Shelley, eds., *The Encyclopedia of American Catholic History* (Collegeville, MN: The Liturgical Press, 1997), 853.

11. James T. Fisher, *Communion of Immigrants: A History of Catholics in America* (New York: Oxford University Press, 2002), 43.

12. For Shriver, see Scott Stossel, *Sarge: The Life and Times of Sargent Shriver* (Washington, DC: Smithsonian Books, 2004).

13. *The Star-Ledger*, May 9, 2004, and May 20, 2004.

14. Mario Matthew Cuomo, "Religion, Belief, and Public Morality" (delivered September 13, 1984), at www.americanrhetoric.com/speeches/mariocuomoreligiousbeliefs .htm (accessed March 6, 2008)

15. Cited in Jonathan D. Sarna and David G. Dalin, *Religion and State in the American Jewish Experience* (South Bend: University of Notre Dame Press, 1997), 73.

16. *The Jewish Community Study of New York: 2002 Highlights* (New York: UJA-Federation of New York, 2002), 17. A study of the Pittsburgh Jewish community, also conducted in 2002, found that 37 percent of Jews lived in the suburbs. These and other local community studies referred to below are available on the same website as the NJPS, www.jewishdatabank.org/index.cfm.

17. Organizations dedicated to Jewish culture (many of them Holocaust memorials) are spread somewhat more evenly around the country with 39 in the Middle Atlantic region and 19 elsewhere. Still, the Middle Atlantic's preeminence was marked in 2000 by the establishment of the Center for Jewish History, in New York City. Describing itself as the "Jewish Library of Congress," the new center brought together under one roof the American Jewish Historical Society, previously located on the Brandeis University campus near Boston, and four independent New York organiza-

tions: the YIVO Institute for Jewish Research (devoted to the cultural heritage of Yiddish-speaking, east European Jewry), the Leo Baeck Institute (focusing on the history of German Jews), the American Sephardi Federation (dealing with Jewish communities of Iberian origin), and the Yeshiva University Museum.

18. The only major exception—and it certainly is major—is Saul Bellow, the Canada-born Chicagoan who became the first American Jew to win the Nobel Prize for literature.

19. Stephen J. Whitfield, *In Search of American Jewish Culture* (Hanover, NH: University Press of New England [for] Brandeis University Press, 1999), 61.

20. The key institutions of all three are now located in New York City. (Two smaller branches are headquartered in Philadelphia: Reconstructionism, a naturalistic, nontheistic reinterpretation of the Jewish experience, and Jewish Renewal, a nondenominational movement known for its stress on spirituality, music, and meditation.) Reform's Union of American Hebrew Congregations and Central Conference of American Rabbis relocated from Cincinnati to New York in the middle of the twentieth century and the East Coast branch of its seminary, Hebrew Union College, is now more consequential than the Cincinnati campus. The comparable institutions of Conservative Judaism—the United Synagogue, the Rabbinical Assembly, and the Jewish Theological Seminary, were established in New York—the last of these a particular fixture of New York City Jewish life since its founding in 1886. Orthodox Judaism, a more dispersed movement, now comprises three major New York-based synagogue groups: (from left to right) the Union of Orthodox Jewish Congregations of America, the National Council of Young Israel, and Agudath Israel of America. Its most important rabbinical organization is the Rabbinical Council of America and its most important educational institution is Yeshiva University, whose rabbinical seminary, undergraduate colleges, and graduate schools have to a large extent shaped American Orthodox Judaism. The two most important Hasidic groups are based in Brooklyn—Satmar, which has as little as possible to do with other Jews and denies the legitimacy of the secular State of Israel, and Lubavitch, also known as Chabad, which engages in extensive outreach to Jews all over the world and whose continued allegiance to its deceased leader, Rabbi Menachem Mendel Schneerson, has drawn criticism from some who consider the movement a messianic cult.

21. Egon Mayer, Barry Kosmin, and Ariela Keysar, *American Jewish Identity Survey 2001* (New York: City University of New York, 2001) at www.gc.cuny.edu/studies/studies_index.htm (accessed March 6, 2008).

22. Mitra S. Kalita, *Suburban Sahibs: Three Immigrant Families and Their Passage from India to America* (New Brunswick, NJ: Rutgers University Press, 2003), 8.

CHAPTER 4

1. Quoted in Nancy Tatom Ammerman, *Baptist Battles: Social Change and Religious Conflict in the Southern Baptist Convention* (New Brunswick, NJ: Rutgers University Press, 1990), 39.

2. Quoted in Andrew Manis, *Southern Civil Religions in Conflict: Black and White Baptists and Civil Rights* (Athens: University of Georgia Press, 1987), 65.

3. Herman Talmadge, *You and Segregation* (Birmingham: Vulcan Press, 1955), 76.

4. A. L. Strozier, "The Battle of the Giants," *Alabama Baptist 120*, July 14, 1955: 8, 16; from the *Congressional Record*, 83d Congress, 2d session, May 27, 1954: 7257, quoted by Numan V. Bartley, *Rise of Massive Resistance* (Baton Rouge: Lousiana State University Press, 1969), 118–19; Robert Sherrill, *Gothic Politics in the Deep South* (New York: Grossman Publishers, 1968), 217.

5. *Christian Recorder*, February 14, 1863; See also Clarence E. Walker, *A Rock in a Weary Land: The African Methodist Episcopal Church During the Civil War and Reconstruction* (Baton Rouge: Louisiana State University Press, 1982), 41–42. Walker specifically argues that the AME's philosophy of racial uplift was part of its civil religion.

6. Vincent Harding, "Fighting for Freedom with Church Fans: To Know What Religion Means," in Larry G. Murphy, ed., *Down by the Riverside: Readings in African American Religion* (New York: New York University Press, 2000), 474.

7. King, Martin Luther, Jr., "A Testament of Hope," *Playboy*, January 1969: 234, quoted in Kenneth L. Smith and Ira G. Zepp, *Search for the Beloved Community* (Valley Forge: Judson Press, 1974), 127; Fred Shuttlesworth interview with Andrew M. Manis, March 10, 1984 (Manis, "The Civil Religions of the South,") Charles Wilson Regan and Mark Silk, Religion and Public Life in the South: In the Evangelical Mode (Lanham, MD: Rowman and Littlefield, 2005), 168. See also Andrew Manis, *A Fire You Can't Put Out: The Civil Rights Life of Birmingham's Reverend Fred Shuttlesworth* (Tuscaloosa: University of Alabama Press, 1999).

8. Carl Kell and L. Raymond Camp, *In the Name of the Father: The Rhetoric of the New Southern Baptist Convention* (Carbondale: University of Southern Illinois Press, 1999), 120–121.

9. The amendment read: "Equality of rights under the law shall not be denied or abridged by the United States or by any state on account of sex."

10. Paul W. Weyrich, a conservative activist long interested in mobilizing evangelicals, convened a meeting in Washington for evangelical leaders to address the Jones situation. See Randall Balmer, *Thy Kingdom Come: An Evangelical's Lament* (New York: Basic Books, 2006), 14–17.

11. Jerry Falwell, *Listen, America!* (New York: Doubleday and Company, 1980), 150, 185.

12. Bob Allen, "Couple Says IMB Won't Appoint Missionaries with Woman Pastors," *Associated Baptist Press News*, September 12, 2002, Volume 02-83.

13. "Church Notes," *Religion in the News* 6, no. 1 (Spring 2003).

14. See John C. Green, "The Undetected Tide," *Religion in the News* 6, No. 1 (Spring 2003).

15. Andrew W. Billingsley, *Mighty Like a River: The Black Church and Social Reform* (New York: Oxford University Press, 1999), 81.

16. *New York Times*, December 21, 2003.

17. *Atlanta Journal Constitution*, March 1, 2004, April 1, 2004; *New York Times*, March 1, 2004, April 1, 2004; *Atlanta Journal-Constitution*, November 11, 2004.

18. C. Eric Lincoln and Lawrence H. Mamiya, *The Black Church in the African American Experience* (Durham: Duke University Press, 1990), 176–82.

19. *Seven Promises of a Promise Keeper* (Colorado Springs: Focus on the Family Publishing, 1994), 153.

20. *Boston Globe*, February 15, 2006.

21. Lisa San Pascual, "The Social Gospel Lays an Egg in Alabama," *Religion in the News* XX (Spring 2003).

22. Martin Luther King, Jr., *The Wisdom of Martin Luther King In His Own Words* (New York: Lancer Books, 1968), 23, 41, 64, 75.

23. "Summertime—the Story," at www.callaloo.co.tt/spectacle/atlanta/summer.html (accessed March 7, 2008).

CHAPTER 5

1. Ray Waddle, "Book Explores Religion, Public Life in the 'Southern Crossroads,'" *EthicsDaily*.com, April 1, 2005.

2. J. R. Graves, *The Watchman's Reply* (Nashville: Tennessee Publication Society, 1853), 20, 60.

3. Graves, *Watchman's Reply*, 14–15.

4. Norris also served as titular head of a major fundamentalist church in Detroit.

5. Barry Hankins, *God's Rascal: J. Frank Norris and the Beginnings of Southern Fundamentalism* (Lexington: University Press of Kentucky, 1996), 3–4, 176; Oran P. Smith, *The Rise of Baptist Republicanism* (New York: New York University Press, 1997), 33–34.

6. Samuel S. Hill, Jr., "The Southern Baptists: Need for Reformulation, Redirection," *Christian Century* 80 (January 9, 1963), 39–42.

7. Sydney Ahlstrom, *A Religious History of the American People* (New Haven: Yale University Press, 1972), 871.

8. Grant Wacker, *Heaven Below: Early Pentecostalism and American Culture* (Cambridge, MA: Harvard University Press, 2001), 222.

9. Jeffrey Toobin, "Ashcroft's Ascent," *New Yorker*, April 15, 2002.

10. "Feminism and Appropriate Roles for Women," The Assemblies of God Perspectives—Contemporary Issues, on website of Assemblies of God USA at www.ag.org/top/Beliefs/contempissues 03 feminism.cfm (accessed March 10, 2008).

11. George E. Pozzetta, "Nativism," in Samuel S. Hill, *Encyclopedia of Religion in the South* (Macon: Mercer University Press, 1984), 530.

12. Randall M. Miller, "A Church in Cultural Captivity: Some Speculations on Catholic Identity in the Old South," in Randall M. Miller and Jon L. Wakelyn, *Catholics in the Old South: Essays on Church and Culture* (Macon: Mercer University Press, 1999), 36–37.

13. Randall M. Miller, "Roman Catholicism," in Charles Reagon Wilson and William Ferris, *Encyclopedia of Southern Culture* (Chapel Hill: University of North Carolina Press, 1989), 1308.

14. See Timothy Matovina, "Latino Catholics and American Public Life," in Andrew Walsh, *Can Charitable Choice Work?: Covering Religion's Impact on Urban Affairs and Social Services* (Hartford: The Leonard E. Greenberg Center for the Study of Religion in Public Life, 2001), 59–65.

15. United Methodist News Service (NMNS) Press Release, November 2, 1998; also see www.umaffirm.org/jcnono.html.

16. "UMNS Report on Annual Conferences, Arkansas Conference, June 11–14, 2003," at umns.umc.org/acreports/Arkansas.htm; UMNS Press Release, June 27, 2003.

17. American Baptist Press (ABP) Press Releases, March 4, 1998, and August 22, 2001.

18. Bobby Jindal, "Atheism's Gods," *This Rock* 6, No. 2 (February 1995).

19. John Maginnis, "Jindal Throttles Back His High Energy Style," *Times-Picayune*, June 13, 2007.

CHAPTER 6

1. For focused discussions of Hawaii and Nevada, see Wade Clark Roof and Mark Silk, eds., *Religion and Public Life in the Pacific Region: Fluid Identities* (Lanham, MD: AltaMira Press, 2005). See in particular chapter 5, George J. Tanabe, Jr., "*Pono* and *Kapu*: Righteousness and Taboo in Hawaii."

2. Walter Nugent, *Into the West: The Story of Its People* (New York: Alfred A. Knopf, 1999), 351.

3. Carl Abbott, *The Metropolitan Frontier: Cities in the Modern West* (Tucson: University of Arizona Press, 1993), 182–84.

4. Zygmunt Bauman, *Liquid Modernity* (Malden, MA: Blackwell Publishers/Polity Press, 2000), 8.

5. Catherine Albanese, "Religion and American Experiences," *Church History* 57 (1988): 345.

6. Moses Rischlin, "Immigration, Migration, and Minorities in California: A Reassessment," *Pacific Historical Review* 41 (1972): 76.

7. Elden Ernst, "Religion in California," *Pacific Theological Review* (Winter 1986): 46.

8. Elden G. Ernst (with Douglas Firth Anderson), *Pilgrim Progression* (Santa Barbara, CA: Fithian Press, 1993), 53.

9. Cited in James P. Gaffney, "The Anatomy of Transition: Cathedral Building and Social Justice in San Francisco, 1962–1971," *Catholic Historical Review* 70 (1984): 60.

10. Anita M. Caspary, *The Crisis of the Immaculate Heart Community of California* (Collegeville, MN: Liturgical Press, 2003), 5.

11. Michael Kanin, as quoted in Deborah Dash Moore, *To the Golden Cities: Pursuing the American Dream in Miami and L.A.* (New York: Free Press, 1994), 21.

12. Neil C. Sandberg, *Jewish Life in Los Angeles: A Window to Tomorrow* (Lanham, MD: University Press of America, 1986), 125.

13. Quote from Moore, *To the Golden Cities*, 269.

14. George M. Marsden, *Reforming Fundamentalism: Fuller Seminary and the New Evangelicalism* (Grand Rapids, MI: William B. Eerdmans Publishing, 1987), 21.

15. Marsden, *Reforming Fundamentalism*, x.

16. Lisa McGirr, *Suburban Warriors: The Origins of the New American Right* (Princeton: Princeton University Press, 2001), 53.

17. McGirr, *Suburban Warriors*, 20.

18. Quoted in Denis Voskuil, *Mountains in Goldmines: Robert Schuller and the Gospel of Success* (Grand Rapids, MI: William B. Eerdmans Publishing, 1983), 42.

19. Donald E. Miller, *Reinventing American Protestantism: Christianity in the New Millennium* (Berkeley: University of California Press, 1997), 11.

20. Michael Lienesch, *Redeeming America: Piety and Politics in the New Christian Right* (Chapel Hill: University of North Carolina Press, 1993), 11.

21. R. Stephen Warner, "Approaching Religious Diversity: Barriers, Byways and Beginnings," *Sociology of Religion* 59 (1998): 193–216.

22. "Terhangeles: Capital, Culture and Faith," presented at the Religious Pluralism in Southern California Conference, University of California at Santa Barbara, May 10, 2003.

23. Phillip E. Hammond and David W. Machacek, *Sokka Gakkai in America: Accommodation and Conversion* (Oxford: Oxford University Press, 1999).

24. Interview with David W. Machacek, quoted in Machacek, "New Players and Patterns," Wade Clark Roof and Mark Silk, Religion and Public Life in the Pacific Region: Fluid Identities (Lanham, MD: Alta Mira, 2005), 99.

25. Council of American-Islamic Relations website at www.cair.com/AboutUs/Vision/Mission/CorePrinciples.aspx (accessed March 10, 2008).

26. Theresa Watanabe, "A Clinic in Critical Condition," the Los Angeles Times, November 18, 2000.

CHAPTER 7

1. *The Pacific Northwest Pulpit*, compiled by Paul Little (New York: The Methodist Book Concern, 1915).

2. Robert W. Service, "The Law of the Yukon," in John William, ed, *Canadian Poets*. (Toronto, Canada: McClleland, Goodchild & Stewart, 1916), pp. 364.

3. Ken Kesey, *Sometimes a Great Notion* (New York: Viking, 1964), 21.

4. David M. Buerge and Junius Rochester, *Roots and Branches: The Religious Heritage of Washington State* (Seattle: Church Council of Greater Seattle, 1988), 216.

5. Steve Maynard, "Pope's Words Won't Break Local Bonds," *Tacoma News Tribune*, July 23, 2007.

6. See Doug Dye, "For the Sake of Seattle's Soul: The Church Council of Churches, the Nikkei Community, and World War II," *Pacific Northwest Quarterly* Volume 93, No. 3. (Summer 2002): 127–36.

7. Washington Association of Churches Homepage at www.thewac.org (accessed March 10, 2008)

8. Quoted in Dye, 73.

9. Mission Statement, Ecumenical Ministries of Oregon website at www.emoregon .org/about_us.htm (accessed March 10, 2008).

10. Interfaith Creation Festival website at www.interfaithcreationfest.org/index.html (accessed March 10, 2008)

11. "The Columbia River Watershed: Caring for Creation and the Common Good," *An International Pastoral Letter by the Catholic Bishops of the Region*, at www.columbiariver.org/files/pastoral-english.pdf, 23 (accessed March 10, 2008).

12. Statement on the home page of the Interfaith Creationfest 2007, www.inter faithcreationfest.org.

13. See William Cronon, "The Trouble with Wilderness; or, Getting Back to the Wrong Nature," in William Cronon, ed., *Uncommon Ground: Rethinking the Human Place in Nature* (New York: W. W. Norton & Co., 1995), 69–90.

14. The limited number of respondents in the Pacific Northwest in the Akron/Pew survey means that these findings should be taken as suggestive more than determinative.

15. See William M. Lunch, "The Christian Right in the Northwest: Two Decades of Frustration in Oregon and Washington," in John Green, Mark Rozell, and Clyde Wilcox, eds., *Marching Toward the Millennium: The Christian Right in the States 1980–2000* (Washington, DC: Georgetown University Press, 2003).

16. Quoted in James K. Wellman, Jr., *Evangelical vs. Liberal: The Clash of Christian Cultures in the Pacific Northwest* (New York: Oxford University Press, 2008).

17. Emilio Gentile, *Politics as Religion* (Princeton: Princeton University Press, 2006), xv. Here Gentile is at pains to distinguish civil from political religion, which is altogether more hegemonic in seeking to monopolize the allegiance of the citizenry.

18. The "State of Jefferson" is a mostly rural area of southern Oregon and northern California that, several times since the nineteenth century, has been proposed as a separate state.

CHAPTER 8

1. Shelley Roberts, *Remaining and Becoming: Cultural Crosscurrents in an Hispano School* (Mahwah, NJ: Lawrence Erlbaum Associates, 2001), 44–46.

2. *Salt Lake Tribune*, February 3, 2003.

3. Robert Gottlieb and Peter Wiley, *America's Saints: the Rise of Mormon Power* (New York: G. P. Putnum & Sons, 1984), 96.

4. *Los Angeles Times*, November 15, 2007.

5. Amy Sullivan, "Mitt Romney's Evangelical Problem," *Washington Monthly*, September 1, 2005.

CHAPTER 9

1. For some of the best information on these groups, with some attention to the Midwest, see R. Stephen Warner and Judith Witner, eds., *Gatherings in Diaspora: Re-*

ligious Connections and the New Immigration (Philadelphia: Temple University Press, 1998).

2. For discussion, see James L. Guth, John C. Green, Corwin E. Smidt, and Lyman A. Kellstedt, "Partisan Religion: Analyzing the 2000 Election, *Christian Century* (March 21–28, 2001): 18–20.

3. The data for this section was taken from *Census 2000* (Washington DC: U.S. Dept. of Commerce, Economics, and Statistics Administration, U.S. Census Bureau, [2001] electronic resource) and the *Official Catholic Directory for the Year of Our Lord 2002* (New York: P. J. Kennedy, 2002).

4. Kathleen Neils Conzen, *Making Their Own America* (New York: Berg, 1990), 5, 33, 2.

5. William G. Howell and Paul E. Peterson, *The Education Gap: Vouchers and Urban Schools* (Washington: Brookings Institution, 2001), 213 (where they discuss religion and support for vouchers) and 254 (for the quote).

6. Terry M. Moel, *Schools, Vouchers and the American Public* (Washington, D.C.: Brookings Institution Press, 2001), 213.

7. Mary Hanna, "Bishops as Political Leaders," in *Religion in American Politics*, Charles Dunn, ed. (Washington: Congressional Quarterly Press, 1989), 76.

8. John T. McGreevy, *Catholicism and American Freedom* (New York: W. W. Norton, 2003), 285.

9. Paul Wilkes, "Education of an Archbishop," *New Yorker* (July 15, 1991): 49.

10. Mary E. Bendyna and Paul M. Perl, Political Preferences of American Catholics at the Time of Election 2000 (Washington, D.C.: Center for Applied Research in the Apostolate, 2000), 30–32.

11. Mary E. Bendyna and Paul M. Perl, Political Preferences, 34 William V. D'Antonio, James Davidson, Dean Hoge, and Katherine Meyer Anderson, American Catholics (Walnut Creek, CA: AltaMira, 2001), 95 and 49.

12. Ibid., 96 and 49.

13. Bendyna and Perl, Political Preferences, 34.

14. Website of the Department of Peace and Justice for the Archdiocese of Chicago, at www.archchicago.org/departments/peace_and_justice/peace_justice.shtm [Access date needed]

15. *New York Times*, November 1, 2006, 1.

CHAPTER 10

1. For an extended account of this larger story (without the regional dimension) through the 1980s, see Mark Silk, *Spiritual Politics: Religion and America Since World War II* (New York: Simon and Schuster, 1988).

2. *Secret Proceedings and Debates of the Convention Assembled at Philadelphia, in the Year 1787, for the Purpose of Forming the Constitution of the United States of America* (Richmond, VA: Wilbur Curtiss, 1839), 89–90. The fashion, at least in the convention, seems to have been to hold religion at arm's length—evidenced by the tabling of Benjamin Franklin's motion to begin every day's session with prayer. James Madison,

The Journal of the Constitutional Convention, in Gaillard Hunt, ed., *The Writings of James Madison* (New York: G. P. Putnam's Sons, 1902), III, 309–311.

3. *Newport Herald*, September 9, 1790, reprinted in Judith M. Buddenbaum and Debra L. Mason, *Readings on Religion as News* (Ames, IA: Iowa State University Press, 2000), 65

4. *Connecticut Courant*, June 7, 1802.

5. *Kline's Carlisle Weekly Gazette*, October 7, 1795, quoted in David W. Robson, "College Founding in the New Republic, 1776–1800," *History of Education Quarterly* 23 (1983): 335.

6. "Farewell Address," transcript of final manuscript, 20; see gwpapers.virginia .edu/farewell/index.html.

7. Ibid.

8. Mercy Warren, *History of the Rise, Progress and Termination of the American Revolution* (Boston: Manning and Loring, 1805), III, 403–404.

9. Lester J. Cappon, ed., *The Adams-Jefferson Letters: The Complete Correspondence Between Thomas Jefferson and Abigail and John Adams* (Chapel Hill: University of North Carolina Press, 1988), 338–40.

10. Sarah Barringer Gordon, *The Mormon Question: Polygamy and Constitutional Conflict in Nineteenth-Century America* (Chapel Hill: University of North Carolina Press, 2002), 74.

11. Daniel L. Dreisbach, ed., *Religion and Politics in the Early Republic: Jasper Adams and the Church-State Debate* (Lexington: University of Kentucky Press, 1996), 49. Adams did drop a footnote to make clear that he was using *established* "in its usual and not in its legal or technical sense."

12. The extent to which Mormonism was seen by many Americans as beyond the pale—even after the LDS Church officially foreswore polygamy, was evident in the massive public opposition to the seating of Reed Smoot in the U.S. Senate in 1906. For an account of this fascinating episode in American religious history, see Kathleen Flake, The Politics of American Religious Identity: The Seating of Senator Reed Smoot, Mormon Apostle (Chapel Hill: University of North Carolina Press, 2004).

13. *New York Times*, July 23, 1952; J. B. Matthews, "Reds and the Churches," *The American Mercury* (July 1953): 13.

14. Will Herberg, *Protestant-Catholic-Jew* (Garden City, NY: Doubleday, 1960 [1955]), 38.

15. Thomas J. Carty, *A Catholic in the White House: Religion Politics, and John F. Kennedy's Presidential Campaign* (New York: Palgrave MacMillan, 2004), vii–viii.

16. Martin Luther King, Jr., *Why We Can't Wait* (New York: Harper, 1964), 96–100.

17. For an account of the episode, see Mark Silk, *Spiritual Politics: Religion and America Since World War II* (New York: Simon and Schuster, 1988), 160–67.

18. See Alexander Gordon, "The Real Man Without a Country," *Religion in the News* 5, No. 2 (Summer 2002).

19. For a comprehensive treatment of religion gaps in voting patterns, see John Green, *The Faith Factor: How Religion Influences American Elections* (Westport, CT: Praeger, 2007).

20. These numbers, produced by John Green, differ a little from the original exit poll numbers on two counts. First, the issue priorities here are taken as a percentage of the respondents who actually gave an answer to the question (92.3 percent of those polled). Second, the national exit poll data were re-weighted to match the actual election results by region. Thus, the original figure of 21.7 percent for the moral values voters comes out as 23.7 percent in this analysis. The following discussion draws from John Green and Mark Silk, "Why Moral Values Did Count," *Religion in the News* 8, No. 1 (Spring 2005).

21. Two regions were outliers in this regard: The Mountain West had by far the largest proportion of moral values voters, largely due to the high number of Latter-day Saints; New England had more such voters than the other Kerry regions. These results may reflect sampling error that appears to have exaggerated the numbers of Latter-day Saints in the Mountain West and evangelicals in New England. However, it could be that both groups turned out in especially high numbers in 2004 because of the issue of same-sex marriage. This was especially the case in New England where the legalization of civil unions (Vermont) and same-sex marriage (Massachusetts) had occurred.

22. See Mark Silk and John Green, "The GOP's Religion Problem," *Religion in the News* 9, No. 3 (Winter 2007); "Why Moral Values Did Count," *Religion in the News* 8, No. 1 (Spring 2005).

23. On Huckabee as Missionary Baptist, see William Lindsey, "Huckabee's Baptism," *Religion in the News* 10, No. 3 (Winter 2008).

RELIGION BY REGION SERIES

AltaMira Press
Co-published with the Leonard E. Greenberg Center for the
Study of Religion in Public Life at Trinity College

Mark Silk and Andrew Walsh, Series Editors

Bibliography

BOOKS

Anderson, John W. and William Friend, eds. *The Culture of Bible Belt Catholics*. New York: Paulist Press, 1995.

Botham, Fay and Sarah M. Patterson. *Race, Religion and Region: Landscapes of Encounter in the American West*. Tucson, Arizona: University of Arizona Press, 2006.

Carroll, Brett E. *The Routledge Historical Atlas of Religion in America*. New York: Routledge, 2000.

Engh, Michael E. *Frontier Faiths: Church, Temple, and Synagogue in Los Angeles* Albuquerque: University of New Mexico Press, 1992.

Ernst, Eldon G. with Douglas Firth Anderson. *Pilgrim Progressivism*. Santa Barbara, California: Fithian Press, 1993.

Evans, Eli N. *The Provincials: A History of Jews in the South*. New York: Atheneum, 1973.

Francaviglia, Richard V. *Believing in Place: A Spiritual Geography of the Great Basin* Reno, Nevada: University of Nevada Press, 2003.

Frankiel, Tamar. *California's Spiritual Frontiers: Alternatives to Anglo-Protestantism, 1850–1915*. Berkeley: University of California Press, 1988.

Franklin, Wayne and Michael Steiner, eds. *Mapping American Culture*. Iowa City, Iowa: University of Iowa Press, 1992.

Gastil, Raymond D. *Cultural Regions of the United States*. Seattle: University of Washington Press, 1975.

Gaustad, Edwin Scott and Philip L. Barlow. *New Historical Atlas of Religion In America*. New York: Oxford University Press, 2000.

Harvey, Paul. *Redeeming the South: Religious Cultures and Racial Identities Among Southern Baptists, 1865–1925*. Chapel Hill: University of North Carolina Press, 1997.

Heyrman, Christine Leigh. *Southern Cross: The Beginning of the Bible Belt.* New York: Alfred A. Knopf, 1997.

Hill, Samuel S., ed. *Religion in the Southern States.* Macon, GA: Mercer University Press, 1983.

────── and Charles H. Lippy, eds. *The Encyclopedia of Religion in the South.* 2d ed. Macon, Georgia: Mercer University Press, 2001.

Iwamura, Jane Naomi and Paul Spickard, eds. *Revealing the Sacred in Asian and Pacific America.* New York: Routledge, 2003.

Jacobson, David. *Place and Belonging in American.* Baltimore: Johns Hopkins University Press: 2002.

Jones, Loyal. *Faith and Meaning in the Southern Faith Uplands.* Urbana and Chicago: The University of Illinois Press, 1999.

Leonard, Bill J. *Christianity in Appalachia.* Knoxville: The University of Tennessee Press, 1999.

Charles Lippy, *Bibliography of Religion in the South.* Macon, Georgia: Mercer University Press, 1985.

McCauley, Deborah Vansau. *Appalachian Mountain Religion: A History.* Urbana: The University of Illinois Press, 1995.

Maffly-Kipp, Laura. *Religion and Society in Frontier California.* New Haven: Yale University Press, 1994.

Manis, Andrew. *Southern Civil Religions in Conflict.* Macon, Georgia: Mercer University Press, 2001.

Mauss, Armand L. *The Angel and the Beehive: The Mormon Struggle with Assimiliation* Urbana: University of Illinois Press, 1994.

Mathews, Donald G. *Religion in the Old South.* Chicago: University of Chicago Press, 1977.

Meinig, Donald W. *The Shaping of America: A Geographical Perspective on 500 Years of History, Volume 3: Transcontinental America, 1850–1915.* New Haven: Yale University Press, 1995.

──────, *The Shaping of America: A Geographical Perspective on 500 Years of History, Volume 2, Continental America, 1800–1867.* New Haven: Yale University Press, 1992.

──────, *The Shaping of America: A Geographical Perspective on 500 Years of History, Volume 1, Atlantic America, 1492–1800.* New Haven: Yale University Press, 1986.

Montgomery, William E. *Under Their Own Vine and Fig Tree: The African-American Church in the South, 1865–1900.* Baton Rouge: Louisiana State University Press, 1993.

Moore, Deborah Dash. *To the Golden Cities: Pursuing the American Jewish Dream in Miami and L.A.* Berkeley: University of California Press, 1994.

Noble, Allen G., ed. *To Build a New Land: Ethnic Landscapes in North America.* Baltimore: Johns Hopkins University Press, 1992.

Nostrand, Richard L. and Lawrence E. Estaville, eds. *Homelands: A Geography of Culture and Place Across America.* Baltimore: Johns Hopkins University Press, 2001.

O'Connell, Nicholas. *On Sacred Ground: The Spirit of Place in the Pacific Northwest.* Seattle: University of Washington Press, 2003.

Ownby, Ted. *Subduing Satan: Religion, Recreation and Manhood in the Rural South, 1865–1920.* Chapel Hill: University of North Carolina Press, 1990.

Schoenberg, Wilfred P. *A History of the Catholic Church in the Pacific Northwest.* Washington, D.C.: The Pastoral Press, 1987

Sherrill, Roland A. ed. *Religion and the Life of the Nation: American Recoveries.* Urbana: University of Illinois Press, 1990.

Szasz, Ferencz M. *Religion in the Modern West.* Tuscon: University of Arizona Press, 2000.

Wilson, Charles Reagan, ed. *Religion in the South.* Jackson, Mississippi: University Press of Mississippi, 1985.

—— *Baptized in Blood: The Religion of the Lost Cause, 1865–1929.* Athens: University of George Press, 1980.

SCHOLARLY ARTICLES, BOOK CHAPTERS, AND DISSERTATIONS

Boles, John B. "Religion in the South: A Tradition Recovered." *Maryland Historical Magazine* 77, no. 4. (Winter 1982): 388–401.

Brauer, Jerald T. "Regionalism and Religion in America." *Church History* 54, no. 3. (Spring 1985): 366–78.

Brauer, John Thomas. "Stability and Change in United States Religious Regions, 1980–2000." University of Kansas Doctoral Dissertation, 2006.

Ernst, Eldon. "American Religious History from a Pacific Coast Perspective." Pp. 3–39 in *Religion and Society in the American West,* edited by Carl Guarnari and David Alvarez. Lanham, Maryland: University Press of America, 1987.

Goff, Philip. "Diversity and Region." *Themes in American Religion and Culture.* Chapel Hill: University of North Carolina Press, 2004.

Hill, Samuel. "Religion and Region in the United States." *Annals of the American Academy of Political & Social Science* 480. (1985): 132–141.

Hunt, Matthew O. and Larry L. Hun. "Regional Religions?: Extending the 'Semi-Involuntary' Thesis of African American Religious Participation," *Sociological Forum* 15, no. 4. (Dec. 2000): 569–94.

Killen, Patricia O'Connell. "The Geography of a Religious Minority: Roman Catholics in the Pacific Northwest," *U.S. Catholic Historian* 18, no. 3. (Summer 2000): 52–87.

McGuire, Meredith B. "Religion and Region: Sociological and Historical Perspectives." *Journal for the Scientific Study of Religion* 30, no. 4D (1991): 544–547.

Maffly-Kipp, Laurie. "Eastward Ho! American Religion from the Perspective of the Pacific." Pp. 127–48 in *Retelling U.S. Religious History,* edited by Thomas A. Tweed, Berkeley: University of California Press, 1997.

Mathews, Donald G. "We Have Left Undone Those Things Which We Ought to Have Done: Southern Religious History in Retrospect and Prospect." *Church History* 67, no. 2. (June 1998): 305–25.

Nordquist, Philip A. "Lutherans in the West and Northwest," in *New Partners, Old Roots*, edited by Heidi Emerson. Takoma, Washington: J&D Printing, 1986.

Quinn, Michael D. "Religion in the American West," in *Under an Open Sky Rethinking America's Western Past*, et al. editor William Cronon. New York: Norton, 1992.

Shibley, Mark. "Religion in Oregon: Recent Demographic Currents in the Mainstream." *Pacific Northwest Quarterly* 83, no. 3. (July 1992): 82–87.

Shortridge, James. "A New Regionalization of American Religion." *Journal of the Scientific Study of Religion* 16. (June 1977): 43–154.

Shipps, Jan. "Region and Regional Culture in America" in *Can Charitable Choice Work?*, edited by Andrew Walsh. Hartford, Connecticut: Leonard E. Greenberg Center for the Study of Religion in Public Life, Trinity College: 2001.

Silk, Mark. "Defining Religious Pluralism in the United States." *Annals of the American Academy of Political and Social Science 2007* 612. Pp. 64–81.

Stump, Roger W. "Regional Divergence in Religious Affiliation in the United States." *Sociological Analysis* 45, no. 4. (Winter 1984): 283–299.

Szasz, Ferenc and Martha Connell Szasz. "Religion and Spirituality." Pp. 359–90 in *Oxford History of the American West*, et.al. edited by Clyde A. Milner II. New York: Oxford University Press, 1994.

Wentz, Richard E. "Region and Religion in America," *Foundations* 24, no. 2. (April-June 1981).

Zelinsky, Wilber. "An Approach to the Religious Geography of the United States: Patterns of Church Membership in 1952." *Annals of the Association of American Geographers* 51. (June 1961): 139–193.

Index

Abbott, Carl, 109

Abington Township v. Schempp, 212

abortion: African Americans in the South and, 80; Midwest Catholics and, 200; New England Catholics and, 49, 58, 59–60; South Dakota's referendum on, 201–203; Southern Crossroads' conservatism and, 101

Abyssinian Baptist Church (New York City), 23

Adams, Jasper, 208

Adams, John, 208

African American Catholics, 196

African American denominations: biracial community groups in the South, 81–82; biracial congregations in the South, 82; biracial social justice campaigns in the South, 82–83; civil religion and, 68; civil rights and, 68–70; founding of, 67–68; imitated by the religious right, 79; Midwest, 186, 188–89; New Jersey, 21; Pacific Northwest, 10; passivity around social issues, 69; Pentecostals, 6; political engagement and, 79–80; politics in the South and, 79–81; religion in the South and, 67–70; Washington, D.C., 24. *See also* African American Protestants

African American Muslims, 131

African American Protestants: conservatism in the Southern Crossroads, 100, 103; ecumenicalism and, 51; Midwest, 12, 183; New England, 4, 51; the South, 5; Southern Crossroads, 6–7

African Americans: biracial social justice campaigns in the South, 82–83; demographics in the South, 63; New England, 41; religion in the South and, 67–70

Ahlstrom, Sydney, 91

Aitken, Robert, 129

Alabama, 79, 82–83

Alaska: childhood hunger, 151; environmental spiritualism and, 146–47; evangelicals, 148; in the Pacific Northwest region, 1

Albanese, Catherine L., 110

Albuquerque, New Mexico, 159

Alfred E. Smith Memorial Foundation Dinner, 30

Alger, David, 138

Alinsky, Saul, 98, 197

Allen, Catherine, 74

Allen, Richard, 67, 68

Allen African Methodist Episcopal Church (New York City), 23

Nebraska, 191
Nelson, Jonathan, 139
Nevada, 2, 111, 125
New Age spirituality, 173, 213
New Amsterdam, 15
New England: Catholics, 42–43, 44–49, 57–62; church–state relations and, 207, 211–12; civil religion in, 55–56; conservative Protestants, 51–55; demographics, 41–42; local government and, 56; mainline Protestants, 42–43, 49–51, 56–57; pluralism and, 55; religious demographics, 3–5; significant religious characteristics of, 42–43; trends of change in, 43–44
New England Baptist Association, 52
New England Baptist Convention, 52, 53
New Hampshire, 45
New Jersey: Catholics, 28; early colonization, 15; Indian Americans, 37–39; Protestantism, 21
New Life Church (Colorado Springs, Colorado), 177
New Mexico: Asian immigrants, 162; Catholics, 10; historical overview of, 158–62; migration and, 10–11; politics and, 178
New Netherland, 15
New Orleans, Louisiana, 224
New Orleans Protestant, 96
"new paradigm churches,"123
New Religious Movements, 213
New Spirituality, 142–43
New York: early colonization, 15; foreign-born population, 125; Jews, 32, 33; Protestants, 19
New York City: Catholics and Jews, 27; Irish Catholics, 25–26; Jews, 27, 33, 37; Protestants, 22–24
Nicolay, Jan, 202–3
Nine Houses of Gaia, 143
Nones: Pacific Northwest, 9; Pacific region, 8
nonprofits, 51
Norris, J. Frank, 88–90

North, Oliver, 75
North American Air Defense Command, 174
North Dakota, 200
Northern Baptists, 170
Northwest Coalition Against Malicious Harassment, 138–39
Northwest Coalition for Human Dignity, 139
The Northwest Fall Equinox Festival, 143
Northwest Texas Conference, 103
nuns, 96
Nussbaum, R. Max, 119

Obama, Barack, 227
O'Brien, Henry, 48
Ockenga, Harold, 53
O'Connell, William, 48
O'Connor, John, 24
O'Connor, Sandra Day, 226
Ohio: 2006 gubernatorial election, 203–4; Protestants, 191
oil drilling, in Alaska, 146–47
O'Keeffe, Georgia, 161
Oklahoma: "Bone-Dry Law," 97; Catholics, 98–99; Republicans, 105; secular politics, 105
Oklahoma City bombing, 131
Oklahoma Conference of Churches, 99
"Old Fashioned Revival Hour," 121
old-growth forests, 145
Olympic Games of 1996, 83–84
O'Malley, Sean, 46, 60, 62
Orange County, California, 122, 123
Oregon: childhood hunger, 151; Death with Dignity Act, 153; environmentalism and, 147; evangelicals, 148
Oregon Christian Alliance, 152
Oregon Natural Resource Council, 145
Orthodox Judaism, 35, 36–37
outreach ministries, 95

Pacific Northwest: anti-government millennialists, 144; civil religion,

About the Authors

Mark Silk is the founding director of the Leonard E. Greenberg Center for the Study of Religion in Public Life and Professor of Religion in Public Life at Trinity College in Hartford. A historian by training, he was a reporter, editorial writer, and columnist for the *Atlanta Journal Constitution*. He is the author of *Spiritual Politics: Religion and America Since World War II* and *Unsecular Media: Making News of Religion in America*, and was co-editor of the Center's *Religion by Region* series. He also edits the Center's magazine, *Religion in the News*, and its blog, *Spiritual Politics*. He is a graduate of Harvard College and holds a Ph.D. from Harvard University.

Andrew Walsh has been associate director of the Leonard E. Greenberg Center for the Study of Religion in Public Life since 1997. He was co-editor of the Center's *Religion by Region* series. A former reporter for the *Hartford Courant*, he is a historian of religion in America and holds degrees from Trinity College and Yale Divinity School, as well as a Ph.D. from Harvard University.